THE DE GAULLE NOBODY KNOWS

THE DE GAULLE NOBODY KNOWS

An Intimate Biography of
Charles de Gaulle

BY

ALDEN HATCH

HAWTHORN BOOKS, INC., *Publishers*

NEW YORK

FIRST EDITION, *November, 1960*

To
ROGER VAURS
who expended so much
time, energy and good will
in preparing the way
for this book

ACKNOWLEDGMENTS

I am most grateful for the assistance of many French men and French women who, even during days of crisis, gave me unfailing courtesy and unstinted help. Among them were: General Charles de Gaulle, President of the French Republic who, though protocol prevented his giving me an interview, did me the honor of receiving me as a guest at the Élysée.

Also, Minister of Justice Edmund Michelet; Minister of Information Louis Terrenoire; Minister of Culture André Malraux; President of the Council of Foreign Affairs, National Assembly, Maurice Schumann; former President of the Council René Pleven; former Minister for the Sahara and Deputy Premier Jacques Soustelle; Alphonse Juin, Marshal of France; members of General de Gaulle's personal staff, Colonels Gaston de Bonneval and Geoffroy de Courcel, Messieurs Olivier Guichard and Pierre Lefranc; Madame Geneviève de Gaulle Anthonioz; Director of Press Relations, Élysée, M. Jean Chauveau; Director of Press Relations, Foreign Office, M. Pierre Baraduc; Director of the French Information Service (U.S.) Roger Vaurs, and Assistant Director Mademoiselle Yvonne Daumarie; Director of Information, Radio-Diffusion-Television Française M.

René Thibault; Count and Countess Alexandre de Saint-Phalle; M. Henri Daniel-Rops, *Académie Française;* M. Albin Chalendon; Charles Vioud (known in the Resistance as Landais); M. François Bondy, Editor of *Preuves;* M. Scott Charles, Director of the Congress for Cultural Freedom; Brigadier General John P. Condon, U.S.M.C.; M. Charles Orengo, formerly editor of *Plon* and now at *Hachette;* Count Jean de Madre; Madame Thérèse de Drouas; M. Théodore d'Arnaux; Madame Charles Saint; M. André Nemo, vice consul, and Mme. Monique Polgar, press attache, both with the French Embassy Information Division, New York.

＊ ✤ ✤

CONTENTS

[9]

CONTENTS

❧ ⚜ ❧

LIST OF ILLUSTRATIONS

[11]

LIST OF ILLUSTRATIONS

General de Gaulle in January, 1946, escorting his daughter Elisabeth to the church where she was married.

Charles, Yves and Jean, the three children of General de Gaulle's eldest son Philippe.

De Gaulle on the Government bench, in the National Assembly, the day of his investiture as the last Premier of the IVth French Republic (June 1, 1958).

Crowd at Tamatave, Madagascar, welcomes de Gaulle in July 1960.

The illustrations listed above appear between pages 196 and 199.

President de Gaulle before a joint session of Congress, April 25, 1960, with Vice President Nixon in background.

President and Mme. de Gaulle pose with their dinner hosts, President and Mrs. Eisenhower.

Prime Minister Khrushchev presenting President de Gaulle with a model of the "lunik" on his visit to France in March, 1960.

President de Gaulle with Prime Minister Macmillan and President Eisenhower at the abortive Paris "summit" conference in May, 1960.

The illustrations listed above appear between pages 230 and 233.

THE DE GAULLE NOBODY KNOWS

CHAPTER ONE

❧ ⚜ ❧

"I AM FRANCE"

SIXTY YEARS AGO, in a big old-fashioned apartment in the city of Paris, four young boys were playing with their lead soldiers. They were fighting real battles based on Napoleon's victories. Each brother represented a different nation. Ten-year-old Charles assigned them their roles. "You, Xavier, are Austria," he said. "Jacques is Prussia. Pierre is Italy. Of course, I am France."

Today more than ever Charles de Gaulle is France. Yet to most Americans and many Frenchmen he is an enigma. If even his own countrymen are confused, it is natural that to the rest of the world de Gaulle appears as a cold, egotistical man, whose unpredictable thoughts are concealed behind the impassive mask of his jutting profile. In the words of French Academician, Henri Daniel-Rops, "In his public image he is a monolithic figure."

That is, of course, de Gaulle's intention. To his mind, the man who represents France must stand on a lonely pinnacle wrapped in grandeur. "Where I am," he says, "a man must have neither friends nor enemies."

De Gaulle has, of course, many bitter enemies; but he neither regards nor treats them as such. In fact he has, at times, invited his bitterest antagonists to join his government. He has no intimate friends. He is surrounded by old comrades of Fighting France and the Resistance—his aides, his ministers, and most of the principal figures of his government—but though he cherishes and loves them, they could not be called intimates. Perhaps his closest friend is brilliant, burning, André Malraux, author, ex-communist, Resistance fighter, and now Minister of Culture. In the realm of the Gaullist mystique, he is de Gaulle's philosopher and, yes, friend. Only he may burst into the Presidential sanctum unannounced. But the last man who called de Gaulle "Charles" died at Christmastime, 1959—his brother Pierre.

As to de Gaulle being incomprehensible, that is sheer nonsense. The whole course of his life runs as straight as one of the new French pipelines across the Sahara. His every act and every word are designed to carry out his single-minded purpose to restore France to greatness, without which, according to him, she is not France.

De Gaulle has made no mystery of this; he has poured it out in all his books. What confuses his supporters—and his enemies —is the fact that though he has a single objective, he takes many roads to achieve it.

His identification with France began when he first learned the significance of his name—de Gaulle, *of France*. All his life he seemed to have a prevision of the role he was to play and to be preparing himself for it. As a small child kneeling beside his bed in his woolen nightshirt, he prayed to Our Lady that he might be allowed to do something great for France, "no matter what, but something great."

Long before World War II began he adopted as his personal emblem the double-barred Cross of Lorraine, Saint Joan's Cross. For this man is as great a mystic as St. Augustine, and as incurably romantic as Don Quixote. He could write: "In my emotional moments I thought of France as the princess in the fairy stories, or the Madonna in the Frescos. . . ."

But unlike Cervantes' Foolish Knight, de Gaulle never tilts at windmills. Beneath his romanticism lies a streak of Gallic realism often expressed in acrid comments or biting wit. His realism keeps him from confusing the desirable with the possible. That is why he offered the French colonies their choice of independence or life within the "French Community," a political and economic union similar to the British Commonwealth. Knowing that it was hopeless to try to hold them by military might, he took the only sensible course. It is also the reason he promised Algeria the right of self-determination, to the horror of his conservative supporters, the anger of the Army, and rebellion in Algiers. "We could hold it by force," he said, "but that would not endure."

It was de Gaulle's realism, not the fantasy of grandeur, that insisted on France's successful nuclear experiments. One day at the Elysée he said, "In the present military circumstances no nation can pretend to a place in the councils of the great powers unless it has the atomic bomb."

Then his lips twitched in a quarter-smile and a cat's-paw of humor ruffled his pale blue eyes. "Even if it is a very little one," he added.

Another confusing aspect of de Gaulle is that he is always remembering the past and thinking of the future. To him the present is merely a moving point in the flow of time. As one of his opponents, Pierre Boutanz, truly said, "De Gaulle is a man of yesterday—and of tomorrow."

Naturally, this is frustrating to people living in the present. De Gaulle has at last really become France, but he did not just spring full-fledged from the loins of his goddess. His thoughts, his mystique, and his common sense were all conditioned by the special circumstances in which he grew up, and the fortunes and trials of the adventurous life he led before he began his great adventure. But the finest workmanship will not temper a blade unless the steel is worthy. To know this is the beginning of understanding the man, who by his moral grandeur three times has saved his beloved France, the first time from her enemies; the second from her friends; and the third time from herself.

CHAPTER TWO

⚜ ⚜ ⚜

"A CERTAIN ANXIOUS PRIDE . . ."

CHARLES ANDRÉ JOSEPH MARIE DE GAULLE was born on November 22, 1890, in the manufacturing city of Lille, near the Belgian border of France. His place of birth had little relevance in his life. The de Gaulles had been Parisians for more than two hundred years. Before that they lived in Normandy and Burgundy.

It was his mother's family, the Maillot-Delannoys, who lived in Lille, and de Gaulle was born there only because Madame de Gaulle went home to her mother to have her baby.

Sometimes, a man seems to gather in his person all the virtues and faults of his ancestors. De Gaulle is such a man. The formative influences of his character began many centuries before his birth. A convenient date might be 1415. According to an old chronicle, cited in the de Gaulle family history, on October 25 of that year, near the forest of Agincourt, "between nine and ten in the morning, the Admiral of France . . . and the Sire de Gaule (*sic*) with a thousand men of the élite, charged to disperse the English archers."

The Sire de Gaule, who had advised his commander-in-chief not to fight from his disadvantageous position at Agincourt, was one of the few who escaped that fatal field. With his small band of retainers, he fought a rear-guard action against the English over the same route General Patton's armor followed from St. Lo to Carentan. When de Gaule was finally surrounded and captured by forces outnumbering his by 100 to 1, English King Henry V offered to take him into his service. Rather than take the oath of fealty to an alien king, Jean de Gaule chose exile. His estates were confiscated and himself declared "traitor and felon." Thereby, he set a precedent that his far distant kinsman followed.

The de Gaulle family came to Paris in the middle of the eighteenth century. The general's great-great-grandfather, Jean-Baptiste de Gaulle, was a king's-counsel and attorney for the Parliament. When the French Revolution broke out he, of course, remained loyal to King Louis XVI. He and his son, Phillipe, were thrown into prison and marked for the guillotine. Only the fall of Robespierre saved the family from being truncated.

In spite of the perilous times in which he lived, Jean-Baptiste did so well at the law that when he died in 1798 he left his widow and four children a fortune of 841,000 French pounds, which has enabled this frugal family to live in comfort ever since. But not in idleness.

De Gaulle's grandfather, Julien-Philippe de Gaulle, was the first historian of note in the family. As a little boy during Napoleon's Hundred Days in 1815, he had seen the Emperor acclaimed by the workmen in the Faubourg St. Antoine; had heard them beg Napoleon for arms with which to fight the enemies of France. Having thus seen a moment of history, he devoted his life to writing it, producing such major works as his *New History of Paris* and *Life of St. Louis*.

Madame Julien-Philippe de Gaulle (born Maillot) was also a historian, a most unusual profession for a lady of that era. Thus de Gaulle got a double dose of the historical virus, further compounded by the fact that his father, Henri de Gaulle, and both his uncles continued the literary-historical vein.

Henri de Gaulle also resumed the soldierly tradition of the family. When the Emperor Napoleon III declared war against

Prussia in 1870, he became a sergeant in the Garde Mobile de la Seine.

By the time Sergeant de Gaulle's regiment was mustered in, the ineptitude of the French generals and the chaotic conditions of supply had already lost the war. Marshal Bazaine was surrounded at Metz and the Emperor was in trouble at Sedan. In uniform but *without* guns, the Garde Mobile was rushed forward to join the Army of Marshal MacMahon at Châlon. They arrived just in time to retreat by train to Vincennes, outside of Paris.

At Vincennes they learned that Napoleon III had surrendered a great French Army at Sedan. The German troops were flowing up the fine straight roads of France toward Paris.

The Garde Mobile was hastily supplied with breech-loading *Chassepot* rifles. They had two practice firings to learn the mechanism of these new-type weapons. Then, as the veteran Prussian troops encircled the fortified city, the Garde Mobile was ordered to defend the Porte St. Denis. Henri de Gaulle must have noted the closed circle of history, for he knew that a year or so before Agincourt, the Sire de Gaule had been charged with the defense of this same ancient gateway against the Duke of Burgundy.

Held at bay by the star-shaped bastion of casemented, heavily-gunned forts linked by earthworks which defended Paris, the Germans settled down to starve out the city. It was almost the last great classic siege of history. As rations grew shorter, the defenders stared with hungry eyes at the fields of vegetables growing between the lines. Sergeant de Gaulle volunteered to lead a bean-picking platoon into that lush no-man's land. A German sniper winged him in the arm. So close to home was he that, after having his wound bandaged, he was in his father's house that night.

Henri de Gaulle soon went back to his regiment for the final desperate months of the siege. He was promoted by casualty until he took command of his company, of which all the other officers had been killed or wounded. On January 21, 1871, he was fighting in the Rue Montfort under the shadow of the East Fort when news came that the city had surrendered.

Charles de Gaulle grew up during the longest peace France has known in two centuries. Frenchmen called it "the sick peace," because of the frustrations of living in a defeated nation, two of whose finest provinces, Alsace and Lorraine, had been annexed by the victors.

Henri de Gaulle had married his cousin Jeanne Maillot. With their five children, Xavier, Agnès, Charles, Jacques, and Pierre, the de Gaulles lived in a big, high-ceilinged apartment at 3 Place Saint-François-Xavier in the old Paris of the Left Bank. It had a little wrought-iron balcony from which the children could look across the square to the ancient church of Saint-François-Xavier where they went to Mass every Sunday and holy day.

Madame de Gaulle had two moving passions in life, piety and patriotism, which her husband shared. Their children were imbued with a living faith in God and so deep a love for France that it became for all of them the central theme of their existence. Charles de Gaulle remembers his mother telling of her despair when, as a girl, she saw her father and mother burst into tears at the news of Bazaine's surrender; while his father's stories of the heroic defense of Paris made the siege a vivid personal experience. In his memoires he wrote: "To my three brothers, my sister, and myself a certain anxious pride in our country came as second nature."

As he grew older, de Gaulle loved to walk through the beautiful city which is the heart and soul of France. The solemn, lanky little boy, dressed in a French sailor suit with its red-striped blouse and a beret with a red pom-pom, wandered about Toulouse-Lautrec's frivolous city of opera and ballet and balls, and glittering demi-mondaines driving through the Bois in four-horse landaux with a monkey turning cartwheels on the jump-seat—the Paris which was a symbol of gaiety and profligacy to all the world.

What de Gaulle remembered about it were "the symbols

of our glory—night falling over Notre Dame, the majesty of evening at Versailles, the Arc de Triomphe in the sunshine, and the conquered battle flags quivering in the vault of the Invalides." A brilliant review for the Czar of Russia at Longchamps, with straight lines of blue-coated, red-trousered infantry tipped by the wicked glitter of polished bayonets; the horse artillery with their clanking guns and the *cuirassiers* in shining breastplates and plumed helmets made his heart balloon with pride. While the sight of the black-draped statue of the lost city of Strasbourg in the Place de la Concorde filled him with overwhelming sadness.

Even at an early age he was upset by the loss of French prestige when the Government appeased England by giving in to her aggression at Fashoda. The disgraceful conviction of Captain Alfred Dreyfus as a spy, with its overtones of anti-Semitism, and the French generals' attempts to surpress the evidence which eventually cleared Dreyfus' name, made an impression on de Gaulle that he never forgot; for it was a stain on the honor of the Army of France.

✳ For all his love of Paris, de Gaulle has always liked country-living better. In summertime his whole family used to go to their family farm at La Ligerie in the valley of the Dordogne. One compartment of the train was filled to overflowing with de Gaulles. As they all piled out on the weed-grown platform of the little station, de Gaulle, clutching a History of France, would swing his prominent, sensitive beak to savor the lovely summer scents of herbage and plowland, blossoms and green leaves receiving and giving the benefice of the sun. Before he even unpacked he would be off careering over the familiar fields on his long stilt-like legs and jumping the little laughing brooks.

✳ The summer he was thirteen he organized the neighboring farmer boys into a troop of scouts—before Sir Baden Powell was heard of in France—and took them on a camping trip which was, in fact, a campaign. Though most of the boys were older than de Gaulle there was no question of who was in command, a thing made easier by the fact that he was already taller than most eighteen-year-olds. Their logistics were planned as carefully as an army's, their bivouacs were as orderly.

For amusement they divided into opposing armies and refought famous battles. Those that France had actually won, followed the facts; but historical accuracy suffered severely when a defeat like Agincourt was replayed, for de Gaulle, always commanding for France, revised the faulty strategy and won.

The campaign was brought to an untimely end when the farm boys were recalled to get in the harvest. It is probable that they found it a nice rest after campaigning under de Gaulle.

War and politics were far from being the only subjects of discussion in the de Gaulle's Paris household. Henri de Gaulle was an erudite, traditional gentleman with a scholar's high forehead and delicate aristocratic features. He was professor of philosophy, mathematics, and literature at the Jesuit College in the nearby Rue de Vaugirard. He ruled his family with what Madame Anthonioz describes as "austere tenderness," and imbued them all with a wide ranging appreciation of literature and philosophy. On holiday afternoons he often took them to the theatre to see the classic dramas of the Comédie Française, "Around the World in Eighty-Days," or the new tragedies in verse by Edmond Rostand. One of Charles de Gaulle's favorite plays was L'Aiglon, Rostand's romantic dramatization of the last days of Napoleon's son.

The de Gaulles read the plays of Shakespeare, Goethe, and the German poets, in French translations. They could get into exciting family arguments about the science-fiction of Jules Verne or the philosophy of Friedrich Nietzsche or Henri Bergson. The latter was a friend of the de Gaulle family and sometimes came to their apartment. The realism of Bergson's method of reasoning appealed to Charles' logical mind and he was one of two men who have profoundly influenced de

Gaulle's personal philosophy. The other, much later, was André Malraux.

His family say that Charles was the most argumentative of them all, an eager but contrary student, at one moment shy and silent; and the next ready to do battle. He learned best what he taught himself; and any proposition which appeared illogical to him would be dismissed with his favorite expression, "It's absurd!"

He might have applied that phrase to his own appearance in those days, and perhaps mentally did so, for he has a keen sense of the ridiculous. He grew so tall so fast that his sleeves and trousers could never quite close the gap, and his nose grew fastest of all. He had golden brown hair, a long, thin face, and pale blue eyes that could look as dull as a duck pond on a foggy day or blaze like the blue flame of the arc lights on the Champs-Élysées.

De Gaulle has often been accused of having no sense of humor. "If he could laugh," someone has said, "he would be a really great man."

Actually, in his teens, he loved to work up elaborate practical jokes and laughed uproariously when someone fell into one of his booby traps. He could even laugh at himself in the days before it became a kind of *lese majesté* to do so.

Now, he seldom laughs but often smiles, with that small, subtle twitch of his lips; and his humor is refined to the biting phrases by which he strips the pompous of pretense. Recently one of his aides, harassed by a typical bureaucratic snafu, muttered, "Death to all fools!"

Dead-pan de Gaulle remarked, "What a vast program!"

Except for a particularly pious moment when seven-year-old de Gaulle toyed briefly with the notion of being a missionary in some French colony, there was never any doubt in his mind as to his career. From the time he entered Stanislas College, he was pointed for St. Cyr, the West Point of France. His father, now prefect of students, was, of course, delighted by his choice. Indeed, all the de Gaulle boys became officers in the French Army, although Charles was the only career soldier.

One of de Gaulle's classmates in school was a stocky brown-eyed boy with a shock of thick, dark hair, in whom the flame of patriotism burned as brightly even as in him. His name was Georges Guynemer. Though their contrasting physiques made them look like all the long-and-short-of-it cartoons, their spirits were in accord.

At Stanislas, de Gaulle did well though not brilliantly. His best education was always self-administered. One lesson he taught himself well. It was a quotation from a book written by his uncle, Charles de Gaulle, called *The Awakening of a Race:*

"In a camp surprised by a night attack, when everyone fights alone against the enemy, no one asks the rank of him who first raises the flag and gives the first call to rally . . ."

Young de Gaulle copied the quotation in his note book and remembered it until the day when it became exquisitely appropriate.

If de Gaulle did only well at Stanislas, well was good enough. For in the strange malaise which seems to affect the French people just before every great war, the Army had become very unpopular. This was due in part to the Dreyfus scandal and the abortive attempt of General Boulanger to establish a military dictatorship; and in part to easy times and high living. As a result, the number of applicants for St. Cyr had dropped from over 2,000 in the nineties to only about 700 in 1909.

That year de Gaulle was graduated from school and accepted by St. Cyr. But first, according to a sensible rule just promulgated by the Army, he had to do one year of military service in the ranks. He was mustered into the Thirty-third Regiment of Infantry stationed at Arras. This chance appointment also had a profound effect in shaping his life.

✣ ✤ ✣

CHAPTER THREE

DE GAULLE AND PÉTAIN

T HE Thirty-third Infantry was a proud regiment with the resounding names of Austerlitz, Wagram, and Moscow on its battle flags. Stationed at Arras, the ancient capital of Artois on the Scarpe River, it was quartered in a particularly ugly, brick barracks. The prison-like structures surrounded a long, narrow parade ground whose only adornment was a tall, thin flagpole.

De Gaulle was issued the heavy, dark-blue tail coat, baggy, red trousers and forage cap of a *poilu,* and assigned to the Ninth Company commanded by a Captain Tugny, who had not the slightest prevision that a reflected gleam of immortality would thereby touch him.

In fact, Captain Tugny acquired a certain distant dislike for his tall, ungainly recruit. Aside from the fact that de Gaulle, sticking up from the ranks like that flagpole, ruined the symmetry of the company on parade, he was undeniably sloppy. In a hurry to get on with his military education, he was impatient with routine and spit and polish, of which he only later realized the value. His precociously developed sense of destiny always gave him a feeling that rules were for other people. This made him a prickly sort of private to have under one's command. Later, one of his superiors characterized him as "the most undisciplined man in the Army."

However, de Gaulle did get along very well with the tough young sons of miners and farmers who were the conscript bulk of the regiment. While breaking the bread of comradeship with them he carefully studied their likes and dislikes, especially their gripes against the Army. Later he remembered and applied those lessons well.

Though the history of the regiment was proud, its morale was low. The malaise affecting the top brass in Paris seeped all the way down, as it always does. This distressed de Gaulle, who organized a series of impromptu lectures on his favorite topics—the glories of France and the value of "the military spirit, the art of soldiers, and their virtues, which are part of the capital of humankind." The amazing thing is that he induced quite a few of his comrades to listen to him.

Meanwhile, he continued his self-education in the fine library in the ancient Abbaye de Saint-Waast, rich in books and manuscripts collected by generations of monks. Along the banks of the Scarpe he studied the terrain of the famous siege of Arras in 1654 and mentally corrected the strategic errors of those great opposing captains, the Prince de Condé and the Vicomte de Turenne.

De Gaulle took no more kindly to the rather primitive instructions in military science than he had taken to the formal teaching at Stanislas. Outmoded regulations enraged him. So did foolish orders. "Absurd!" he muttered. His attitude endeared him neither to his drill masters nor his officers.

As a result, when his year of service was ended he was still a private. When asked why he had not promoted de Gaulle, Captain Tugny remarked, "Do you want me to make a sergeant of a boy who would only feel at ease as Constable of France?"

When de Gaulle entered it in 1910, the Special Military School at St. Cyr was an unexpectedly gracious military academy, quite unlike the forbidding, medieval crenelations and gloomy mountains of West Point. It stood at the end of the

[27]

cobbled main street of the village of St. Cyr, which was only about eighteen miles from Paris. The entrance was through an intricate, wrought-iron gate, over which Napoleon's eagle spread its wings. Yellow-gray, seventeenth-century buildings with gracefully arched windows and mansard roofs, surmounted by a multitude of chimney pots, surrounded a series of grassy courtyards in which grew tall, old trees with widespread branches. The main barracks of the *Cours Napoléon,* facing south, had on its wall a giant sundial surmounted by the Imperial Arms. In front of it stood a statue of the Emperor in his famous frog-tailed uniform.

The chapel, where de Gaulle spent a good deal of time, soared tall and narrow at the edge of an escarpment which looked over the lovely, lush, French fields to the dark and gentle forest of Versailles.

The Germans spitefully bombed this pleasant place to pieces in World War II.

The atmosphere of vanished glories and present military honor raised de Gaulle's patriotic fervor to incandescence. To his love of France was added a passion for the Army, for which he had, in truth, a vocation in the religious sense of the word. Such flaming idealism made him dreadfully vulnerable in future days when its honor appeared compromised.

However, he did not like routine military studies any better at St. Cyr than he had at Arras. One of his biographers, Gaston Bonheur, calls him "a student without a master."

The fact is de Gaulle knew that the tactics and maneuvers so dear to the old men were designed for other times and other wars. In particular, he was being taught to fight the Franco-Prussian War all over again. An example of rigid thinking came when he talked about the possible use of the airplane in war. The commandant dismissed that foolish idea with the comment, "They are all right for sport. For the Army, zero!"

However, de Gaulle did make a serious effort to get good marks. He intended to rank in the upper third of his class so that he might have the privilege of choosing his outfit when he was graduated. This was not too difficult, since his phenomenal memory enabled him to record a printed page on his brain simply by reading it once. Even today, he writes his speeches out carefully, then abandons the manuscript and talks them, word for word, without notes.

No longer was he sloppy in appearance, though he could not help looking odd. In his full-dress uniform, with its plumed helmet, he looked as tall and thin as a steel windmill. His great jutting nose might almost have been a wind vane. There being nothing else to do about that nose, he made fun of it. His most popular performance was reciting Cyrano de Bergerac's famous "nose speech" to his own outsize proboscis.

He also enjoyed amateur theatricals and contributed some corny comedies of his own authorship to the gaiety of the Saint-Cyrians. A surviving program of one of their plays depicts him in a tattered frock coat, loud, striped trousers, and a Mad Hatter's stovepipe. He is listed as M. Salhuile (Mr. Dirty Oil).

In spite of his enthusiastic, if dubious, dramatics, de Gaulle was not especially popular at St. Cyr. He was strangely shy, and over-compensated with the coldness which became a habit, and later a deliberate method. His classmates called him the tall asparagus, and Le Grand Coq; and even ruder names.

But he grappled a few friends to his soul, among them Jacques de Sièyes, with whom he often sat on the grass of the courts and passed the long, summer evenings talking about past and future battles and the philosophy of leadership.

Another close friend was brilliant, carefree Alphonse Juin, a short, pink-cheeked, blue-eyed boy with enormous energy, who was graduated first in the class. Juin attained scholastic distinction so effortlessly that he had plenty of time left over for deviltry. He and de Gaulle were famous hell-raisers, with their outrageous practical jokes and their rowdy singing and shouting on the special train that left the Gare Montparnasse in Paris every Sunday night for St. Cyr.

On Saturdays the cadets were allowed to go to Paris for the week-end, and that train back was especially dear to Saint-Cyrians. In their memories it stood for the carefree comradeship of youth, the place where they were all exhuberantly free together before military discipline clamped down as they passed through Napoleon's gates.

"See you at the station!" they would shout on Saturday as they scattered to their homes. And on Sunday, as they gathered from all quarters of city, they greeted each other as boisterously as though they had been separated for months instead of hours. Many of them remember de Gaulle dashing through the station with his long legs flying, shouting to his friends as he made the train with a shaved second to spare.

In 1912, de Gaulle was graduated from St. Cyr in the upper third of his class, as he had planned. Rejecting the more glamorous cavalry, he chose to return to the Thirty-third Infantry. A new colonel had taken command. As soon as he was settled in his small room, which promised the luxury of solitude after the noisy dormitories he had occupied there and at St. Cyr, young de Gaulle, full of ardor and prompted by courtesy, "put on his clean white gloves" and went to call on his commanding officer.

At his knock the door swung open, revealing a slender man with a hawk nose, nesting in a bushy military mustache, and fierce dark eyes. "The Colonel is not receiving," said Colonel Philippe Pétain. And slammed the door.

Thus began the curiously intricate relationship between Charles de Gaulle and Philippe Pétain, which might have been predestined by the Greek god of tragedy.

Their next encounter was hardly more fortunate. On the fourteenth of July de Gaulle was leading his platoon in the Bastille Day parade in Arras. One can imagine his happy pride as he strode along in his new, blue, dress uniform, knee-length, blue, frock coat with its single epaulette and its double-row of shiny buttons, his plumed kepi and his glittering sword carried at exactly the correct angle, followed by the long, straight lines of his well-drilled men.

Colonel Pétain, mounted on a glossy charger, came trotting along the column, sharply peering at the swinging ranks for any possible faults. Some impulse made him cut sharply across the line of march and de Gaulle's platoon marched into him. As he tried to straighten out the humiliating tangle, de Gaulle heard the Colonel roar, "Lieutenant de Gaulle, you are confined to quarters for eight days."

For once it is doubtful that de Gaulle enjoyed solitude. Added to the agony of having looked a fool before the whole regiment was a burning sense of injustice.

However, he received word the following Sunday morning that the Colonel had rescinded his arrest. He made a mad dash for the Paris train and flung himself into a compartment. In it sat Colonel Pétain, his eyes snapping with amusement. "Well, young man, you didn't think you'd catch this train," he said.

"On the contrary, *mon Colonel*," said de Gaulle cooly, "I was sure of it."

"How could you be?"

"Because my punishment was unfair, and I knew that the Colonel was a just man."

So began their friendship.

Friendship has a firm foundation in mutual respect, and a meeting of minds. Pétain liked his young lieutenant for his youthful ardor and quick grasp of military principles. De Gaulle responded with a kind of hero-worship of the older man of whom he later wrote: "From him I learned the principles of leadership . . ."

In their off-duty walks along the river bank they talked as equals, and, even in public, de Gaulle sometimes challenged his senior's opinions. On one occasion Pétain, lecturing a group of officers on the famous Siege of Arras, criticized the Prince de Condé for not having followed up an advantage. De Gaulle impetuously interrupted him, saying: "But Turenne might have cut him off. The Prince was right not to risk it. After all he saved Arras."

Instead of pulling rank, Pétain applauded this sortie, and when the lecture was over he took de Gaulle affectionately by the arm and walked out with him.

In fact, at this time Pétain had a very flexible mind, and was far ahead of the thinking of the generals in Paris. He told his officers that, "The General Staff assures us that nothing can resist a bayonet charge. But today it is fire power that kills, and this fact must be the basis of all our tactics."

De Gaulle was in complete agreement with this doctrine. For the primitive machine guns of the Franco-Prussian War were now highly developed instruments of death and, to his mind, spelled the doom of massed bayonet charges.

Despite his questing mind and advanced thinking, Pétain was apparently nearing the end of his military career. An announcement came through that he was to be made a Commander of the Legion of Honor. All his officers gathered in the big, echoing assembly room of the barracks for the ceremony. But they were not elated. Everyone of them knew that the decoration was the kiss of death often awarded as a sop to officers who were to be passed over for promotion. "Now he'll never make general," they told each other; and stood in disconsolate groups wondering how to phrase their congratulations without irony; for they were very fond of their commander.

They need not have bothered. Pétain stormed into the room, and before anyone could open his mouth, said abruptly, "Messieurs, I thank you. They have not done me justice!"

❧ ⚜ ❧

THE GREAT WAR

ORLD WAR I was a revolution, as de Gaulle truly called it—a revolution in the lives of all mankind and, especially, a revolution in military science. It started with a kind of febrile gaiety. As the great modern German armies gathered on her frontiers in August, 1914, France threw off the lethargy of the "sick peace." Her people united with an ardor worthy of her greatest days. The mobilization of millions of men was accomplished with hardly a hitch. Where the authorities expected a 13 per cent rate of slackers, the actual rate was only 1-1/2 per cent. Recruiting offices were stormed by eager volunteers.

The troops paraded to the trains under a deluge of flowers like the Battle of Roses of Nice. Laughter and song were more frequent than tears, while soldiers and civilians alike shouted "Revenge at last! On to Berlin!"

In mid-August, 1914, from the Vosges Mountains and the plateau of Lorrain to the country of the Meuse and the plains of Charleroi, 1,200,000 French went into action with superb élan. Their general orders were, "Forward, to hurl the enemy back wherever he is found!" That proud advance was brutally smashed in three bloody days.

[33]

What happened to the grand strategy is graphically depicted in miniature by de Gaulle's personal experience. We know exactly what it was like because he described it himself.

On August 15, 1914, the Thirty-third Infantry of the Second Division went into action near Dinant. Like the lead soldiers of his childhood days, de Gaulle's men were still brilliantly uniformed in their baggy, red trousers and long, blue coats, intolerably heavy under the August sun. Leaving the road along which they had been slogging, they were deployed in the flat, open fields. At the word of command the long, knife-like bayonets were fixed. Trumpets sounded their clear, heart-lifting call; big battle flags whipped in the wind, and the whole, bright, steel-tipped line ran forward. It was a magnificent spectacle, like Austerlitz, and Solferino, and Gettysburg and all those other battles long ago.

De Gaulle, long-striding ahead of his company, knew one high moment of elation. But there was something wrong with the picture. No massed ranks of enemy troops were waiting for the shock. He was charging across an apparently empty field toward mole tracks of fresh-turned earth stretching endlessly to right and left.

Bullets began to whistle past, rare at first, almost hesitant then multiplying. Suddenly the enemy fire became adjusted, concentrated. The hail of bullets, the thunder of bursting shells grew to a tremendous raging storm that scythed down those close ranks of men. By habit, de Gaulle's brave young farmers and miners went on, leaving behind the still and writhing bodies, doubtly pathetic in their gay uniforms, until the tempest became too great for any habit or courage or discipline to breast, and the ones who were left dropped on their faces and sought shelter among the heaps of dead and wounded.

De Gaulle wrote, "In the twinkling of an eye it appeared that all the virtue in the world could not prevail against fire power."

He had been one of the first to fall.

De Gaulle's summation of his personal experience is

typical: "No doubt histories . . . may give an appearance of logic to a thousand confused events. But the actors at the moment had but a single thought, 'It's absurd!' "

From his hospital bed he followed on the maps the German armies' advance to the Marne and the dramatic victory by which old, white-mustached Marshal Joffre stopped them and hurled them back. It was a tremendous credit to the French Army that, after the terrible shock of arms which had brought them from the flush of confidence to the verge of disaster, their discipline and morale enabled them to retreat, reform and fight again, victoriously.

Of Marshal Joffre, de Gaulle wrote: "It was the good fortune of France that Joffre, having engaged the sword badly, did not lose his equilibrium. He had formerly believed in the doctrine of the military schools. . . . But, discerning that his only recourse lay in himself, he freed himself from theories and confronted events with his powerful personality."

By the time de Gaulle recovered from his wound, the French —and the Germans, too—were learning to fight a modern war. The long lines of trenches, foul as open sewers, extended from Switzerland to the sea. In them the war of movement completely bogged down. No longer did the Thirty-third wear their comic-opera uniforms. Instead they were clothed in an inconspicuous shade called "horizon blue," which soon became muddy brown. There were no more brilliant battle scenes, no banners, and no trumpets; only the mud and the lairs in which men lived and died like animals. In 1915, 1,350,000 Frenchmen were killed or wounded. But the French *poilu,* his pride and confidence restored by the victory of the Marne, fought on grimly, muttering his new slogan, *"On les aura!"*—"We'll get them!"

Captain de Gaulle rejoined the Thirty-third as adjutant. He is said to have memorized every name in the muster role of the regiment. It was now commanded by Lieutenant Colonel Boudhors, a thin, scholarly man who was brave without bravado and as indulgent with his men as he was severe with himself. An immediate friendship sprang up between de Gaulle and his new colonel, who many years later said, "As for me, I have been a Gaullist since 1915."

That was a lucky year for de Gaulle. He was merely blown up by a mine at Mesnil-les-Hurles. He survived. All his brothers were now serving in the French Army, and his father had rejoined as a major in the Transport Corps. They too survived.

By the time de Gaulle recovered from his second wound, the most frightful carnage in all history was taking place around Verdun, where the army of German Crown Prince Frederick William was trying to break the hinge of the whole French line by sheer weight of numbers. General Pétain commanded the citadel, and his troops proudly boasted, "They shall not pass!" As de Gaulle wrote later, "On the day they had to choose between ruin and reason, Pétain was promoted . . ."

On his return to duty, de Gaulle was given command of the Tenth Company. Shortly afterward, in February, 1916, the Thirty-third was ordered to relieve the regiment holding Fort Douamont, the most exposed position in the lines defending Verdun. A liaison officer must go ahead. Colonel Boudhors recorded that, "In view of the gravity of the situation and the importance of the mission, I thought that only Captain de Gaulle could fill it. . . . Due to him everything went well, and if the thirty-third was splendid at Douamont, it was due less to its colonel than the clairvoyance of the captain of the Tenth Company."

The Thirty-third arrived at Verdun in motor trucks on the eve of the Crown Prince's desperate effort to take Forts Douamont and Vaux. De Gaulle immediately resumed command of his Company and led them into the lines in the shattered forest on a hillside between Douamont and Vaux. They had forty-eight hours to settle in before the storm broke.

It began with the frightful classic barrage that always preceded an attack. For hours on end great guns and small poured out such a torrent of shells that the sick ground heaved and spewed its entrails into the air, while the blinded, deafened *poilus* waited between life and death for the blow that would annihilate them. Then, behind a rolling curtain of fire, the gray-green hordes stumbled through the smoke and dust, appearing among the broken trees as vague, terrible wraiths of the forest. De Gaulle recognized French helmets and for an instant was fooled into thinking them reinforcements. But the Germans were wearing helmets taken from the dead of Douamont.

In seconds the enemy was crashing through the forest on all sides and behind them. De Gaulle realized they were surrounded. It was swords and bayonets now, and short-fused grenades, elemental combat and no room to shoot. De Gaulle rallied a handful of men and led a charge to break out of the enemy ring. A bayonet pierced his thigh and the battle swept over him.

When he came to his senses, de Gaulle was being carefully carried to the rear of the German lines. He grimaced with irony as he recognized one of the solicitous stretcher bearers as the man behind the bayonet.

In absentia, in a German prison, de Gaulle was made a Chevalier of the Legion of Honor, with this citation:

"The Captain de Gaulle . . . who had a reputation for his high intellectual and morale value, when his batallion suffered a fearful bombardment and was decimated and surrounded on all sides, led his company in a furious assault and ferocious hand-to-hand fighting. This was the only solution he judged compatible with his sense of military honor. He fell in the melée. An officer without peer in all respects.

"Philippe Pétain
"General Commanding."

Naturally, de Gaulle was a most intractable prisoner and a nasty problem to a whole series of German Kommandants. He made five attempts to escape as he was shuttled around Germany to five different prisons. From the emergency dressing station near Verdun, he was sent in a hospital train across Germany to the prison hospital at Friedberg. There the excellent German doctors patched him up so well that he was equal to his first break for freedom. He got through the barbed wire around the hospital, only to be pulled down by police dogs.

His next stop was at Roseberg, where he spent long hours secretly making himself an imitation German uniform. It was a remarkably poor fit. The sleeves hit a little below his elbows and the trousers flew at half-calf. In this comic costume he was easily recognized, and captured.

Each time de Gaulle was caught, he was thrown into solitary confinement. Cramped in a small cell, solitude brought not solace but black despair.

From Roseberg he was transferred for a while to Sczuczyn, near the Polish Border. Fifty officers were lodged in the dusty loft of a granary whose lower floor was jammed with hundreds of Russian prisoners. There he met small, wiry Louis Parent, whose life later became linked with his.

Apparently he did not remain at Sczuczyn long enough to formulate a plan of escape, for his next attempt took place at the fortress castle of Magdebourg. One of his cellmates was Roland Garros, the famous French aviator, who proved to be a most stimulating companion. Garros and de Gaulle conceived a plan to tunnel out through the solid rock. By day they loafed and slept, by night they dug like moles with improvised tools and the added hazard of having to conceal the debris of their labors.

The work had to be done in utter silence, but the loafing included long and interesting conversation in which de Gaulle added to his military education all Garros knew about the use of aircraft in war. He became familiar with the names and characteristics of the latest fighters and bombers, which seemed so terrifying then and look so toylike now. French Spads, and Nieuports and Farmans were compared with German Fokkers and Gothas, or British Camels and de Havilands, and all their possible uses were explored, though neither Garros nor de Gaulle, at that time, envisaged aircraft as anything but auxiliaries, certainly not as a decisive instrument of war.

Thus de Gaulle received knowledge of immense value by this close association with Garros, though its immediate object was frustrated by the discovery of the tunnel long before it

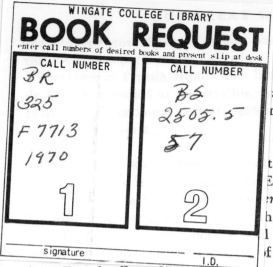
A R

...ely decided to break up ...shipped off to Kavalier- ...eventually escaped, and ...as sent to Fort IX (Re- ...n at Ingolstadt, on the

...t famous of the German ...English as "The Escapers' ...rge de la Fille de l'Air." ...h, were ringed by a moat, ...l and yet another moat. ...f its erection, ill-omened for a French officer—1870.

De Gaulle's arrival caused a minor riot. As he entered the inner courtyard the international crowd of officer-prisoners, French, English, Russian, Italian, and Belgian, poured out of the casemates and, following their tradition, formed a double line of honor, cheering and shouting, "Have you anything to hide? You will be searched. Throw it to us!"

The guards yelled harshly, *"Raus! Raus!* Break it up!"

A Sergeant came raging out, ordering everybody to attention. He was greeted by hoots and catcalls, and ironic shouts of, "On to Verdun! On to Verdun! Slacker!"

Pale with fury, the sergeant drew his revolver and pointed it at de Gaulle's middle. Towering over the German, de Gaulle walked steadily toward him with a half smile, saying softly, *"On les aura!"*

De Gaulle was delighted to find one old friend in his dormitory-cell—Louis Parent, from Szczuczyn. Parent described the life in Fort IX:

There were ten men in our room, which was about forty feet long by ten feet wide, in a casemate of the fort. On one side were two barred windows looking over the moat. There was always a sentry under the windows. We had camp cots, a few

[39]

naked electric light bulbs and a little coal stove to cook on. We were allowed five kilos of coal a week; it was very cold.

The Germans gave us very little food—soup with a few grains of meat in it. Once every ten days we got a ration of meat. We lived on packages of food sent us by our families through the Red Cross.

One time someone sent us a bear's foot. That was good. We ate it marinated and also had a little joke on the Germans which de Gaulle thoroughly enjoyed. We told them it was a man's foot. Somehow the story got back to England and Winston Churchill rose in the House of Commons to accuse the Germans of making their prisoners eat human feet.

Parent says that de Gaulle was very temperamental. When the black mood was on him he might remain icily aloof for days without speaking to anyone. At other times he talked so brilliantly that all the prisoners gathered around to hear him interpret the military situation, reading between the line of the German Communiques to sift the truth from their distortions.

At other times he lectured on past battles; analyzing them to learn where the great offensives designed to break the stalemate of trench warfare had failed. Of Verdun he said, "They shall not pass! They shall not pass because they did not pass. Not that Verdun was impregnable; but the weak point of the German offensive, like our own, was that it wasted itself in attacks without result. Had they had the means for a complete breakthrough, we would have been in a bad spot."

When he learned of the success of the British tank attack at Cambrai, de Gaulle was tremendously excited. He recognized the potential of armored vehicles far more completely than he did that of aircraft; which was true of his thinking even in World War II. "The instrument for the breakthrough is found," he said. "A war of maneuver becomes possible again." And he added, "On the ground and in the air, as on the sea, war will become a function of the motor . . ."

Despite his moodiness, perhaps even because his aloofness gave him prestige, de Gaulle was much respected at Fort IX, where he was nicknamed "The Commodore." French Air Force General de Goÿs, himself a forceful character with a bold nose, black mustache, and dark, piercing eyes, says, "The escapers were in a sense a picked group, the incorrigible élite of all the allied armies. In that milieu de Gaulle was the most difficult prisoner, in spite of his youth. There were generals, colonels, majors, of all arms and armies, many of them older than he, yet he imposed himself upon us by the force of his temperament, his intelligence and his character. Though I was forty and he but twenty-seven, I often came to consult him about my problems.

"In return I was able to do something for him. I had concealed on me a phial of yellow powder, which, if you swallowed it, turned your skin yellow. Then you could report sick and go to the hospital from which there was a better chance of escaping. One day de Gaulle came to me and said, 'Give me a chance to escape, too. Give me some of your yellow powder.' "

General de Goÿs obliged him, and de Gaulle swallowed a good dose. Cavernous from prison diet, with his skin bright yellow, de Gaulle must have been a frightening spectacle. The Germans hurried him to the hospital from which he duly escaped. That time he got almost to the Swiss Border before he was recognized and captured.

Parent remembers his return to the cell. Standing in the doorway, very tall and woebegone, de Gaulle said, "Voilà! This is most unfortunate for me. I am too tall."

De Gaulle did not give up—he is not easily dissuaded. He made another abortive jail-break from Fort IX, this time only getting as far as the station. But he did carry out a successful minor operation. The personal possessions of the prisoners were taken from them and kept on a safe in the Kommandant's office. De Gaulle organized a group of a dozen fellow officers to go to the office and demand their things back. Poor Kommandant Hirsch was a rather weak character, all pompous front but with little guts. The prisoners practically surrounded him, all talking at once very rapidly and very angrily, and paying no attention to Hirsch's expostulatory bellows. When he finally called guards to clear the room, the safe had mysteriously disappeared.

De Gaulle was a prisoner of war for thirty-two months. "Those years in prison were a great privilege in the life of my uncle, for they gave him time for reflection," said Madame Geneviève de Gaulle Anthonioz. She did not speak ignorantly, for in World War II she was a heroine of the Resistance and a prisoner in the concentration camp at Ravensbrück.

"There are many elements in the formation of a man's character," she continued. "One of the most important is trial by fire. That was de Gaulle's trial by fire, his forty days in the wilderness. Before that time he was always tense and active, never relaxed. His wounds and his imprisonment were heavy trials for him. But it was most important. It was then that he began to think and to write. When he was released, he had written a good part of his first two books."

It is a striking thing how many of those who have become leaders of their fellow men in thought or action, for good or evil, have ripened to maturity in an enforced period of inactivity. From Homer's blindness, Cervantes' imprisonment, and Voltaire's exile, what great works sprang. And in more modern times certainly Ghandi's incarceration, Winston Churchill's enforced retirement from politics, and Franklin Roosevelt's polio were essential influence on character. On another side, Karl Marx, Lenin, and Hitler all perfected their evil genius in prison.

So it was with de Gaulle, who, like him or not, has surely played a supreme role in his country's history.

As the long years passed and "hope only lived on credit," his health suffered severely but his intellect blazed more brightly. Luckily, though their bodies were starved, the prisoners were allowed to nourish their minds with all the books available in the excellent German public libraries to which they sent their orders each week.

There were many brilliant men among the "incorrigible élite" to help sharpen de Gaulle's mind. Among them Berger-

Levrault, who became a leading publisher; Rémy Roure, the brilliant journalist of *Figaro;* George Catroux, later to have a great career as general, diplomat, and cabinet minister; a very young and very brilliant Cossack, a second lieutenant named Tukhachevsky, who was both an avid listener to de Gaulle's impromptu lectures and a stimulating opponent in argument.

During his final year of imprisonment, de Gaulle devoted himself to a concentrated study of German psychology through the writings of their philosophers and the history of their leaders. His knowledge of the German language, already good, became excellent.

His studies resulted in his book *Discord among the Enemy,* published after the war, in which he analyzed the reasons for the German defeat at the Marne. He argued that it was due to the Nietzschean complex of the German generals, each of whom regarded himself as a superman. Thus, in an army noted for its blind obedience, the generals refused to obey orders and follow the battle plan. Each army commander recognized only his own ambition. This produced a race for glory in which the different army corps plunged forward instead of supporting each other, thereby opening the gaps in the line through which Joffre struck victoriously.

De Gaulle also made a careful study of the German newspapers. Mindful of the relationship between war and politics, he was able to estimate from their tone the strains on the German people. He watched the cracks widening in the monolithic façade of the State, and was able to predict the ultimate Allied victory by these evidences of "discord among the enemy."

But even as hope grew stronger, he suffered one more severe blow. In an old French paper, he read of the death of his boyhood friend, George Guynemer, who had written his name in glory on the skies of France with the smoke and fire of enemy planes shot down. When de Gaulle thought of the chubby little boy who had become France's greatest ace, he put down the paper and wept.

Tukhachevsky found him thus and asked, "Are you sad because of the lost war?"

De Gaulle rose angrily, "But we've won! Already the war is won."

"I mean because it is lost to us, because we are not in it."

De Gaulle acknowledged that this was one reason for his melancholy.

"Cheer up," said Tukhachevsky. "In the future there'll be another war for us."

❧ ⚜ ❧

POST-GRADUATE COURSE IN WAR

IN DECEMBER, 1918, de Gaulle came home to his father's apartment on the Place Saint-François-Xavier. He was skeletal in appearance and weak from semi-starvation, but his superb constitution was unimpaired. In his boyhood room with its wrought-iron balcony he rested his body and healed his soul.

While the great men of the era, Woodrow Wilson, Lloyd George, and the French "Tiger" Clemenceau, with their distinguished advisers, argued about peace and the League of Nations, which would preserve it forever, de Gaulle spent his time reading and thinking and talking about philosophy and history with his father; clarifying his ideas for the books he planned to write.

All the de Gaulles had returned safely from the war. There is a picture of the four brothers, taken at the time of Xavier's wedding. They are extremely smart and dashing in their horizon-blue uniforms and gleaming boots, and their identical, clipped, military mustaches. They all look young and gay, as was fitting on such a festive occasion, with the exception of Charles, whose thin face seems prematurely melancholy.

Though in that euphoric era peace seemed assured for his

time, de Gaulle had no intention of giving up the Army. One of the things that troubled him was that imprisonment had deprived him of experience in the later, more modern techniques of war, maneuvering infantry with supporting tanks, and the tremendous, rapid advances of the final days of victory. A soldier must know all there is to know about fighting, and since a long peace appeared in prospect for France, he determined to seek that lost experience in foreign wars. His curious —and some think, egotistical—sense of destiny assured him that the knowledge would come in handy some day. He wrote: "I was convinced that France would have to go through gigantic trials, that my interest in life consisted in one day rendering her some signal service; and that I would have the occasion to do so."

For a young man looking for a fight there were still opportunities despite, or because of, the efforts of the statesmen walking on the grand terrace at Versailles while the fountains played and the Germans dejectedly signed on the dotted line. For one thing, the huge, inchoate, revolutionary army of Bolshevic Russia was attacking Poland, which had just been restored to nationhood. That afforded an opportunity both idealistic and educational.

De Gaulle got in touch with General Joseph Haller, who was recruiting and training volunteers in France for an expeditionary force to help defend Poland. He was welcomed with enthusiasm and on May 19, 1919 he reported at Sillé-le-Guillaume as a captain in the Fifth Division of Polish Chasseurs.

About a month later Haller's little army started on the long train trip across Germany. It was a weary journey, due to the disorganization of the Reich's railroads. De Gaulle found it infinitely depressing to look upon the gray face of a defeated nation. Poland, despite her mortal danger, was exhilerating by contrast, brave people looking hopefully toward the future.

The Fifth Polish *Chasseurs* detrained at Novo-Georgiewsk just in time to take part in the operations around Volhynie. It was very educational. Polish Marshal Joseph Pilsudski conducted a campaign in high style that gave the Red offensive a very bloody nose.

The Bear withdrew to lick his wounds and that great peace-maker, Russian winter, imposed his icy truce. De Gaulle returned to Paris on leave.

When the ice thawed on the Vistula, the tide of war rolled in again. This time a great Russian offensive drove to the suburbs of Warsaw. Hastily, France dispatched a military mission under her most brilliant young general, Maxime Weygand, who had been Generalissimo Ferdinand Foch's Chief of Staff. De Gaulle hurried back to the wars, and received command of a mixed force of tanks and infantry.

The Polish plains were ideally suited to mechanized warfare as was sadly demonstrated some nineteen years later. They presented a rare opportunity for de Gaulle to experiment with his unorthodox theories, correct errors, and develop new techniques. He may be said to have earned his degree in the school of the great offensive by which Marshal Pilsudski, under Weygand's tutelage, broke the Russian front and hurled the red tide back in rout.

De Gaulle's handling of his mixed force was so spectacular that it won a citation from General Weygand and the Cross of St. Wencelas from a grateful Poland. It also won him a professorship at the new Polish School of War at Remberton outside of Warsaw. In a former camp of the Imperial Russian Guard, de Gaulle lectured to all ranks of Polish officers, post-graduate students of the art of war.

In the Polish campaign the reckless use of coincidence, which dramatizes de Gaulle's life story in a way no serious writer of fiction would dare to perpetrate, appears again. Weygand, who gave him that war citation, was, like Pétain in 1940, one of the architects of the surrender of France, so bitterly opposed by de Gaulle. In addition, the commander of the huge, defeated, Russian Army, at twenty-eight the youngest general in the Russian service, probably the youngest army commander in the world, was a former Cossack lieutenant named Tukhachevsky.

[47]

The *Salon d'Automne* was quite a contrast to the bleak Polish plains. All fashionable Paris was there, drinking tea and looking at the strange pictures by the mad modern painters. Even their names seemed odd—Braque, Raoul Dufy, Rouault, and a joker named Pablo Picasso. But some people said they were the coming men.

De Gaulle did not care for the paintings—his inclination in everything but war was conventional. But he did like the looks of a slim, willowy girl with dark hair and wonderful gray eyes who was sitting with her parents at one side of the room. In the crush for tea at the buffet, he encountered one of those useful young men who know everybody. "Who is that charming young girl sitting by the wall over there?" he asked.

The young man flicked his eyes, avoiding a stare with practiced politeness, and said, "That is my cousin, Mademoiselle Yvonne Vendroux of Charleville. Would you like to be presented to her?"

De Gaulle said that it would be agreeable to him, and carrying their tea cups, the two young men moved across the room animatedly discussing the pictures to maintain the pleasant fiction of a completely casual approach. De Gaulle was presented to Monsieur and Madame Vendroux and then to their daughter. Not unintentionally he found himself sitting next to Mademoiselle Vendroux. Conversation was a trifle difficult. She was a shy girl, very prim and proper—*bien élevée,* the French would say.

De Gaulle was also very shy in society and more than a little awkward. He was sitting in one of those rickety folding chairs apparently essential to the enjoyment of art, with his kepi balanced one one bony knee and his tea cup on the other and his mind at dead center, responding in monosyllables to the attempts of the older Vendrouxs at conversation. Things might never had gone any further than that.

Napoleon once said, "Give me lucky generals!" De Gaulle has always been that, perhaps never more so than when a sudden nervous movement tilted his tea cup and sent it sliding off his knee. As the tea splashed over Yvonne Vendroux's dress, he looked so gawky and so horrified she burst out laughing. She was very pretty when she laughed.

What could a polite young man do but buy a bouquet and call on the Vendrouxs the next day at their hotel. He was far more at ease and interesting in a small salon with two or three people than in a social mob. The Vendrouxs began to like him; even his shyness was an asset in their eyes after the impolite boldness of the post-war young. Yvonne found him charming. It is quite likely that she perceived, under his intellectual assurance, his carefully concealed vulnerability.

The call resulted in an invitation to stay at *Septfontaines*, the Vendrouxs' magnificent estate in the rugged Ardennes Mountains. De Gaulle undoubtedly enjoyed himself, hunting with Yvonne's two brothers in the splendidly wild, sweet-smelling forest. Until his eyesight failed him nearly forty years later, never if he could help it did he miss *la grande battue des sangliers*, the great hunt of the wild boars, at *Septfontaines*.

He also enjoyed talking with Yvonne in the evenings when the whole family sat around one of the great fireplaces that warmed the chateau. In her own home her timidity disappeared. She unaffectedly enjoyed de Gaulle's discourses on history and philosophy. The word discourse is carefully chosen, for even by a fireside he was more apt to lecture than to converse. But Yvonne's ardent young mind found it a relief from hunting talk and social chatter. Even then she listened very well.

So their courtship began, although the story of their meeting, often repeated, may be apocryphal. Of course, nothing would have come of it had it not been a very suitable match, since all concerned were *bien élevés*. The Vendrouxs were rich biscuit manufacturers from Calais, a typical bourgeois family attached to the land and *"la vie économique."* They owned a town house in Calais as well as the country place. De Gaulle was comparatively poor but very well born indeed. All the parents beamed. De Gaulle was very much in love. So was Yvonne.

One did not have much chance to be alone with a girl in

France in those days; the dance floor was almost the only place. De Gaulle planned his campaign as carefully as though it were a military operation, though one wonders if he had the same confidence in its success that he did when the factors were such computable things as manpower, logistics, terrain, and fire-power.

In any event he invited Yvonne to the Polytechnic Ball in Paris. It is said to have been during the sixth dance that, waltzing with her rather stiffly, de Gaulle, very formally, asked Yvonne to be his wife. Very formally, for she was still extremely shy (*timide,* as her people would say), Yvonne said that she would.

They were married in the church of Notre Dame de Calais on April 7, 1921. Their's was the best kind of love, founded on tenderness, trust and admiration. In the extraordinary, difficult, cruel, and glorious vicissitudes of their existence, it never wavered or diminished. There have been only two women in de Gaulle's life—his mother and his wife.

❧ ⚜ ❧

FROM MAYENCE TO COLOMBEY

NO MAN WHO REACHES the pinnacle of life ever stops learning, for to do so is to lag behind the stream of time. The decade of the twenties was a continuous, if less exciting, period of education for de Gaulle. He began it by teaching the cadets of St. Cyr, and there is no better way of learning than teaching.

It was in October, 1921, that he became professor of history at his alma mater. On this subject he was that rarest of pedagogues, an inspired teacher. For not only was his style of lecturing clear and lighted by the gift of phrase, but he identified himself so completely with the ancient glories of France that when he described events a millennium or five centuries past it was as though his pupils were listening to an eyewitness account in all its exciting immediacy.

One may imagine him beginning with a phrase like the opening sentences of his book, *France and Her Army:* "France was made by sword thrusts. Our fathers entered History with the blade of Brennus." If that would not stir aspiring young soldiers, nothing would.

Meanwhile de Gaulle was preparing himself for the Superior School of War, the equivalent of the U. S. Army's General Staff

School. He was ordered there in November, 1922, for the two years' course. As usual he gave his masters a most unhappy time. One of them said, "He has the attitude of a king in exile." Of them all it is probable that the commandant, Colonel Moyrand, had the most embarrassing experience.

At the School of War, following hallowed military tradition, they were teaching the students to fight the last war. To de Gaulle it seemed that it was repugnant to French military minds to take an empirical view of strategy. They were forever trying to work out a formula applicable to all situations. In the pause between world wars this was known to its adherents as "The Method a Priori." It might more aptly have been called, "The Method of Verdun."

"The Method," as it was called for short, envisaged assuming a strong position, setting up fields of fire and waiting for attack, confident that the fire-power of automatic weapons had given the defense an enormous advantage.

De Gaulle thought that, "A belief that one is capable of evading the perils of surprise . . . produces an illusion of power which neglects the mystery of the unknown." He called it "a fatal exaggeration." In prison and in Poland he had already developed an empirical theory of war based on the necessity of suiting action to the prevailing conditions without preconceived ideas. He called it, "The Method of Circumstance."

Virtually his entire two years at the School of War was spent in a running debate with his superiors on the virtues of the two methods. It did not endear de Gaulle to them. Even his colleagues regarded him as a very queer fish. According to de Gaulle's favorite biographer, Georges Cattaui, they experienced a sense of inquietude in his presence. "They obscurely sensed in him many things that were out of the ordinary, they suspected him, envied him and admired him." But they did not like this aloof man "who desired to enclose himself in the silence of a trappist monk," and when he spoke was arrogantly terse.

Of course, in order to graduate at all, de Gaulle had to make formal obeisance to the theory he was being taught, but he did no more than enough to obtain what he called with his small smile, his "sacrament."

Colonel Moyrand was a dedicated disciple of "The Method." This inevitably led to some sharp disagreements with "The Intractable." Nevertheless, he had a sneaking admiration for de Gaulle's brilliance. In fact, he considered it enough worthwhile to give him a sharp lesson. For this reason, in the war games in the summer of de Gaulle's final year, Colonel Moyrand gave him command of the "Blue Army," taking command of the "Reds" himself.

The "campaign" was waged in the foothills of the Alps near Grenoble. The Colonel established his "army" in a carefully prepared position, emplaced his artillery, entrenched his infantry, and laid out fields of fire.

Meanwhile de Gaulle threw out scouting parties which probed the "enemy" position for a possible weakness. When they had reported, he went into action. Throwing conventional tactics to the winds and emitting orders like a machine gun, he sent his astounded regiments careering all over the declivitous countryside, swarming up impossible mountains, sneaking up gullies, feinting and withdrawing until suddenly he snapped the trap, catching the Colonel flat-footed and putting him in the bag.

Colonel Moyrand was apoplectic at what he bitterly called de Gaulle's "unfair tactics." When his torrent of acrimonious expostulation ceased for lack of breath, de Gaulle, dead pan and solemn, said, "But I won."

The argument, continuing after their return to the School of War, spread upward through the echelons until it reached the Chief of Staff. That gentleman decided to get to the bottom of it, and on a tour of inspection, stopped at the School of War. There he arranged a sort of hearing in which the opponents argued their case all over again. When the debate was ended, Chief of Staff Marshal Pétain rendered the verdict: "De Gaulle is right."

But in winning, de Gaulle had lost. Instead of being

sent to the General Staff in Paris, as graduates of the School of War customarily were, he was ordered to the staff of the Army of the Rhine at Mayence, which amounted to a reprimand. On his record Colonel Moyrand wrote: "His spirit is most indocile." This was indubitably true, but in a peacetime army, it was a very black mark indeed.

However it did not distress de Gaulle unduly. At Mayence he was able to pursue his studies in German psychology at first hand. What did disturb him very much indeed was to discover that the French Army appeared to be forgetting its victory, and the Germans their defeat. "As for me," he wrote, "I shall not cease to prepare myself."

De Gaulle was not only dedicated to the Army, but he was extremely ambitious. For a young officer who wanted to make a name for himself in peacetime, the pen was literally mightier than the sword. This much at least had the French Army progressed since the days when Marshal MacMahon had threatened to wipe off the promotion list any officers who wrote a book.

In de Gaulle's first published book, *Discord Among the Enemy*, he explained the German defeat at the Marne, and analyzed the insistence of Admiral Von Tirpitz on unrestricted submarine warfare which had brought the United States into the war with fatal results for Germany. He also went into the final discord in the German High Command in 1918, which had resulted in "the sudden collapse of a people both strong and valiant," who had withstood the heavy burdens of war with "such fortitude, endurance, and capacity for suffering as to command the admiration even of their enemies."

As opposed to the disastrous struggle of German supermen for pre-eminence, de Gaulle wrote, "In a French Garden, no tree tries to smother the others with its shade, the flower beds accommodate themselves to geometric design, and the pool is not ambitious to be a waterfall . . . A noble melancholy pervades all. Perhaps this comes from the idea that each isolated element can shine the better . . ." This would appear to be an over-idealistic simile for the French military hierarchy.

Since there was nothing controversial in this book as far as the French Army was concerned, it won de Gaulle considerable kudos among his superiors. Marshal Pétain, who was now vice-President of the Supreme Council of War, hauled him out of obscurity in the Army of the Rhine to a position on his personal staff where he was charged with making studies for a history of the French Army under the direction of Pétain, himself. This research later formed the basis of de Gaulle's book, *France and Her Army*.

In his little office at 4 *bis* Boulevard des Invalides, de Gaulle's light burned late as he worked on another proposal of the High Command. This was a project for fortifying the Franco-German Frontier. In an article in the *Revue Militaire Française*, December 1, 1925, he wrote, "The map of France reveals her fortune . . ." He pointed out that the Northeast Frontier was not a frontier at all but "a terrible breach" between German territory and the rich valleys of France where, "geography itself organizes the invasion by multiple routes: the valleys of the Meuse, the Sambre, the Escaut and the Scarpe where all the rivers, roads and rails offer guides to the enemy . . ."

De Gaulle proposed fortified strong points at strategic positions, as Louis XIV's great engineer, Vauban, had fortified them 250 years before. His article was very highly thought of by the General Staff and was used as an argument when Painlevé and Maginot built the Maginot Line in which France put her trust in 1940. Fatally, the Maginot Line stopped at the most vulnerable point, the Belgian Frontier.

De Gaulle himself became uneasy at the success of his article, and in January, 1926, pointed out that though permanent defenses were useful, the plan of operations should *not* be purely defensive, but should be left to the commander in the field.

In 1927, Pétain asked de Gaulle to lecture on his ideas at the School of War. On the day of the first lecture the assembly room was full to bursting as de Gaulle, accompanied by Pétain in all his medals and gold-braided insignia of a Marshal of France, mounted the platform. Beside Pétain, de Gaulle looked very young and awkward with his gangling frame, elongated neck and unruly blond hair. But in spite of this and the meager distinction of his rank, those who were there say that he was enhaloed by authority.

Marshal Pétain spoke first with a prevision that the acid years have turned to irony: "Listen, Gentlemen, to Captain de Gaulle," he said. "Listen to him well!" The myth-makers have, since then, added words Pétain did not say: "For the day will come when a grateful France will call upon him."

Abruptly de Gaulle began: "The manner of war, Gentlemen, has essentially returned to the character of contingency . . ."

His lecture was on leadership and his ideal chief was, in fact, a Gaullist. These young soldiers schooled in discipline, listened silently and amazed as he told them, "Those who accomplish great things often pass beyond the appearances of a false discipline. After the naval Battle of Jutland, where British Admiral Jellicoe lost the opportunity to destroy the German Grand Fleet, Lord Fisher, First Lord of the Admiralty, said, 'He has all the qualities of Nelson except one—he does not know when to disobey.' "

One is struck by a certain inconsistency here. *Discord Among the Enemy* showed how the German generals got into trouble by flouting orders. The key must lie in knowing *when* to disobey. De Gaulle always thought he knew the right moment.

After repeating his course of lectures at the Sorbonne, de Gaulle was promoted to major and given command of the Nineteenth Batallion of *Chasseurs* of the Army of the Rhine at Trèves. This violated the traditions that the Chasseurs were always commanded by one of their own. Explaining this reversal, General Matter, Director of Infantry, observed, "We are dealing with a future generalissimo of the French Army."

Despite his difficulties with his superiors, de Gaulle always got along well with his men—of course, they offered him no competition. He genuinely loved and looked after them with all the devotion with which he performed every military duty.

During the bad winter of 1928-29, the Army of the Rhine had an epidemic of influenza. It was a pretty mess, with morale dropping toward zero, as young Frenchmen died by hundreds. However, an investigating committee from the Chamber of Deputies found the Nineteenth Chasseurs in good shape. The rank and file were not ungrateful to their commander. Unofficially they made him an honorary *Chasseur*.

"The Army of the Rhine will not last long," de Gaulle said in 1929 . . . "It appears that Anschluss (the return of the Rhineland to Germany) is near. Then Germany will take back, by force or by agreement, her territories which were given to Poland. After which she will reclaim Alsace from us. That seems to me to be written in the sky."

At a time when Germany was still disarmed and Hitler no more than a crazy demagogue, this sky writing was illegible to most Frenchmen. In any event France was sliding into the same apathy which preceded World War I. The beginning of the Maginot Line—in the Vosges Mountains, where it was least needed—satisfied the materialistic-pacifistic philosophy of a people who, dreaming no more of greatness, were willing to settle for pseudo-security.

After two quiet years of command on the banks of the Moselle, de Gaulle was delighted to be assigned to the Staff of the Army of the Levant. He had a presentiment that some day he would need a detailed knowledge of this part of the world. However, he did not think much of the French Colonial system. To his mind it did not penetrate below the surface of an ancient people and an ancient way of life, and therefore would be as evanescent as wind ripples on the desert sand.

The Arabs, he thought, would never be satisfied with any imposed system or any alien authority, though they would always submit temporarily to superior force. "We should either arrive (at something great) or get out of here," de Gaulle said. And added, "I think there is one man, and only one, who understands Syria and what we should do here. It is Colonel (Georges) Catroux. That is why he has left."

During the nearly two years of his assignment in Beirut,

[57]

de Gaulle made a point of touring all the adjacent territories. Yvonne de Gaulle accompanied him on most of these trips, for she loved to travel. They visited Damascus, Aleppo, Palestine, and Egypt. De Gaulle went as no ordinary tourist but as a student of their particular economies, problems, and terrain; and, especially, of their people, so passive in apparent acceptance of their fate; so turbulent beneath that calm appearance.

Not that he neglected the great landmarks of normal tourism. As devout a Catholic as ever, he was moved unutterably by the sacred shrines of the Holy Land, confirming his faith with the sense they gave him of the very presence of Jesus, Who seemed to have been there so short a time before.

To a man with his strong feeling for history, secular landmarks also had a strong emotional appeal. His favorite was, perhaps, the *Krak des Chevaliers,* that tremendous medieval granite fortress built by the French Knights of St. John of Jerusalem in the fourteenth century. Other places that stirred historical memories were Acre, where Richard of the Lion Heart won—after all he *was* French, though King of England— and Damietta where St. Louis lost half his gallant French Army.

As de Gaulle examined the walls of Jerusalem he saw in his mind's eye the catapults, wooden towers, and scaling ladders crowded by men in armor blazoned by the Crusaders' Cross, and Godfrey de Bouillon leaping alone to the parapet.

The Pyramids, no doubt, reminded him less of Cheops than of Napoleon raising the ardor of his victorious army, that was yet doomed by British sea power, with his famous phrase "Forty centuries of history look down upon you." Nor is there much doubt that de Gaulle's strong streak of realism appraised the Napoleonic adventure as a romantic aberration which failed to reckon with the hard facts of logistics.

In fact, each place he visited and every facet of this tumultuous land of empty deserts and crowded cities impressed upon de Gaulle the brief tenure of western conquest, and laid the foundation of his belief that it could only be held by free association backed by mutual economic interests. That is the logical background of his "illogical" attitude toward the French colonies in Asia Minor and Africa.

The de Gaulles returned to France in 1932. The next few years were probably the happiest of their lives. De Gaulle is not a man who expects happiness, or seeks it, or even wants it very much. In a list of his goals it would occupy the bottom line. Nevertheless, a brief span of it was granted him by circumstances.

Yvonne de Gaulle had followed her husband's fortunes through all his assignments. They had lived in a barracks at Mayence, a little apartment in Paris, barracks again at Trèves and a white Moorish villa in Beirut.

There were three children now, Elizabeth, Phillipe—named for Marshal Pétain—and Anne. Somehow the de Gaulles managed to maintain a close family relationship, a true home, throughout their kaleidoscopic changes of residence. Like the atmosphere of his father's home, de Gaulle's household was austere but tender. One might suppose that his strong young son would be the favorite child of a soldier so conscious of his name and ancestry. But it was little Anne, an invalid almost all of her short life, whom de Gaulle loved best. With her he was all tenderness.

On their return from Syria, the de Gaulles lived in an apartment in the Hôtel Lutétia, on the Boulevard Raspail. It was in the heart of old Paris on the Left Bank, close to the place where he had grown up, and convenient to the Ministry of War. No doubt they could have afforded more luxurious quarters but it suited their way of life very well.

Neither of them cared for entertaining, except for family gatherings. The "Great World," as the French call society, bored them. It is also true that they bored the Great World. Recalling the occasion of one of the few social dinners that the de Gaulles attended in this period, Count Alexandre de Saint-Phalle said, "My wife and I decided that de Gaulle was the dullest dinner companion we had ever met."

At a considerably later date Saint-Phalle realized that this

[59]

was because the social chatter at the table had simply reduced de Gaulle's active brain to a comatose condition.

Though the apartment on the Boulevard Raspail suited the de Gaulles well enough as a temporary residence, they both felt that it was time to put down some roots. They loved going to Yvonne's family home in the Ardennes, where de Gaulle enjoyed the hunting in the fall and long solitary walks in the forest at all seasons. So they began to look for a country house. They were agreed that it should not be in a gentle, smiling countryside, but in some rough and lonely place.

After considering several places none of which seemed quite right, in 1936, they bought an estate called *La Boisserie* at Colombey-les-Deux Eglises in the province of Haut-Marne. It was on the edge of the Champagne district of Lorraine about 150 miles from Paris.

La Boisserie was a small, ancient manor house containing about a dozen rooms. The façade was severely simple. At one end was a square tower with a pointed roof where de Gaulle had his study. There were at first few modern conveniences, which troubled the de Gaulles not at all; and a great loneliness which they loved.

De Gaulle's own description of it throws a shaft of light on the inner man he so carefully conceals. "It is my home," he wrote. "This part of Champagne is impregnated with calm; vast and sad horizons; nearby woods, cultivated fields, and melancholy wasteland; in the distance stand the ancient mountains, time-worn and resigned . . . (My house) is situated high on a plateau marked by a wooded hill where it passes the centuries amid the lands cultivated by their inhabitants. Though I am careful not to impose myself on them, they surround me with a discreet friendship. I know their families; I esteem them and I love them.

"Silence fills my house. From the tower . . . I look westward for a distance of fifteen kilometers without seeing a single building. Beyond the plain and the woods my eyes follow the long descending slopes of the Valley of the Aube and rise again to the hills beyond. From one high place in my garden, I look on the savage deeps where the forest envelops the place like the sea beating against a promontory . . . meanwhile in the little park, the trees are almost always green and when the flowers planted by my wife fade, they are soon reborn.

"When I walk in one of the neighboring forests, Les Dhuits, Clairvaux, Le Heu or La Chapelle, their somber depths submerge me in sadness, but suddenly the song of a bird, the sunlight on the foliage or the burgeoning of a copse remind me that life, wherever it appears, fights a battle it has never lost . . ."

Deep were the roots de Gaulle put down, but not so deep that he hesitated for an instant to tear them up when exile became the path of honor.

CHAPTER SEVEN

"THE ARMY OF THE FUTURE"

On his return from Syria in 1932, Major de Gaulle had been appointed Secretary General of the Supreme Council of National Defense. This was the strongest key post a man of his rank could attain, for he was in a position to pass on the agenda of the meetings of the council, and organize the material upon which their decisions were based. His appointment was evidence of the respect in which his intellect was held by the top brass, and the continued confidence of Marshal Pétain. It was, in fact, the high tide of their friendship.

That same year de Gaulle published his second book, *Le Fil de l'Epée* (The Edge of the Sword), which he dedicated to Pétain. It was a disquisition on the techniques of military leadership and the qualities necessary to a chief. The book was written in a style that was at once highly intellectual, (with quotations ranging from Socrates to Anatole France) romantically idealistic, and very practical. In other words it was pure de Gaulle.

"The great warriors," he wrote, "have always been conscious of the role and value of instinct. Alexander called it his 'hope', Caesar his 'luck' and Napoleon his 'star'; was it not simply their certainty of a particular gift which . . . put them sufficiently *en rapport* with the realities to dominate them? (They) gave an impression of a natural force which could command events. As Flaubert said of the young Hannibal, he was already clothed in 'the indefinable splendor of those who are destined for great enterprises.' "

Reading between the lines, one can see that de Gaulle proposed to clothe himself in these same garments, and he frankly describes how it is done. "One must assure oneself of (prestige)," he wrote, "or at least develop it. . . . First of all there is no prestige without mystery . . . It is necessary that in the projects, the method, and the spirit an element must reside which others cannot understand and which intrigues them. Certainly it is not done by shutting oneself in an ivory tower inaccessible to subordinates. On the contrary, empire over souls requires that they see you, and that each one thinks himself seen by you. But one must maintain a reserve, keep a secret surprise. . . .

"Nothing heightens authority more than silence. . . . To speak is always to delay thought, weaken ardor; in short to disperse oneself when action requires concentration . . . Evangelical perfection does not lead to empire. The man of action can do nothing without a strong dose of egotism, pride, endurance, and guile . . . but he must use them to realize great things . . ."

In his recipe for military greatness, de Gaulle insists that the soldier should not use his power to overthrow the State, nor should the politician interfere in generalship. Either brings disaster, as it did at last to Napoleon: "After Austerlitz comes Waterloo."

"Reserve, character, greatness, these conditions of prestige, impose an effort that repels most people . . . and produces what Faguet calls, 'The misery of great men' . . ."

De Gaulle likewise admits that persons who assume these characteristics are uncomfortable to have around in peacetime. They are bound to be unpopular and this, too, adds to their loneliness.

It is different in time of war. "In action no more censors!

[63]

All hopes, all wills orient themselves toward (the Chief) as the iron to the magnet. When the crisis comes, it is he whom they follow . . . Reciprocally, the trust of the lowly exalts a man of character . . ."

In writing of a leader's loneliness de Gaulle spoke from personal experience. Indeed, the picture of a great man which emerges from de Gaulle's book, with all its hauteur, reserve, and craft, together with a high sense of integrity and honor and the emphasis on the chief's function of inspiring the mass of his people to their utmost heights of endeavor, might be called, "Self Portrait."

In an era when the atmosphere of France was so pacifistic that "soldier" was almost a dirty word, de Gaulle's paean to military glory was unlikely to be a best seller. Bonheur describes its reception as "like a yawn in the bedchamber at the hour of the siesta."

Behind the dingy door of his little office in a long corridor of the Ministry of War, de Gaulle was already thinking hard about another book which had a far greater impact, though regrettably not in France. It was called *Vers l'Armée de Métier, (Toward a Professional Army),* which was published in English as, *The Army of the Future.*

Though de Gaulle wrote the book himself, as its trenchant style clearly shows (he modeled his literary methods on Victor Hugo's maxim, "Concision in style, precision in thought, decision in life"), it was partly conceived by a sort of brain trust which he gathered around him. They were Lieutenant Colonel Emile Mayer (retired) who had been a friend of Taine and a comrade of Joffre and Foch; and whose age had only sharpened the edge of his mind; Rémy Roure, a veteran of Fort IX, now a leading journalist on the great paper *Le Temps;* Mayer's son-in-law, M. Grunebaum-Ballin, who had a finger in every political pie; Publisher Berger-Levrault, also lately of Fort IX, and another journalist, Lucien Nachin.

This little group met every Monday evening at the Brasserie Dumesnil, a bistro on the corner of the Boulevard Montpar-

De Gaulle as a boy. © S.C.A. Courtesy, French Embassy Information Div.

As a cadet at St. Cyr. © S.C.A. Courtesy, French Embassy Information Div.

The house in Lille where de Gaulle was born. © Voix du Nord. Courtesy, French Embassy Information Div.

St. Cyr before its destruction by the Germans in World War II. *Courtesy, Fren* *Press and Information Service.*

Captain de Gaulle in 1915.
© *S.C.A. Courtesy, French* *Embassy Information Div.*

De Gaulle as a tank officer in 1940. *Courte* *French Embassy Information Div.*

nasse and the Rue de Rennes. Sitting under the glaring lights on banquettes and cane-bottomed chairs at their favorite corner table, they talked gravely of their fears for the French Army chained to the immense concrete works of the Maginot Line and immobilized by the mentality of Verdun.

Often they were joined by various generals, colonels, philosophers and journalists who came to listen to the brilliant talk and contribute fresh ideas. On the anvil of that table covered with red-checkered tablecloth, bottles of wine and mineral water, and the excellent inexpensive food, the form of the "Army of the Future" was hammered out.

Back in his office, at a desk covered with models of tanks, mobile guns, troop-carriers and other motor-driven accessories of military might, de Gaulle worked out the organization of the Armored Corps. He pondered the philosophy of its reason for being and its strategic use on long nocturnal walks through Paris in whose deserted, shadowy streets he found the solitude he always needed for reflection.

The premise which gave the book its French title was that the techniques of handling complex mechanical equipment could not be taught to conscripts in a couple of years. Both the Navy and the Air Force were manned by technicians who made careers in them. It was only logical that to handle its complex new weapons, the Army, too, must have a group of career soldiers, with all the knowledge, ability, and *esprit de corps* that comes to a permanent military organization.

The book was a plea for a motorized armored corps manned by 100,000 professional soldiers, forming a mobile striking force to back up France's fortifications and her mass conscript army; and to carry the war to the enemy if need be. With the Maginot Line as her shield, the motorized army would be the sword of France.

As de Gaulle pointed out, if her army could not move from behind the Maginot Line, France was valueless as an ally to the smaller nations like Belgium, Poland, and Czechoslovakia, who relied upon her for support. If they were attacked all the French Army could do was to sit in their monstrous underground fortresses, helplessly whirling the turrets in which their magnificent cannon were rooted to earth, glaring at the enemy.

De Gaulle worked out in meticulous detail the components of his mobile army—the exact number of tanks, motorized infantry, artillery, heavy and light, anti-aircraft guns, communication sections, tactical air support, photo reconnaissance, etc., etc. In doing so he drew on his immense historical knowledge and made special studies of every modern development. Most important of all, he illumined it by his imaginative forecast of the strategy and tactics of a truly modern war.

No one will claim that de Gaulle was the only person thinking along these lines. Colonel George Smith Patton, Jr., U.S.A., had similar ideas, so did General J. F. C. Fuller in England, General Giulio Drouchet in Italy and General Hans von Seeckt in Germany—especially von Seeckt. But no one else had thought it through so thoroughly. *Vers l'Armée de Métier* was, in fact, not only a brilliant argument for such an army, but a complete manual of its composition and use in war.

The book was published in 1934. In France it sold 750 copies at fifteen cents apiece. But in Germany it sold 7,000 copies and became required reading for the German General Staff, who even had it read aloud to Hitler. When German General Heinz Guderian formed the First Panzer Army its composition followed de Gaulle's specification almost exactly. As one disgusted French general remarked the day after the Fall of France, "The Germans bought victory for fifteen cents."

While he worked on his book de Gaulle, of course, was carrying out his regular military duties. These included what he called "weaving the Penelope web" of a plan for the industrial mobilization of France. Convinced that modern war required a total national effort, de Gaulle made careful studies of other nations' plans for industrial mobilization and discovered that his own country was lagging far behind in this field. His blueprint for remedying this situation was finally passed, in somewhat truncated form, by the National Assembly in 1936, under the spur of Germany's aggressive rearmament under Hitler.

Another project on which de Gaulle worked was the composition of an international army, which M. Paul-Boncour proposed in Geneva in 1932 for the League of Nations. Needless to say, it would have been a highly mobile modern force like de Gaulle's theoretical Army of the Future. Naturally nothing came of it.

De Gaulle was on the Staff of the Secretary General of the Supreme Council of the National Defense for five years (1932-1937) under *fourteen* French governments. It was disheartening work. His research on industrial mobilization showed him the great resources of the nation, and the feeble will of the politicians to use them. De Gaulle recognized that it was not altogether their fault. It was not that they lacked intelligence or patriotism—some of them, he says, were "men of incontestable value and great talent." But hardly would a premier take office when everybody, including his own party and his own cabinet, would begin conspiring against him. His short time in office would be occupied by a political high-wire act that everyone knew could not last. With such rapid shifts of government a continuous military policy was impossible.

Meanwhile, Hitler came to power and, in October, 1933, broke with the League of Nations and began a tremendous drive to rearm Germany. His plan for creating armored divisions became known to French Intelligence in November, 1934. It was sheer agony to de Gaulle to watch helplessly, "the enemy of tomorrow endowing himself with the means of victory while France was still without them."

It was then that de Gaulle entered politics, by the back door so to speak. With his circle of the Brasserie Dumesnil, he determined to make a drive to have the French National Assembly adopt his plan for the Army of the Future. He knew he was putting his long neck out, for the Army would not look kindly on an officer who went over the heads of the General Staff to civilian authority.

De Gaulle's first step was to enlist journalistic allies. This was successful. Perhaps the strongest of them was André Pirroneau of the *Echo de Paris,* but many others joined in. The next move was to secure a political sponsor. Paul Reynaud seemed the logical choice. A paradox among aging French politicians, he was a man with "his future before him"; a man with an open inquiring mind.

The contact was made early in 1935, and de Gaulle called on Reynaud in his office at 5 Place du Palais Bourbon behind the Chamber of Deputies. He found Reynaud seated behind a big table-desk covered with African sculpture which he collected. The deputy was a short, squat man with a dark olive skin and a vaguely oriental tilt to his eyes. With him was his intelligent young assistant, Gaston Palewski. The tall soldier and the little statesman felt an immediate bond between them. Reynaud had read de Gaulle's book, and was intensely interested. Furthermore, he was deeply concerned for the safety of France.

That first talk was followed by many others. Reynaud was willing to propose the plan in the Chamber, even though he knew he would be sticking his short neck out. But he said, "I must have ammunition." De Gaulle supplied him with plenty of that.

On March 15, 1935, Reynaud launched the plan which might have saved France and, indeed, avoided World War II, in an emotional but lucid oration in the chamber of Deputies. De Gaulle, sitting in the visitors' gallery, was filled with admiration for the brilliance with which the dynamic little deputy expounded his ideas. "Let us make a hypothesis there is a war tomorrow and Belgium is invaded," Reynaud said; and his dark eyes snapped as he added, "That is not without precedent.

"If we have not the means to give her help immediately in covering her eastern frontier, what will happen? It is possible that the thing will happen, which has happened before. It is possible that her army will be thrown back to the sea.

"For us that would mean 350 kilometers of open frontier on the north for France to defend. Is there anyone here who will accept in advance the thought of seeing the richest provinces of France again invaded and torn from our country?"

Then clearly and concisely he showed how a mobile armored army of 100,000 men at comparatively little cost, would alleviate the peril. At the end of his speech Reynaud said very solemnly and with a prescience that even he could not know: "If we do not have this armored corps, all is lost."

Naturally the whole idea was far too sensible to arouse the enthusiasm of the politicians. It is hard to blame them. The plan was loaded with political dynamite. For in suggesting a professional army, even part of an army, it challenged the ideal of the citizen-soldier dear to the hearts of French liberals ever since the French Revolution and the great days of General Hoche's victories over the professional armies of all the kings and emperors of Europe's old regime.

But in the end it was not the politicians who killed the new army, but the generals. They were shocked, embarrassed, and horrified. They rushed into print with categorical contradictions of de Gaulle's theories. General M. E. Debeney stated unequivocally that the great battle would take place in the northeast on the Maginot Line and the problem was simply to defend. General Weygand in the *Revue des Deux Mondes* argued that the plan would divide the Army into two parts and added: "Two armies—not on your life!" As for the offensive function, Weygand said, "We already have a mechanized, motorized, and mounted reserve. There is nothing to create; everything exists."

A whole series of Army-inspired articles, whose titles explain themselves, ran in *Le Figaro*: "Tanks are not Invincible;" "The Weakness of Tanks;" "Where Politicians Go Wrong."

While conservatives raved, the Socialists were even more agonized. Their idea was that aggressive Germany might go in for Panzer armies, but peaceful France had no need of offensive forces. They seemed afraid that if they had them, they might be tempted to use them. Léon Blum, later the Popular Front Premier, wrote, "Down with the Professional Army!"

Marshal Pétain decided to have his say. He said it in a preface to General Chauvineau's book, *Is An Invasion Still Possible*. The Marshal stated with all the weight of his authority and the conviction of his experience that tanks and aircraft did not change the basic factors of warfare and that the security of France lay in a continuous front buttressed by impregnable strong points. In an historical paradox it could be said that France lost World War II because the Germans did not pass at Verdun.

In 1936, Hitler sent his new army marching into the Rhineland. Under the Treaty of Versailles this part of Germany west of the Rhine had been demilitarized. The German move broke their treaty obligations. It was at once a defiance and a test of allied resolution. The French Government was for fighting. Appeasement-minded British Prime Minister Stanley Baldwin urged caution.

At a dinner of Veterans of Fort IX, Maitre Louis Parent saw his old comrade, Lieutenant Colonel de Gaulle. "What do you think?" he asked.

"All the information we have indicates that Hitler is bluffing," de Gaulle answered. "In spite of England's fears we should march in and throw them back across the Rhine!"

For a fact, as we know now from captured German documents, it was a desperate bluff. Hitler planned to shoot himself if the French marched. As Louis Parent says, "It was our last chance."

Hitler's move, which brought Strasbourg once more within range of German guns, sent a shock wave through complacent France. De Gaulle considered it the one good thing from a bad situation. As the politicians scurried around impelled by the national concern for defense, he had hopes of getting the Reynaud bill, which had lain in committee for over a year, to the floor of the Chamber. Lieutenant Colonel Mayer took him to see the new Popular Front Premier, Léon Blum. The meeting took place in the big, ornate office of the Premiers of France in the Hotel Matignon, the magnificent, wall-enclosed palace of Prince de Talleyrand, on the very day in October, 1936, that King Leopold of Belgium denounced the treaty of alliance with France, giving as his reason that France was powerless to help his country. "In practice," the King said, "given what modern mechanized forces are capable of doing, we would be alone in any case."

Under this shock, Blum was extremely cordial, and spoke of his great interest in de Gaulle's ideas.

De Gaulle, remembering *Down with the Professional Army*, said, "And yet you opposed them."

Blum acknowledged the hit with a smile, "One sees things differently when one becomes head of a government," he said.

Then they talked about the possibility that Hitler would march on Vienna, Prague, or Warsaw. "What do you think will happen in that case?" Blum asked.

"It's very simple," de Gaulle said ironically. "We'll mobilize. Then, peering between our battlements, we shall watch the enslavement of Europe."

"Does that mean you think we should send an expeditionary force to Austria, or Bohemia, or Poland?" Blum asked sharply.

"No," said de Gaulle. "But if the Wehrmacht advances along the Danube or the Elbe, why shouldn't we go to the Rhine? While it's deploying on the Vistula, we could take the Ruhr. In any event, the mere fact that we *could* do so would probably prevent these acts of aggression. But our present system forbids us to stir. The armored corps, on the contrary, would incline us to do so . . ."

Blum agreed that it would be terrible if France's allies were overrun, but he argued that Hitler could not hold his conquests unless France were crushed. "How would he manage that?" Blum demanded. "Even you must admit that though our system is badly adapted for attack it is excellent for defense."

"I cannot admit anything of the sort," de Gaulle replied. And he pointed out that the absence of mechanized force had just lost France the Belgian alliance.

"At least our defenses will protect our own country," the Premier argued.

"Nothing is less certain," said de Gaulle. "Even in World War I there were breakthroughs. Look at the progress made in tanks and aircraft since then. They can smash the line at any chosen point. Once through they can thrust far behind our lines with their fast-moving armor. If we also have armor we can repair the breach. If not all will be lost."

The interview, which was supposed to be for fifteen minutes, lasted three hours. Blum spoke of the great new credits which were going to be voted for defense.

"Yes," said de Gaulle disconsolately. "We are going to spend as much money as we need for an armored corps. But we won't have it."

"That is up to the War Department," Blum pointed out. "It is the affair of M. (Edouard) Daladier (Minister of War) and General (Maurice) Gamelin."

"Allow me to think," de Gaulle said stiffly, "that the national defense is the affair of the Government."

While they talked, the telephone had been ringing constantly —someone needed an O.K. for a paper, an important person who wanted a favor, a dozen small details of administration or politics.

As de Gaulle took his leave the telephone shrilled again. With infinite weariness Blum gestured toward it. "Do you think it is easy for the head of the Government to judge a complicated plan like yours, when he cannot have five minutes for consecutive thought?"

De Gaulle left him thus. In his heart was pity for the distracted man who was trying to do his best under an impossible system; but hope he had none.

As everybody had foreseen, Reynaud's bill to create a mechanized corps was voted down at the insistence of the General Staff. The fact is it never had a chance. As was also foreseen, de Gaulle's career was again damaged. Even before his last effort, at a meeting of the Supreme Council, Minister of

War General Maurin had said to him, "Goodbye, de Gaulle! Where I am there is no place for you!"

To his visitors Maurin fulminated, "De Gaulle's got himself a tame writer—Pirroneau—and a gramaphone—Reynaud. I shall send him to Corsica!"

As de Gaulle puts it, "While making the thunder rumble, General Maurin had the magnanimity not to launch the bolt." However de Gaulle's promotion to Colonel was held up. Meanwhile he attended the War College. Finally, in December, 1937, de Gaulle was promoted to colonel, over Chief of Staff General Gamelin's dead body, so to speak. The promotion was put through by the new Minister of War, Daladier, who though opposing de Gaulle's ideas, recognized his ability and integrity.

Colonel de Gaulle was given command of the new 507th Tank Regiment. If he could not have his armored corps, he was determined to have the best tank regiment in the French Army.

❧ ⚜ ❧

AGINCOURT TO THE SEA

THE FRENCH GENERALS derisively nicknamed de Gaulle "Colonel Motor." However, there was one thing that he put ahead of the internal combustion engine; that was morale. A way to inspire *esprit de corps* in an armored regiment was to personalize their tanks by giving them resounding names like warships; for to his mind they were the armored cruisers of the land. In choosing them he leaned heavily on British admiralty style nomenclature—*Typhoon, Tornado, Terrible....*

The christening ceremony on the parade ground at Metz was attended by the commanding officer of the division, Major General Henri Honoré Giraud, a fire-eating, hell-for-leather type whom de Gaulle admired for his dash if not for his political acumen.

After the tanks had been baptized in foaming champagne, came the review. The long line of polished monsters rumbled over the dusty plain, de Gaulle riding high in the turret of the lead tank. Above his head from the whipping radio mast flew the standard he had chosen for his regiment—the double-barred Cross of Lorraine.

It was not Franklin Roosevelt who first likened his difficult ally to Joan of Arc; it was de Gaulle himself. In an interview with Eric Hawkins of the *New York Herald-Tribune* in the black winter of 1940, he said, "I am like Joan of Arc." Adding with his little quarter smile, "Only *I* have no army."

As the Cross of Lorraine flying in the dusty sunshine at Metz showed, his identification with "the Maid" went far back of that. In fact, it went back to his childhood and his youth; and more recently to the small baroque church where at Mass every Sunday he and Yvonne sat, not in the front pew as was proper for the Squire of Colombey, but close under the stained glass window consecrated to St. Joan. Like Joan, he was mystically informed of the role he was to play.

Colombey was between Metz and Paris (it had been chosen partly for this reason), so Yvonne de Gaulle lived there most of the time her husband commanded the 507th. He was able to spend nearly every week-end in the home he loved so dearly; walking in the little park and his "somber forests;" writing in his tower study; enjoying the peaceful evenings with his children; and bringing his brothers and his mother there for the close family gatherings that were the only social occasions he really enjoyed.

These were precious days and he knew it; made more radiant by the fact that they would be so brief. For he was certain that beyond the mountains to the east forces were gathering fast that would bring her heaviest trial to France and tear the pleasant pattern of his life apart.

In 1938, de Gaulle published the last of his pre-war books, *La France et Son Armée*. It was a history of the French Army, its techniques, its glories, and its failures, written with the deep emotion of a passionate heart. His final apostrophe to the French people tells us still more of his own nature, and of the proud and terrible anxiety he felt for France:

> "Unhappy people, who carry the heavy burden of their sorrows for century after century without flinching. Ancient people, whom experience has not freed from their vices, but in whom the sap of new hopes forever rises. Strong people...

Ah! great people made for example, enterprise, and combat, always in the spearhead of History, whether as tyrant, victim, or champion; and whose genius, by turn negligent or very terrible, is faithfully reflected in the mirror of their army."

Lieutenant Colonel Mayer edited it, the last service he rendered his beloved younger friend. On the morning he finished revising the galley-proofs, Mayer wrote on his engagement pad, "Today. My death."

They found him at his desk with the last pages in his hand.

No book, however passionately inspired, could shake the French people from their torpor; not even the writing in the German sky of the Luftwaffe planes and the Panzer divisions in full panoply marching through the streets of Berlin and on to Vienna to force Anschluss (union with Austria) could do that. French politicians, even French generals, seemed like so many rabbits watching with dread fascination the snakes of German armored divisions coiling over Eastern Europe.

"Without surprise but not without pain," de Gaulle read of the weak-kneed surrender at Munich, the rape of Czechoslovakia and, finally, the Nazi attack on Poland in September, 1939. It was particularly agonizing to see the Panzer armies he had in a sense invented, slashing Poland to pieces. France and England, driven at last to the course of honor, declared war on Germany. But the French Army was stuck with its feet in Maginot concrete, and even England's oceans were but half held against the Nazi submarines.

De Gaulle believed that a French attack on the Ruhr was feasible while the Wehrmacht was busy in Poland. Instead he was not even allowed to keep his own armored regiment together. His tanks were parcelled out among infantry divisions.

That long winter of the phony war was one of discontent to de Gaulle. While most of the leading French statesmen and generals prophesied, not without satisfaction, a stalemate, de Gaulle thought it but a lull, while Germany gathered fearful force for the spring deluge. On January 26, 1940, he made one final effort to get attention for his views. He presented an elaborate secret memorandum to the eighty principal persons in the High Command and the Government, analyzing the German victory in Poland and discussing their intentions and capabilities. It was a dark picture which might yet be remedied if the High Command would gather its armor together in a striking force instead of dispersing it as adjuncts to the infantry.

As everyone knows, nothing much happened. Even so brilliant a journalist as M. Brisson, editor of *Figaro*, said to de Gaulle, "But don't you see, we have already won a bloodless Marne?"

On a visit to Paris de Gaulle dined in Paul Reynaud's apartment on the Rue de Rivoli with Léon Blum. "What's your prophecy?" Blum asked.

De Gaulle said, "The only question is whether the Germans will attack westward to take Paris or (in spite of their pact with Russia) strike eastward to take Moscow."

The two politicians whom de Gaulle respected most were simply incredulous.

However, two armored divisions had been formed in 1939; but even these were designed to act with the infantry. In his passion to get something done, de Gaulle paid a visit to Generalissimo Gamelin at his headquarters in the Chateau of Vincennes.

It was a curious atmosphere for the Commander-in-Chief of an Allied Army of some five million men. In a quiet setting which reminded de Gaulle of a monastery, the Generalissimo, looking like a faded photograph of a World War I general, was surrounded by a few staff officers. Actual command of the armies in the field was exercised by General Georges, while in his ivory tower at Vincennes, Gamelin lived a life of studious contemplation which gave de Gaulle "the impression of a savant testing in a laboratory the chemical reactions of his strategy."

The Generalissimo told him that two more armored divisions, the Third and Fourth, would be formed and said, "You will have the honor of commanding the Fourth Armored."

De Gaulle's immobile face flushed with pride at being chosen to command a division, though only a colonel. He thanked

[79]

Gamelin, who said, "I can understand your satisfaction. As for your misgivings, I don't believe they are justified."

Then with maps and intelligence reports Gamelin proved, to his own satisfaction, that the expected German attack would shatter itself against the concrete face of France.

But if the Commander-in-Chief was satisfied, the French people were not. As usual they expressed their apprehension by overturning the Government of Premier Daladier. On March 23, 1940, President Albert Lebrun asked Paul Reynaud to form a government. Reynaud sent for de Gaulle to help him write a policy statement to present to the Chamber of Deputies. De Gaulle drew up a short, clear statement which Reynaud accepted without change. Then he went to the Palais Bourbon to hear the new Premier's speech and the debate on confirming his government.

It was there, on that day, that de Gaulle was shocked into a distaste for parliamentary government—as opposed to the American presidential form—which has only been strengthened by his subsequent experiences in politics. Then he was still comparatively naive, an innocent idealist, half unwilling to believe the things he saw. As he walked through the marble corridors of that building dedicated to democratic ideals he heard the rustle of intrigue, whispers of defeatism, even treason.

The debate was appalling. With the nation in deadly peril, de Gaulle saw deputy after deputy rise, not to speak words of encouragement or even constructive criticism, but to whine about what they called the injuries done them by Reynaud's new coalition. Only Léon Blum, who had been offered no place in the cabinet, spoke with grandeur. Due to him, Reynaud's government was confirmed by a majority of one vote in over five hundred.

Afterward, Edouard Herriot, who as President of the Chamber, officially announced the vote, said to de Gaulle, "The fact is, I am not very sure that it had even that."

A mortal sickness afflicted the French Government, and the High Command as well, paralyzing action and will. Since the nonaggression Pact between Russia and Germany the large

Communist Party had openly opposed "The imperialists' war." The ultraconservatives, headed by Pierre Laval, looked on fascism as the wave of the future. It was whispered that when Reynaud's government fell Laval would call in Pétain and form a government to make a deal with Hitler.

Though octogenarian Marshal Pétain was in Madrid as Ambassador to Spain, he cast a gigantic shadow over French politics. Tens of thousands of copies of a sinister pamphlet fluttered through the streets of Paris. The first page showed a picture of Pétain at Verdun with the caption, "Yesterday—A Great Soldier." Next came a picture of him as Ambassador: "Today— A Great Diplomat." On the final page was a huge, shadowy figure of the old Marshal filling the entire scene; and under it simply: "Tomorrow?"

The smell of treason hung on the soft spring air.

To command even his single vote majority, Paul Reynaud had been forced to keep former Premier Daladier in his cabinet as Minister of National Defense and War Minister. This made it impossible for him to establish his authority. Daladier balked him at every turn. Reynaud wanted to make de Gaulle Under Secretary of State in charge of the War Committee. He sent an emissary to Daladier to sound out his feeling. Furiously Daladier said, "If de Gaulle comes here, I shall leave this office, go downstairs, and telephone M. Paul Reynaud to put him in my place."

That would have meant the fall of Reynaud's government. De Gaulle went back to his tanks.

Five weeks later the blow fell. After taking Norway and Denmark in April, Hitler launched his armored might against France on May 10, 1940. On that very day, while the Stuka dive bombers were screaming down to disrupt transport, scatter infantry, and smash artillery emplacements, *Le Journal* published one of Marshal Pétain's most senile pronouncements: "Direct action by enemy aerial forces in battle is an illusion. . . ."

[81]

Following the line of least resistance, two Nazi Panzer armies smashed across neutral Belgium and in four days broke the jerry-built extension of the Maginot Line at twice-fatal Sedan and at Dinant where de Gaulle had received his baptism of fire. The Battle of France was all but lost before more than a tenth of the great static French Army fired a shot. France had 3,000 tanks and 800 motorized machine guns—the Nazi had no more—but because these were dispersed they were useless.

The question remains why Germany adopted the new techniques so brilliantly while equally intelligent French generals remained wedded to old-fashioned theories. It was not only that a dictatorship can move more quickly and efficiently than democracy; it was also that France was full of victorious generals who naturally inclined toward the methods which gained them glory. Germany, with no winning generals, started from scratch. The logic implicit here would indicate that if a victorious nation wishes to maintain a progressive military establishment it should shoot all its winning generals. The idea does not lack merit.

After the miasmas in the political badlands, action came as a relief to de Gaulle. "Battle, even if disastrous, takes a soldier out of himself."

On May 11, the day after the blitz began, de Gaulle was ordered to take command of the Fourth Armored Division, which did not yet exist. "I felt very proud," de Gaulle says, "at finding myself called upon to command a division, though I was only a colonel." On May 15, he went to get his instructions from General Doumenc and General Georges at G.H.Q. It was another of those curious interviews.

In the faded brick Chateau de Montry, with the scent of roses heavy on the air, General Georges received his new division commander. He was "calm, cordial, and visibly overwhelmed." His instructions were pitifully simple. The High Command was trying to form a new front on the Aisne River. De Gaulle, with his division operating alone from Laon, was to hold them off, buy time in any way he could.

"Why not, even now, mass all our armored divisions together?" de Gaulle asked.

General Georges smiled wanly. "We are doing that," he said. "The First was annihilated in Belgium. The Second was smashed in transport on the Oise. The Third fought gloriously in bits and pieces and was overwhelmed. Yours is all that is left."

Then he visibly pulled himself together and said briskly, "Voilà, de Gaulle! You have long held the ideas the enemy is putting into practice. Now is your chance to act!"

There was no time to lose. De Gaulle dashed to Laon that night and established his headquarters in the nearby village of Bruyères. The next morning he collected an embryo staff and set out on a personal reconnaissance in an open staff car. It was a disheartening experience.

Just beyond the Serre River masses of German troops and armor were marching westward toward St. Quentin, with small flanking detachments between Laon and the river. The narrow roads were jammed with refugees choking in their own dust that hung like fog on the hot May air. Mixed with them were bands of French soldiers, disorganized, and disarmed. De Gaulle, standing tall and terrible in his car, demanded what they were doing there. They told him pitifully that they had been swept up by the enemy's flying mechanized columns. The Nazis had shouted contemptuously, "Throw your guns away and get the hell out of here. We haven't time to take prisoners."

That was the first bitter taste of defeat in de Gaulle's mouth. It was one thing to be told the army was beaten; another to see these panic-stricken, bedraggled men. He wrote:

"Then at the sight of those bewildered people and of those soldiers in rout, and also at their tales of the enemy's contemptuous insolence, I felt myself uplifted by illimitable fury. Oh, it was too stupid!"

And he thought, "The war is beginning as badly as possible. Therefore it must go on. For that the world is wide. If I live I will fight, wherever I must, as long as I must, until the enemy is defeated and the stain on my country washed clean." He

[83]

notes that, "All I have managed to do since was resolved upon that day."

De Gaulle decided to attack the next morning with whatever force he had. During the night three battalions of tanks, one heavy, the other two consisting of light Renaults, arrived in the railroad yards at Laon. They were unloaded in the darkness, and in the dawnlight of May 17, roared up the narrow roads between sweet flowering hedges toward the enemy. Most of the tankmen had just been introduced to their machines, some drivers had never handled a tank before. The single battalion of infantry traveled in ordinary busses. But ahead of them rode de Gaulle, his long body sticking high out of the turret of the lead tank which flew his standard of the Cross of Lorraine.

This scratched-up armored corps hurled confusion into the ranks of an enemy grown careless with easy conquest. It smashed convoys and cleared out nests of snipers, boring right through the heart of the German advance. By afternoon the enemy was reacting. Squadrons of Stukas came screaming down. De Gaulle had nothing to beat them off, but the column kept on in a hell of dust and smoke to the junction town of Montcornet.

They killed hundreds of the enemy and took 130 prisoners. These and the others the Fourth Armored took in the next few days were almost the only German prisoners taken in the whole Battle of France.

The next day de Gaulle continued rampaging around the countryside, thrusting toward Crécy where in 1346 the English under Edward III had first used artillery to surprise the French. That night de Gaulle received reinforcements of two squadrons of light tanks and the 322nd Artillery Regiment. So on May 19, at dawn, forward! That day de Gaulle engaged the main strength of the German Panzers coming after him across the Serre. By evening, word came that the High Command had established the new line back on the Aisne. De Gaulle withdrew his battered division.

During one of those violent days two old comrades from Fort IX met. Louis Parent tells how he was fighting with a dismounted cavalry regiment and heard that de Gaulle was nearby. "I went to a little country café where de Gaulle was expected. They said he would arrive about nine in the evening.

"I returned at that hour. In the big room of the café there he was with his officers. They had been fighting all day and they were all terribly thirsty. I pushed through the noisy, smoky room to his table, where he greeted me without surprise—nothing was surprising in those days—and made me sit next to him on the banquette. Naturally, I asked, 'How do you think it's going?'

"Without false hopes or despair, de Gaulle answered, 'My dear Parent, all I have to say to you is that this will be a very long business.' "

Meanwhile, in a desperation move, General Gamelin had been replaced as Generalissimo by General Weygand. The High Command made new plans, but they had no hope or will to win, for their whole system of doctrine and organization was falling apart, paralyzing their minds.

In Belgium the whole British Expeditionary Force of 500,000 men, with 300,000 of the flower of the French Army, was cut off and retreating on Dunkirk. King Leopold of Belgium was thinking of surrendering the Belgian Army.

Meanwhile the Fourth Armored was moving westward. From the moment of its birth in the railroad yards of Laon it had never stopped marching and fighting. But, since it was the only outfit doing anything constructive, it had been heavily reinforced. On May 26 it reached the English Channel, having passed close by Agincourt. Orders came to attack the pivot of the German line at Abbeville. That same day de Gaulle was promoted to brigadier general, the highest rank he ever held in the French Army.

De Gaulle decided to begin the battle that very evening. At 6 P.M. the tanks went forward. That night and all the next day they advanced breaking the Nazi lines. German Major Göehring wrote, "A profound terror of the tanks got into the bones of our soldiers . . ."

[85]

De Gaulle had lost 30 tanks, but he could write, "All the same, an atmosphere of victory hovered over the battlefield. Everyone held his head high. The wounded were smiling. The guns fired gaily. Before us, in a pitched battle, the Germans had retired."

Of course it could come to nothing. In the Battle of France no other ground was won but this sliver of land, 14 kilometers deep. The Fourth Armored fought for three days more before it was relieved by the Fifty-first Scottish Division and pulled back to refit.

De Gaulle had not commanded his battle in the conventional modern manner from a headquarters bunker; he could not, nor did he want to. He had no radio network and could only issue orders to the echelons by sending motorcycle dispatch riders, or, as he said, "Above all, going to see them myself." He was in the thick of the fight all day, every day, sticking up out of the turret of his tank like a flagpole, naked to shells, shrapnel and machine gun fire.

There is a photograph of him taken at this time in the battle dress of the tankers. Looking at it you might say, "Ah, there he is at last in modern dress—a modern man." Look more clearly at that sharp Norman profile, the arrogant lift of the head, the mustache grown long from lack of barbering, drooping a little; and at those pale blue eyes, fierce and fixed on a far, honorable goal. The belted leather tunic seems not so different from a surcoat worn over chain mail, and the dish-shaped helmet could be but a different fashion in knightly headgear. A modern man? At least, he was mounted on a tank.

CHAPTER NINE

❦　⚜　❦

THE CALVARY OF FRANCE

On June 1, de Gaulle had an appointment with Generalissimo Weygand. It was another of those military interviews which followed a bizarre but identical pattern. The Chateau de Montry still drowsed in soft rose-drenched air. Weygand, like his predecessor, was calm and cordial. In fact this was the professional attitude in disaster of all French generals, like the fixed smile on the face of a trapeze artist or a doctor's bedside manner. The latter is the better simile for they were, in fact, attending the deathbed of France.

Weygand was also overwhelmed. "I shall be attacked on June 6, on the Somme and the Aisne," he said, "by twice as many German divisions as I can muster. That means the prospects are poor. If things don't go too fast. If I can get the French troops saved from Dunkirk back in time . . ." If this, if that, and if some other unlikely piece of luck, "We have a chance. If not . . ."

De Gaulle left him with a heavy heart. He knew that here was a broken man, who had no will "to face destiny alone—the harsh, exclusive, passionate characteristic of a Chief."

At least Weygand's intelligence service was good. On June 5, de Gaulle heard the Germans were attacking on the Somme.

[87]

He went to ask for orders from General Frère, commanding the Eighth Army. Not unexpectedly he found General Frère calm and cordial. And he was brutally frank.

"We're sick," he said. "Rumor has it that you're to be a minister. It's certainly late in the day for a cure. Oh, de Gaulle! At least let us save our honor!"

Rumor was right. On June 6, de Gaulle received a message from Premier Reynaud that he had been appointed Under Secretary of State for National Defense. He instantly realized the other politicians' acceptance of him was the measure of their desperation.

In Reynaud's office in the War Ministry, de Gaulle met the Premier that night. All the lights were out, and heavy, silver, three-branched candelabra gave a soft, unreal illumination to the scene. Reynaud explained that he had taken Marshal Pétain into his cabinet. "Better to have him inside than out," he said cynically.

"I am afraid you'll be forced to change your opinion," de Gaulle said somberly.

That candlelit interview was the beginning of the time of desperation. The honor of France had been de Gaulle's passionate concern all his life. Her fall was his Calvary. Realism told him that the battle was lost, but he also knew that France need not be. For ten nightmare days, while the Army crumbled and the Government fled from town to town down the dusty, refugee-choked roads, he tried to save the State.

His hope was Reynaud, the squat little man with the slanting eyes, who still believed in France. His opponents were his one-time friend, Marshal Pétain, old and frightened, but still avariciously grasping for power, General Weygand, a man with his mainspring broken, who told de Gaulle that "My only hope is that the Germans will leave me enough men to maintain order," and their evil genius, former Premier Pierre Laval, who believed in Hitler more than he did in France. On their side, too, softly sapping her lover's resistance, was Reynaud's mistress, Madame Heléne de Portes, who believed in Pétain.

De Gaulle's plan was to fight and fight and never stop fighting, no matter what the odds. He wanted to make Paris a gigantic fortress defended from suburb to suburb and street by street "in the belly of Paris." When the capital fell, he proposed to retreat into Brittany, hold it as long as possible, and from there move the Government, the remains of the Army, and the great unscathed French fleet to North Africa and fight on from there.

While he was with Reynaud, the Premier enthusiastically agreed. Each time de Gaulle was obliged to leave his side, Reynaud fell under the influence of the defeatists.

On June 9, de Gaulle flew to England to carry Reynaud's promise to Churchill that France would fight on; and to get British help in transporting French troops to North Africa. He was accompanied by Roland de Margerie and Lieutenant Geoffrey de Courcel. The latter was an ardent young man, tall and slender, with a long, esthetic rosy face. He gave an impression of both vigor and elegance. He had been chosen for the mission because he spoke English with an impeccable Oxford accent.

De Gaulle and Churchill met for the first time in the Prime Minister's famous study at No. 10 Downing Street. Only four days before, Churchill had made the greatest fighting speech of modern times when he told Parliament that Britain would fight "On the beaches and in the fields . . ."

At that first meeting these two men, so unlike in appearance and temperament, so very much alike in courage and tenacity, found themselves en rapport. De Gaulle decided instantly that under such a man, England would never surrender. To him, Churchill seemed "equal to the rudest task, provided it also had grandeur." Churchill has recorded almost the same thought about de Gaulle. Whatever their quarrels since, these two never lost the mutual respect which was engendered that day.

Beyond that gain, and it was a great one, however distant its benefits, the meeting accomplished nothing. After conferring with British Minister of War Anthony Eden and Chief of Staff Sir John Dill, de Gaulle's airplane, darting and twisting like a moth in a sky full of sparrow-hawks, carried him uncertainly back to Paris. It landed at Le Bourget about nine-thirty, picking its way among fresh bomb craters. Hardly had de Gaulle reached his office when he was summoned to Reynaud's home for a midnight conference. The Germans had broken through everywhere. Paris was about to fall.

June 10 was a day of agony. Italy declared war. The Germans crossed the Marne. That evening the French Government fled from Paris. During the few scattered hours de Gaulle had spent in his office at the Ministry of War, he had realized ever more bitterly how complete was the moral collapse of France: "In the midst of a prostrate and stupified nation, behind an Army without faith and without hope, the machine of Government was turning in irremediable confusion."

When the Government left Paris confusion was compounded. De Gaulle traveled to the temporary Government Headquarters at Briare over roads choked by frantic refugees with their belongings piled on everything from Rolls-Royces to pushcarts. A dense, yellow fog, which the fleeing people thought was poison gas, added to their panic. It seemed as though all France was on the run.

At Briare the Government was installed in a lovely chateau— in what beauty of surroundings and ironic scenes of grandeur was the tragedy played out! However, it lacked certain necessities for a headquarters. There was, for example, only one telephone, located in the downstairs lavatory.

As de Gaulle entered the gallery of the chateau he saluted Marshal Pétain, whom he had not seen since 1938. "So you're a general," Pétain said, looking at the two stars on his kepi. "I don't congratulate you. What good is rank in defeat?"

Meaningfully de Gaulle replied, "But Monsieur le Maréchal, you received *your* first stars in the 1914 retreat. A few days later came the Marne."

"No comparison," growled Pétain.

Winston Churchill came to Briare that day in a desperate effort to bolster French courage. The Army was not impressed.

All Weygand talked about was surrender. Pétain seconded him. Churchill said, "Come, come, Monsieur le Maréchal. Remember the Battle of Amiens in 1918, when things were going so badly. I visited you at your headquarters then. . . . A few days later the front was re-established."

Pétain rasped, "Yes. You English were done for. But I sent forty divisions to rescue you. Today it's we who are smashed to pieces. Where are *your* forty divisions?"

In spite of de Gaulle, Paris was declared an open city—undefended. Two days later, June 13, Churchill was back again, this time at Tours, thus far had the peripatetic Government of France slid down the slope of disaster. No one even met the British Prime Minister at the airport. In a borrowed car, he tried for two hours to find the French Government. Finally, at the Prefecture, he and Reynaud talked in a sweet sunlit garden. To Churchill's words of courage all the Frenchman could say was, "There is no light at the end of the tunnel."

After the conference, Churchill, with Lords Beaverbrook and Halifax, went into the Prefecture. Churchill writes, "As we went down the crowded passage to the courtyard I saw General de Gaulle standing stolid and expressionless in the doorway. Greeting him, I said in a low tone in French, '*L'homme du destin*' (The man of destiny). He remained impassive."

Churchill flew back to England having gained little hope. De Gaulle considered resigning, but Minister of the Interior Georges Mandel, who was still full of courage, talked him out of it: "You have great duties to fulfill, *mon Général,* with the advantage of being, among us all, an untarnished man."

The Germans swept on through Paris, and the Government of France, with a crowd of deputies and journalists, struggled down to Bordeaux, the capital of defeat. De Gaulle's plan for a Breton redoubt had been vetoed by Weygand.

At the Bordeaux Prefecture, on the evening of June 14, de Gaulle talked briefly with Reynaud. As always when he was with him the Premier's courage revived. "If you stay here, you will be submerged in defeat," de Gaulle said. "You must get to Algiers as quickly as possible. Are you resolved on that—yes or no?"

"Yes."

"Then I go to England tomorrow to arrange about shipping. Where shall I meet you?"

Paul Reynaud said resolutely, "In Algiers!"

Before he left, de Gaulle had dinner at the Hotel Splendide. In the dining room jammed by the rag-tag crowd of ministers, politicians, and hangers-on, Marshal Pétain, looking frail and ancient in his oakleaves and stars, was sitting alone at a table. De Gaulle walked over to pay his respects. Words would not come to either man. They shook hands in silence. They never met again.

With young de Courcel, of whom he was becoming ever more fond, de Gaulle drove through the scented night across Brittany. In the morning they sailed from Brest in the destroyer, *Milan*—France had not even one airplane left for him.

As they cleared the harbor they passed the magnificent new French battle cruiser, *Richelieu,* starting for haven in Dakar. Puffs of smoke and the crack guns in her secondary battery saluted the Under Secretary of Defense. The next time she saluted de Gaulle it was with live ammunition from her fifteen-inch guns.

In London, on June 16, de Gaulle had lunch with Churchill and Sir Robert Vansittart of the Foreign Office at the Carlton Club. With them were French Ambassador André Corbin and finance expert Jean Monnet. The first thing Churchill said was, "If France surrenders, what will become of your fleet?"

"Whatever happens the French fleet will not be surrendered," de Gaulle assured him. "Pétain himself would not consent to that. Besides, the fleet is Admiral (Jean) Darlan's fief. A feudal lord does not surrender his fief."

After lunch they adjourned to 10 Downing Street where together they worked out the most magnificent gesture one nation ever made to another. Britain offered France complete union between the two countries—mutual citizenship, mutual economies, and mutual military establishments. The British War

Cabinet, hastily called in session, approved it, and de Gaulle telephoned it to Reynaud.

The French Premier was at first incredulous, then breathless with new hope. When de Gaulle had finished reading the text of the British offer, Churchill took the telephone. "Hello, Reynaud," he said. "De Gaulle is right! Our proposal may have great consequences. You must hold out!"

Later, Monnet tried to persuade Churchill to send the Royal Air Force fighters to France. De Gaulle sat silent, taking no part in the discussion while his colleague argued the case. Regretfully, Churchill said that it was impossible to strip Britain of her last defense against the Luftwaffe.

Then the two Frenchmen took their leave. As they reached the door de Gaulle turned to face Churchill. Standing there very tall and apparently unmoved, he said slowly in English, "I think you are right."

Churchill wrote: "Under an impassive, imperturbable demeanor he seemed to me to have a remarkable capacity for feeling pain . . . Here is the Constable of France!"

De Gaulle flew back to France in Churchill's own Flamingo airplane. When he landed at Bordeaux, he heard the news he dreaded most. The French cabinet had shouted down Churchill's splendid offer. "We are not going to become a British dominion!" "England will have her neck wrung like a chicken in three weeks." Pétain called it, "Fusion with a corpse."

Reynaud had resigned. President Lebrun had sent for Pétain. De Gaulle knew that meant surrender. He said to the British pilot, "Be ready at dawn. I shall return to England."

From the airport, de Gaulle went to a brief, sad interview with an exhausted, shattered Reynaud, who had no illusions as to the fate of France, "A man who had reached the limits of hope." But there was one flicker of spirit left in him. He gave de Gaulle 100,000 francs from his secret funds, saying, "It is not much, but it may help a little."

Then de Gaulle went to see British Ambassador Sir Ronald Campbell and General Sir Edward Spears. The latter decided to fly back to England with him. After that he went to bed. But not to sleep.

It was a night of agony. For this was his last night in France, perhaps forever. He was leaving all that was most dear to him, the very soil and trees and scents of the land that he had passionately adored all his life. His heart was dead within him, and doubt tortured his brain. For no matter how strong his sense of destiny, how sure his voices, there was the weakness of every man in the midnight ebb of strength when faith is shaken and courage falters.

So his exhausted brain whirled on, presenting pictures of Colombey, its beloved park and quiet, healing forests under German heels. What of Yvonne and the children? He had seen them for one brief moment during the last terrible weeks; had told his wife to go to Brittany and, if Reynaud resigned, to join him in England. That very evening he had used his waning influence to send her passports by a messenger.

But mostly he thought about France and the men who had failed her. Later he recorded these impressions. Reynaud? He would have been a good man under the right circumstances, but in these chaotic conditions he had lost control of events.

All through days without respite and nights without sleep the Premier could feel the entire responsibility for the fate of France weighing upon him personally. For a leader is always alone in the face of ill fortune . . .

(Yet) he faced the storm with a steadfastness which did not waver. Never during those days of drama did Monsieur Paul Reynaud cease to be master of himself. Never was he seen to lose his temper, give way to anger, or complain. The spectacle of that man's high value ground down unjustly by too heavy a weight of events was a tragic one . . .

And Pétain? Pétain who had been de Gaulle's hero, his ideal and his beloved friend. Between them there had been so much love and respect. How had this thing happened:

"What a current was carrying him along to what an ineluctable destiny . . . Too proud for intrigue, too forceful for mediocrity . . . he nourished in his solitude a passion for domination . . .

"In spite of everything I am convinced that in other times Marshal Pétain would not have consented to don the purple in the midst of national surrender . . . But alas! Under the outer shell the years had gnawed his character. Age was delivering him over to the maneuvers of people who were clever at covering themselves with his majestic lassitude. Old age is a shipwreck. That we might be spared nothing the old age of Marshal Pétain was to identify itself with the shipwreck of France."

Nor did de Gaulle in his melancholy assessment blame the others too bitterly. The generals, from Weygand down, were schooled in a doctrine of defense that modern inventions had outmoded. They did not lack ability or courage. All they lacked was the character to free themselves from theory and confront events with greatness—and no man can be blamed because he is not great.

As to the politicians, with the exception of Laval's conniving clique, they, too, were men of integrity. "The regime offered . . . the last government of the Third Republic nothing to fall back upon. Assuredly, many of the men in office looked upon capitulation with horror. (But) in reality this annihilation of the State was at the bottom of the national tragedy. By the light of the thunderbolt the regime was revealed in its ghastly infirmity . . ."

Morning came at last, bringing as it does, courage and clarity of mind. To de Gaulle, facing exile alone, it also brought an inspiration. He telephoned young de Courcel. "What are you going to do?" he asked.

"I am going to try to reach Syria," the boy answered.

In a toneless voice that gave no hint that the answer meant anything to him, de Gaulle said, "I am leaving for England in half an hour. Do you want to come with me?"

Without a second's hesitation, de Courcel said, "I do."

"Good," said de Gaulle.

So Free France gained her first recruit.

CHAPTER TEN

⚜ ⚜ ⚜

JUNE EIGHTEENTH

CONTRARY TO WINSTON CHURCHILL's memoirs and some highly romantic accounts of de Gaulle's escape from France, de Courcel says, "There was no mystery about our departure."

They drove quite openly in three cars to the airport where Churchill's plane was waiting. Sir Ronald Campbell was there to see General Spears off, and a member of Reynaud's former cabinet came to wish de Gaulle well. The plane was warmed up normally, and at the last minute de Gaulle walked back to the hangar to get a piece of rope to tie some baggage up. Then the plane headed into the light wind and took off. The only difficulty was that it had not been refueled. The French Government was, literally as well as figuratively, out of gas.

As they flew across the blossoming fields of Brittany the three men in the plane were deeply emotional. De Gaulle sat looking down at France with an expressionless face. The others, respecting his silence, could not guess his thoughts. They were, for once, personal. He was thinking of Yvonne and the children, wondering if they would get away, and of his mother, who had been very ill, in the little Breton village where she had taken refuge with his brother Xavier. The countryside looked green and peaceful, but black oily smoke hung over the forests where he knew they were burning the great munitions dumps before the Nazis came.

The plane passed over La Rochelle and Rochefort where ships were afire in the harbor and, out at sea, beyond, a liner was incredibly sinking in a painted ocean. As they left the coast of France behind, de Gaulle roused himself and began to talk to Spears about the future. He had snapped the book of his memory shut.

One thing he said amazed de Courcel later by its prevision. "I'm sure the United States will eventually enter the war," de Gaulle told Spears. "And also that there will be war between Germany and Russia. Hitler will repeat Napoleon's mistake. The great miscalculation the French Government and our generals are making is in thinking of this as a local war like 1870, when if you are beaten there is nowhere to go and nothing to do but surrender, instead of realizing that this is a world war and there is all the world to fight in."

They had so little gas that they could not sweep far out to sea to avoid possible Luftwaffe fighters, but had to chance an almost direct route, naked to attack. The pilot was relieved when he sighted the Isle of Jersey lying in the Channel haze. He hastily put down on its small airport.

While the plane was being serviced its passengers went into the little office. There they were served the murky brew that is England's national drink. De Gaulle sipped his and made a wry face. It was, quite literally, the bitter tea of exile.

Then they resumed the flight, landing safely at Croyden. And Churchill wrote: "De Gaulle carried with him, in this small aeroplane, the honor of France."

In London de Gaulle and de Courcel went to a small flat in the Hotel Rubens near Hyde Park, which had been offered him by Monsieur Laurent, afterward President of the Bank of Indo-China. It was a mere *garconnière*.

There de Gaulle sat down to think on his next move. "Go on with the war? Yes, certainly." But how best was that to be done? The English thought of it as aid to be given by a handful of Frenchmen to the British Empire. De Gaulle thought that it would be "the end of honor, unity, and independence" if it were admitted that France had surrendered. The nation and the State must be saved. For this it was necessary to bring back into the war, "not merely some Frenchmen, but France. . . ." The first thing was to hoist the colors.

That very afternoon he outlined his ideas to Churchill, who offered him the facilities of the British Broadcasting Corporation. But de Gaulle waited until the news came through that Pétain had asked for an armistice. So it was the next day, June 18, 1940, that de Gaulle assumed France.

At six that evening he made the broadcast that has become perhaps, the most famous speech in the whole history of France. He began right from the shoulder:

> The leaders who for many years have been at the head of the French armed forces have set up a government.
>
> Alleging the defeat of our armies, this government has entered into negotiations with the enemy with a view to bringing about a cessation of hostilities. Certainly we have been, we are, submerged by the mechanical force of the enemy on land and in the air. Infinitely more than their numbers it was the tanks, the airplanes, and the tactics of the Germans which threw us back. But is the last word said? *NO.*
>
> Believe me, nothing is lost for France. The same means which vanquished us will bring us victory some day.
>
> For France is not alone. She has a vast empire behind her. She can make common cause with the British Empire, which holds the seas and is continuing the fight. And like England, she can utilize without limit the immense industrial resources of the United States.
>
> This war has not been ended by the Battle of France. This is a world-wide war. All the mistakes, all the setbacks, and all the suffering do not alter the fact that there are in the universe all the necessary means some day to destroy our enemies. Overwhelmed today by mechanical force, we can conquer in the future by a superior mechanical force. The destiny of the world is there.
>
> I, General de Gaulle, now in London, call on all French

De Gaulle's proclamation to the French people in 1940 after the fall of France. *Courtesy, French Embassy Information Div.*

A TOUS LES FRANÇAIS

La France a perdu une bataille!
Mais la France n'a pas perdu la guerre!

Des gouvernants de rencontre ont pu capituler, cédant à la panique, oubliant l'honneur, livrant le pays a la servitude. Cependant, rien n'est perdu!

Rien n'est perdu, parce que cette guerre est une guerre mondiale. Dans l'univers libre, des forces immenses n'ont pas encore donné. Un jour, ces forces écraseront l'ennemi. Il faut que la France, ce jour-là, soit présente à la victoire. Alors, elle retrouvera sa liberté et sa grandeur. Tel est mon but, mon seul but!

Voilà pourquoi je convie tous les Français, où qu'ils se trouvent, à s'unir à moi dans l'action, dans le sacrifice et dans l'espérance.

Notre patrie est en péril de mort.
Luttons tous pour la sauver!

VIVE LA FRANCE !

GÉNÉRAL DE GAULLE

QUARTIER-GÉNÉRAL,
4, CARLTON GARDENS,
LONDON, S.W.I.

The Casablanca Conference in 1943. General Giraud, President Roosevelt, General de Gaulle, and Prime Minister Churchill. © *U.P.I. Photos.*

General de Gaulle lands in Normandy, June 14, 1944. *Courtesy, French Embassy Information Div.*

The liberation of Paris: leaving the Tomb of the Unknown Soldier. © *Zalewski. Courtesy, French Embassy Information Div.*

De Gaulle decorating Eisenhower (*Croix de la Liberation*), June, 1945. © *S.C.A. Courtesy, French Embassy Information Div.*

officers and men who are at present on British soil or may be in the future, with or without arms; I call on all engineers and skilled workmen . . . to rally to me.

Come what may, the flame of French resistance must not be extinguished. And it will not be extinguished.

Those words, spoken with magnificent effrontery, which was not arrogance, but, in fact, a sense of destiny for which de Gaulle's whole life had prepared him, were flung into the void beyond the small broadcasting studio with its single microphone on a green baize table. Would they be received in his beloved land as the ravings of a madman or as a message of hope?

For many days he did not know. Even now there are few earwitness accounts of how that message was first received. Madame Geneviève de Gaulle Anthonioz has told of how it came to one small Breton village. She was with her parents, the Xavier de Gaulles in Locminé in Brittany. The general's tiny white-haired mother had taken refuge with them.

On that eighteenth day of June, 1940, they sat in a window of their little house with a group of retired army officers watching the first German motorcyclists ride up the cobbled village street to take possession of the town. Madame de Gaulle, so passionately patriotic, was frantic with rage and anguish. The shame to her was not that the Germans had come, she had seen them twice before, but that they came unchallenged. "Why does no one shoot," she cried again and again. "Are we going to let them take France like so many tourists?"

Xavier and the old officers tried to calm her, explaining in hopeless voices that Pétain was surrendering France and there was nothing to be done.

Down the street among the cyclists ran the village priest, robes flapping. He pounded on the door and burst into the room. His eyes were shining with excitement and hope. "I have just heard the most wonderful thing on the radio," he said. "A French general in London says that France is not finished. That the war will go on from our empire and the whole world. The flame of her resistance will never die!"

[101]

The old men looked up, hope fighting scepticism in their eyes. "Who is this general?" one of them asked.

The priest said, "His name is General de Gaulle."

The tiny old lady rushed to him, pulling at his robe. In a voice that soared exultantly over the roar of enemy motors she shouted, "That is my son! That is *my* son!"

Less than a month later, on July 16, 1940, Madame de Gaulle died. Because they feared the propaganda effect of the death of General de Gaulle's mother, the Germans would not permit the news to be made public. But somehow the word spread. Madame Anthonioz says "People came from far, far places, many thousands of them, to pay tribute to her. They brought flowers to put on her grave. They even took stones from it to keep as one might keep a holy relic."

A young Breton fisherman took a photograph of the grave, with its thin headstone in the shape of a Maltese Cross, and of all the flowers. He risked death to smuggle it across the Channel in his fishing boat and sent it to General de Gaulle. Madame Anthonioz says that this was the first knowledge her uncle had of his mother's death. And that great mountain of flowers piled upon her grave and spilling over its bounderies was the first concrete evidence de Gaulle had that the people of France had heard him, and had given him their allegiance; as he had given them back their souls.

CHAPTER ELEVEN

❧ ⚜ ❧

FREE FRANCE

FREE FRANCE WAS two men in two rooms in a second-class hotel in London. It was June 19, 1940. The telephone rang. De Courcel answered it and heard Yvonne de Gaulle's voice. He was so moved to know that she was safe that he could not speak; but silently handed the instrument to de Gaulle. There was no more than a flash of gladness in the General's eyes and not a tremor in his voice as he said cheerfully, *"Voilà!* There you are. Take the next train to London. I'll meet you at Paddington Station."

Madame de Gaulle, though not used to adventures or even to traveling alone, had followed orders very efficiently. With her three children she had started for Brest on June 17. The hired car broke down, so she missed the noon boat. It was torpedoed, and may even have been the liner de Gaulle saw sinking as he flew over the coast of France. Yvonne de Gaulle caught the night boat, the last to sail from Brest, arriving in Plymouth the morning of June 19. She had no idea where her husband was, or even if he was still alive, until their son, Phillipe, showed her his speech of the night before in the English papers.

By evening Free France had thus added a woman and three

children to her population. They needed larger quarters and moved to the Hotel Connaught.

That same evening de Gaulle made another broadcast to France in even stronger terms:

> At this hour all Frenchmen know that the ordinary forms of power have disappeared. In the confusion of French souls and the liquefaction of a government fallen under the servitude of the enemy, I, General de Gaulle, a French soldier and chief, I assume to speak in the name of France.
>
> In the name of France I formally declare the following:
>
> Every Frenchman who is bearing arms has a sacred duty to continue the resistance . . . To relinquish even the smallest sliver of French land to the enemy would be a crime against the Nation . . . And now I speak above all for French North Africa; for an intact North Africa . . .
>
> It is intolerable that the panic of Bordeaux shall spread beyond the seas.
>
> Soldiers of France, wherever you may be, arise!

At the same time de Gaulle was writing to the French governors and military commanders throughout the world, begging them to join him in continuing the fight. According to de Courcel he had not the egotism to imagine himself, the youngest general in the French Army, as the leader of Free France if one of the senior generals would declare himself against the armistice. He even had a faint hope, against all probability, that Bordeaux might at the last moment choose to continue the fight, and had telegraphed offering his services in negotiating transport to North Africa. The reply was a telegram ordering him to come home.

On June 20, he wrote to Weygand, who had taken the "astonishing title of Minister of National Defense", urging him to place himself at the head of the resistance and offering to serve under him. Weygand sent it back with an insulting comment.

On June 30, French Ambassador Corbin, who remained loyal to Pétain's government, delivered an order to de Gaulle from Bordeaux to surrender himself prisoner at St. Michel prison in Toulouse to be tried by the Council of War. Of course, he paid it no heed, so the Council tried him in absentia. They condemned him to a month's imprisonment. This verdict did not satisfy Pétain and Weygand. The latter asked the Council to condemn de Gaulle to death. So it was done.

It was a desperately lonely time for de Gaulle. His entire life had been spent within the framework of the Army, rooted in the soil of his beloved country. That life had suddenly ended. At nearly fifty years of age, he was beginning a fantastic adventure. He wrote that he felt "like a man thrown by fate outside of all the boundaries of his world."

Colonel Rémy describes de Gaulle at this time at a moment when he thought himself unobserved: "I saw a very tall officer wearily mounting the stairs, his head bowed, his hand gripping the iron stair-rail. On his kepi were two bronze stars. His shoulders seemed to be borne down, crushed by the weight of an invisible burden. He seemed a man at the limit of doubt . . . Then he saw me. Instantly he recovered; fixed me with a severe look, and was again calm, cold, impassive, sure of himself, sure of ultimate victory."

But de Gaulle had a source of solace denied to many exiles —the happiness of a home. Soon after Yvonne arrived he found a house in the country near London for his wife and children. It was rather like an English version of his beloved Colombey; about the same size and severely simple with long, small-paned windows that opened on a terraced garden. Yvonne de Gaulle had not lost the knack of a soldier's wife for making a home wherever she found herself.

Her husband spent the week in Seymour Place. The older children, too, were busy. Elizabeth was preparing for college at the convent school of *Les Dames de Sion*. There is a charming photograph, taken after she entered Oxford, of a pretty brown-eyed girl in cap and gown riding her bicycle. Later she studied nursing and helped to found the Red Cross of Lorraine.

Phillipe, who had apparently acquired a taste for the sea during his two nights aboard the Brest Packet, was enrolled at the school for naval cadets aboard the Frigate *Belle Poule*, captured by the British in the Napoleonic wars. Only little Anne was always at home.

Every Saturday that it was possible, de Gaulle took a bus out to the country to spend a brief week-end among the flowers and open fields he loved, refreshing himself with the nearest approach to solitude he could command within emergency call of London. As in France, the de Gaulles, though friendly with their neighbors, had virtually no social life. The General's principal amusement was playing childish games with Anne, making her laugh by singing old French nursery rhymes to her, very much off key.

Another source of comfort to him was the friendly attitude of the English people. René Thibault, who became one of his aides, says, "When we walked together, as we often did, from the Hotel Connaught to the Royal Automobile Club for luncheon, total strangers would stop de Gaulle to shake his hand and wish him well. It touched him and gave him courage.

This personal knowledge of the English is the reason he liked them better than Americans until his recent trip to the United States. While he admired Americans for their spirit, idealism, and courage and, because of their mixture of nationalities, called them the first true Europeans, he never lived among them. But he saw the English under the blitz and learned not only to appreciate their courage and stubbornness, but to feel the warmth of their friendship. This was very important to him.

Free France grew very slowly. On the morning of June 20, George Boris, a noncommissioned officer, arrived at the Hotel Connaught. "I have come to volunteer, *mon Général,*" he said.

"You are strongly welcome," said de Gaulle.

Now there were six Free Frenchmen. A few others drifted in, enthusiastic young officers and unknown intellectuals, but none of the generals or politicians to whom de Gaulle had appealed were willing to join his movement. Most Frenchmen in England did not join either. "You are right, but I am too old," Ambassador Corbin said to him.

"You are wrong," said Jean Monnet.

"We are going to America," said André Maurois, and Henri Bonnet. "We will best serve you there."

But Pierre Cot offered to do anything, "Even sweep the stairs."

With his half-smile de Gaulle observed, "You are too conspicuous for that to be desirable."

The only ones who joined overseas were General Georges Catroux, "the only man who understood the Levant," who was now Governor-General of Indo-China, and General Paul-Louis Legentilhomme commanding on the Somali coast of Africa. They were both kicked out of their posts.

"There is no France without a sword," de Gaulle said. And set out to forge one. His hope of raising an army, even a very little one, lay in thousands of French soldiers and sailors rescued from Dunkirk or on French ships in English ports. He got little help from anyone.

The British High Command would have liked to recruit the French into their own depleted ranks. French General Bethouart, commanding the Light Alpine Division, which had fought with the British in Norway, said that he and his men wanted only to go home to France. However, de Gaulle did get permission to go on a fishing expedition among the French servicemen. The British Government lent him a car.

So with the few junior officers who had joined him de Gaulle went visiting the French cantonments in England. Within a week, a few hundred volunteers were encamped at Olympia, which had been lent by the British. They were a ragged lot, housed in little conical tents like tepees, but they were a beginning.

Then on June 28, he got his first real break. On that day Churchill's government recognized de Gaulle as the "Chief of the Free French." This at least gave him a semi-semi official status, though somewhat more dubious than even that of the governments in exile of Poland, Belgium, Holland, *et al.* He began racing all over England in his borrowed car.

At Trentham Park he struck pay dirt, bringing in most of the Thirteenth Brigade of the Foreign Legion, 200 *Chasseurs Alpine,* two-thirds of a tank company and a few odd gunners and signalmen. Most important of all, worth a division, at least, though no one knew it then, was Captain Joseph-Pierre Koenig of the *Chasseurs Alpine.* At other camps, naval bases, even at hospitals to which French wounded had been taken, de Gaulle rounded up more recruits. His navy was two submarines, a patrol boat and a trawler.

De Gaulle's method of recruitment was far from sentimental or appealing, it was a stern, even harsh call to duty. For that reason it had a tonic effect on Frenchmen seeking Roman virtue in a time of moral collapse. Pierre Lefranc, today chief on de Gaulle's personal staff at the Élysée, gave an example of it in describing his first sight of the man who became his idol:

> I had escaped from France by way of Spain and was being taken to England in the American liner, *Santa Rosa.* It was at Gibraltar that I first met General de Gaulle. He came aboard the ship to talk to us, 1,200 French we were, all escapees. His speech was very short. I do not remember his exact words, but this is the substance of what he said: 'So you have escaped. That is good. But what you have done is nothing. Now you must do everything. Until France is liberated you must never stop fighting!'
>
> Then they played the 'Marseillaise' and he left.
>
> Oddly enough it was more inspiring to us than if he had congratulated us and praised us. He has not changed. He always asks more of people than they can do. And so they do it.

By July 14, Bastille Day, France had a sword—but how short the blade! The First Company of the New French Army, the First Naval Company, and the First Platoon Air Force, wearing their insignia of the Cross of Lorraine, paraded down Whitehall to the World War I Cenotaph, and on to the statue of Marshal Foch, on which de Gaulle placed a wreath. A great crowd broke through the police lines, cheering wildly. Though he looked as impassive as the sculptured figure of the dead hero, de Gaulle's tears were held back only by his adamantine will.

Meanwhile the "Government" of Free France was being organized in offices at St. Stephen's House on the Embankment provided by the British Government. De Courcel was Chief of the "Cabinet." One of its most valuable members was René Pleven, who long afterward became Premier of France. He was in charge of finances. Professor René Cassin was in charge of law and justice, and M. Antoine had civil service. A very valuable addition was young Maurice Schumann who escaped to London on June 30.

Schumann, describing his first interview with de Gaulle at St. Stephen's House, says that he was less austere than at a later time when the battle against his own allies for the dignity of France and the trust of the French people forced him to assume "the rigidity of a symbol."

When Schumann asked him if he thought England would hold out, de Gaulle "tranquilly" replied, "If Hitler were coming to London he would be here already."

Then he added, "In sum, the war is a terrible problem, but one which can be solved. It remains only to gather all France on the right side."

Schumann was immediately put in charge of broadcasting, a post he held almost without interruption until the Day of Liberation. It was his voice that Frenchmen heard throughout those years, ringing over Occupied France in the stirring announcement: "Honor and country! Here is General de Gaulle!"

A theme which de Gaulle had set for the broadcasts was that Germany would surely be beaten in the end. A Schumann contribution was telling Frenchmen, "You do not want to be conquered twice—once *by* the Germans and once *with* them."

Another valuable recruit who turned up on June 30, was Vice Admiral Emile-Henri Muselier, who had escaped by way of Gibraltar. De Gaulle had no illusions about this brilliant but prickly officer who, though very able, had an overgrown ego. He welcomed the Admiral warmly and then, lest he get any false notions that his superior rank entitled him to command, de Gaulle with his coldest, authoritative air said, "Admiral, I shall appoint you to command the navy I am organizing. Put on your uniform and report to me tomorrow."

The Armistice with Germany had been signed on June 22, by General Charles Huntziger in the same railroad car in which he had watched the Germans surrender in 1918. Even though de Gaulle expected it, the terms of the French surrender were more abject than he could have believed any Frenchmen would accept. On July 1, the French "Government" moved to its new capital, Vichy, and there, on July 10, Marshal Pétain was installed as Chief of State, with dictatorial powers, by the huge majority in the National Assembly of 569 to 80.

These were terrible blows to de Gaulle, who assumed an even colder and more arrogant pose in public to conceal his inner grief. But a more piercing blow was struck him by Winston Churchill's Government.

The fifteen days following June 18, 1940, had been the honeymoon of Churchill and de Gaulle. It ended abruptly on July 3. On that day news reached St. Stephen's House that the British Mediterranean Fleet had attacked a squadron of French warships in the Harbor of Mers-el-Kebir in Algeria. At the same time they took forceful possession of all French warships in British ports, and at Alexandria in Egypt.

According to the terms of the Armistice the French Fleet remained under the control of the French Government—this much of honor had Pétain kept. But the British, fearing that the Germans would ultimately get hold of it, had appealed to Admiral Gensoul, commanding at Mers-el-Kebir, to surrender his ships or scuttle them. When the Admiral refused, the British Fleet opened fire and sent in Swordfish torpedo planes, sinking two French battleships and the superb battle cruiser *Dunkerque*. The battle cruiser *Strasbourg* and several cruisers sailed out under a tornado of fire and escaped to Toulon. On July 10, a British torpedo plane damaged the *Richelieu* at Dakar.

In his anguish de Gaulle thought of shaking the dust of England from his heels; but a little reflection showed him that nowhere in the world was there any other dust on which to plant them. In addition, his realistic military sense made him understand British motives. If those great French ships ever fell into German hands, England would be done for, and considering how uncertain the Pétain Government's sense of honor was, it might happen.

Churchill himself was deeply disturbed at having to order the action. He cleverly offered de Gaulle the use of the BBC to declare his point of view. De Gaulle minced no words but neither did he kick over the bucket.

> I shall speak frankly . . . There is not a Frenchman who did not learn with sorrow and with anger that the French Fleet had been sunk by our allies. That sorrow and anger comes from the profound depths of our beings . . .
>
> Also, to the English I say they should not represent this odious tragedy as a naval success . . . Here is what a French soldier declares most plainly to our English allies, that it surely will not increase the world's esteem for them in naval matters.
>
> Finally, addressing myself to Frenchmen, I demand that they consider at the bottom of things the only point of view that finally counts, that is to say the point of view of victory and deliverance . . .

By his extremely intelligent handling of the tragic and delicate situation which might well have ruptured the fragile *entente* between Free France and her only ally, de Gaulle for the first time proved that as a statesman he might be arrogant and unbending, but he would never go beyond what was possible.

However in the next check to his career his performance was somewhat less brilliant.

Not unnaturally Mers-el-Kebir sowed the seeds of mistrust of his ally in de Gaulle's mind. The first thing he did was to set up a Deuxieme Bureau (Secret Intelligence) under Commander Dewavrin, whose cloak-and-dagger alias was "Passy." Though it eventually made a magnificent contribution to the allied cause by the information it gathered in Occupied France, its first purpose was to spy on the British. De Gaulle realized that he could do little to prevent Churchill's Government from doing anything it pleased, but at least he was not going to have any more unpleasant surprises.

For a while things went along remarkably smoothly. By September, 1940, Free France might proudly call itself a nation. It even had some real estate of its own. On August 7, de Gaulle had met with Churchill at Chequers, the Prime Minister's country estate. In an atmosphere of unaffected grandeur, typical of Churchill, congenial to de Gaulle, they had no difficulty in agreeing on the official status of Free France. De Gaulle said that he was willing and anxious for Frenchmen to serve under British generals, but that he must be their Supreme Commander. In 1960 he made an identical statement to General Lauris Norstad, which caused the American staff of NATO to say irritably, "The man is a mystery."

The Prime Minister signed an agreement, acknowledging de Gaulle as the Chief of the Free French everywhere, and promising "the integral restoration of independence and *greatness* (de Gaulle wrote that word in) to France." In effect it recognized that de Gaulle was France. For the first time since Louis XIV an individual could have said, "I am the State."

Free France had a real army, too. On August 23, 7,000 men, *Chasseurs* in their blue berets, Legionaires in white desert kepis, artillery men without cannon, and tankers without tanks, but all of them spoiling for a fight, marched in review before the small, great King of England and the tall great man who was France.

The real estate was acquired during August when The Tchad in Equatorial Africa, Ubangi, the Cameroons, the French Congo, and Tahiti all were taken over by or announced their adherence to Free France.

But trouble was not far behind.

The cause of it was that both de Gaulle and Churchill were raging optimists—they had to be. But in the matter of Dakar they overdid it.

Dakar was the biggest fortified French naval base in West Africa. Besides its strong garrison and heavy, coast-defense guns, several powerful French warships were stationed there, including the newest French battle cruiser *Richelieu*. It was the most important prize south of Casablanca.

It must be admitted that de Gaulle originated a rather hare-brained scheme for capturing or seducing it. His idea was to land an expeditionary force of Free French on the coast nearby and march overland to take it from the rear. His plan had little chance of success, but it could have been a minor failure instead of a grand fiasco.

He mentioned the idea to Churchill in July. It germinated in the Prime Minister's fecund brain and suddenly flowered into a typically Churchillian fantasy. On August 6, the Prime Minister called de Gaulle to Downing Street and outlined his plan with majestic, compelling eloquence. It was to stun the garrison by an overpowering display of naval might:

"Dakar wakes up one morning sad and uncertain," Churchill said. "But behold! by the light of the rising sun its inhabitants perceive the sea to be covered with ships. An immense fleet . . . Some are flying the Tricolor. Others are sailing under British, Dutch, Polish or Belgian colors . . . The envoys of General de Gaulle are brought to the Governor (under a flag of truce). Their job is to convince him that if he lets you land, the fleet retires and nothing remains but to settle between him and you the terms of the capitulation . . . If he wants a fight he has every chance of being crushed . . .

"The Governor feels that if he resists, the ground will give way under his feet . . . Perhaps he will wish, 'for honor's sake', to fire a few shots. But he will go no further. And that evening he will dine with you and drink to final victory."

De Gaulle allowed himself to be seduced by Churchill's flaming imagination. But at Dakar the luck was out, the Star in eclipse, and the compass of destiny awry.

On the morning of September 23, the fleet was off Dakar. It was, indeed, a powerful force—two British battleships, four cruisers, and the aircraft carrier *Ark Royal*. The Free French had done their pitiful best, supplying three sloops (gunboats) two armed trawlers and four freighters carrying troops. General de Gaulle, with General Spears, was aboard the *Westerland* which flew the Cross of Lorraine as well as the Dutch flag. However Governor General Boisson of Dakar had been reinforced by six Vichy French cruisers.

The scene was not at all as Churchill had depicted it. The inhabitants of Dakar were neither inspired nor impressed by the sight of an immense fleet, for the simple reason they could not see it. A dense fog, almost unheard of at this time of year, covered the ocean. In this hot, dripping, dismal murk, the armada maneuvered uncertainly while de Gaulle broadcast an impassioned appeal to the French in Dakar.

Both he and Churchill had badly misjudged the temper of the place. The French Navy was in no mood to surrender. What they considered the treachery of the British attack at Mers-el-Kebir had made them fighting mad. The torpedoing of the *Richelieu* had added to their fury. They were itching to take another crack at His Majesty's Navy, and they could not have cared less if General de Gaulle got in the way of one of their fifteen-inch shells.

The first intimation of trouble was when some French and British airplanes took off from the *Ark Royal* and groped their way through the fog to drop leaflets on Dakar. Anti-aircraft guns in the forts and aboard the *Richelieu* opened up.

There is a photograph of de Gaulle standing on the bridge of the *Westerland* that day. Instead of the familiar two-starred kepi, for the only time in his life, he is wearing a black "Montgomery" beret, under which his great nose juts sternly. He never wore the beret again; it was not his lucky hat.

At about eight o'clock, de Gaulle ordered two motor launches to take his negotiating team into the harbor under a flag of truce. They were led by Commander Thierry d'Argenlieu and Captain Becourt-Foch, grandson of Marshal Foch. Only a year before, Commander d'Argenlieu had been Father Louis of the Trinity, Provincial of the Carmelites of France. He had taken leave of absence from his order to serve Free France.

The fighting father's mission of peace was badly received on the docks of Dakar. He and his companions were allowed to land, but the port commander, blushing with embarrassment, told them that he had orders to arrest them. They hastily scrambled back into their boats and roared out of the harbor. The intransigent Vichyites sped their parting by a burst of machine gun fire and seriously wounded d'Argenlieu.

Right after that Dakar emphasized its disapproval of the proceedings by letting go with everything on hand. Shore batteries and ships, including the fifteen-inch guns of the *Richelieu,* fired blindly through the mist at the allied fleet. A lucky shell crashed into the British cruiser *Cumberland.* At that, Admiral Sir John Cunningham radioed somewhat plaintively, "I am not firing at you. Why are you firing on me?"

The answer was "Retire to twenty-miles distance."

That was too much for a British sea dog, and the great guns of England spouted iron and flame in the general direction of Dakar.

In an amazing display of optimism de Gaulle states that he noted "no real fighting ardor on either side," and that "I did not get the impression that the place was determined on a desperate resistance." So he led some Free French marines to try a landing down the coast. They met an equally inhospitable reception and pulled out.

De Gaulle spent a dismal night aboard the *Westerland.* The next morning the luck was no better. That untimely fog hung on. The French in Dakar and the British ships at sea spent the day blazing away at invisible targets. That night the British Admiral asked de Gaulle to come aboard his flagship, the *Barham.*

It was an unhappy meeting. When de Gaulle climbed up the

[115]

dripping side of the dark gray battleship, he found the British in a morose mood. Admiral Cunningham was for giving up an enterprise for which he could see no future, and Brigadier Irwin, commanding the troops, agreed with him. "But," they both asked, "what will become of Free France if we give up?"

De Gaulle had his answer ready. All day he had been wretchedly standing on the *Westerland's* bridge, apparently unmoved, but shuddering inwardly at the crash of each broadside fired by his allies at fellow Frenchmen. He cared not at all about the hunks of steel that the *Richelieu* was hurling in his direction, but every time the orange flames of British guns stabbed through the mist they struck deep in his heart.

To Admiral Cunningham he said, "I agree with you and suggest that you radio that you are stopping the bombardment at the request of General de Gaulle . . . Whatever happens Free France will continue."

Then he returned to his launch, plunging in the oily swell alongside the *Barham,* while boatswains' whistles shrilled and Barham's officers and men sadly lined the rails in the formal ceremonial to a departing Chief of State.

During the night Churchill radioed Admiral Cunningham to press the attack, so for one more day the bombardment continued. By nightfall the British battleship *Resolution* had caught a torpedo in her belly and was under tow, while two Vichy submarines and a destroyer were sunk and the *Richelieu* hard hit. Cunningham broke off the action.

Steaming toward Duala in the Cameroons aboard the French ship *Commandant Duboc,* to which he had transferred, de Gaulle reached a new low of despondency. There was no question that Dakar was a personal disaster. Radio broadcasts told of an angry British reaction. Vichy was exultant over what their propaganda called "The great naval victory of Dakar." Worst of all, the whole American press was jeering. True, Churchill, who was no fairweather friend, went before the House of Commons to say, "My confidence in General de Gaulle is greater than ever." But world opinion was generally expressed by an Englishman to Maurice Schumann: "It seems your 'great man' is not so very great."

The most unfortunate reaction of all occurred in the brain of President Franklin D. Roosevelt. Then and there he decided that de Gaulle was an adventurer with no real following in France or Africa. No acts of faith or fact by the French people, no display of ability, bravery, or statecraft by de Gaulle could thereafter shake this stubbornly held conviction. Through the years this prejudice poisoned the relationship between two great men who might have been great friends and allies, and swayed American policy toward curious bypaths and strange adventures, engendering deep, unnecessary, bitterness.

De Gaulle appraised all the adverse reactions realistically. He was no man to lie to himself about a reverse. Clear-eyed, he saw that this was a bad business. While his purpose did not falter, he was deeply unhappy. He noted, "In my narrow cabin . . . crushed by heat, I was completing my education in what the reactions of fear could be, both among adversaries taking revenge for having felt it and among allies suddenly frightened by a repulse."

❧ ⚜ ❧

THE LADDER OF AFRICA

A S DE GAULLE STEPPED ASHORE at Duala, he stood on the bottom rung of the ladder of Africa. There was nowhere to go but up. His reception was the beginning of the climb.

Under brilliant sunshine, dazzlingly reflected by the white buildings of the port, an enthusiastic crowd of white and black Frenchmen swayed and tossed in tumultuous welcome. In an open space in front of them a regiment of native troops in white shirts, shorts, long white socks, and rakishly tilted fezzes were drawn up at rigid attention, though their black faces were split by white-toothed smiles of welcome. The Cross of Lorraine was flying beside their regimental colors.

As the tall, thin, figure of their commander in his tropical white uniform and solar topee advanced to greet him, de Gaulle recognized Colonel de Hautclocque, who will be known as long as the history of France is read by the *nomme de guerre* he had assumed to protect his family in Occupied France— Leclerc. The depression of the dismal fog-bound hours at Dakar fell from de Gaulle's shoulders like a rain-wet coat. Here were Free French troops on Free French soil, the first his feet had touched since he left Bordeaux.

From the docks, de Gaulle drove through wildly cheering crowds to the *Palais du Gouvernment,* where civil servants, French Colonists and native chiefs crowded around him, "swimming in a flood tide of patriotic optimism."

Thence he flew in a small French airplane to all the African territories which had acknowledged his leadership. Free France nearly lost its Chief when the single engine of his Potez 540 quit enroute to Fort Lamy in the Tchad, and it crash-landed in a swamp.

Extricating himself and his party, he went on to Fort Lamy, where Negro Governor Félix Eboué, who had been the first of all the African leaders to join Free France, affirmed his loyalty and confidence once and for all. To Fort Lamy also came Four Star General Georges Catroux, flying over a thousand miles of hostile desert from Cairo, Egypt, to pledge his allegiance and acknowledge de Gaulle's authority. Catroux said, "You have gone beyond the ladder of rank and are invested with a duty that has no hierarchy."

From Fort Lamy de Gaulle flew to the distant desert outposts where he told a handful of resolute troops that he expected them eventually to fight their way up to the far off Mediterranean and link up with the British in expelling the Nazis and Italians from North Africa. They looked astounded by what sounded like a military hallucination. But when the time came they did it.

At Brazzaville, where de Gaulle arrived on October 24, he planned with General Eduard de Larminat the attack on nearby Gabon, which was holding out for Vichy. Free French and Vichyites were already in contact there, exchanging a few shots and plenty of arguments. On November 5, Lambaréné was taken and on November 9, Libreville, the capital, surrendered, after a sharp fight, to a force commanded by Leclerc and Koenig backed up by a naval squadron under d'Argenlieu, who had hardly recovered from his wounds. Now the Cross of Lorraine flew over all of Equatorial Africa.

But it was the poorest part of the French Empire, dependent on outside sources for virtually all manufactured things. De

[119]

Gaulle appointed René Pleven Secretary General to straighten out its economic tangle and arrange financing in England and the United States.

Meanwhile, at Brazzaville on October 27, he announced the formation of the Defense Council of the Empire to which he appointed Catroux, Muselier, Cassin, Larminat, Leclerc and other faithful leaders. His announcement also contained a sacred promise, which he kept:

> It is necessary that a new power should assume charge of the direction of the French war effort. Events have imposed on me that sacred duty. I shall not fail it.
>
> I will exercise my powers in the name of France and only to defend her, and I make the solemn promise that I will render an account of my actions to the representatives of the French people as soon as it is possible to do so freely.
>
> To assist me in my task I now bring into being as from to-day an Empire Defense Council.
>
> Officers, soldiers, and citizens of France, at this very moment infamous or senile chiefs are trying to hand our Empire over to the enemy. . . .

It was true. Pierre Laval had become Premier under Pétain; and on October 24, at Mentoire, the old Marshal had concluded an accord with Hitler that was almost an alliance.

On November 17, de Gaulle flew back to England. As the low flying plane skimmed through the ocean mist and rain, he was planning the long climb up the ladder of Africa. Great were the obstacles in his way, greatest of all the barrier raised by some of his own countrymen. But he had faith in himself; faith that in his favorite phrase from Chateaubriand, he would be able "to lead the French there by dreams."

London was in the midst of the blitz. The war in Africa had been serenity itself compared to the nightly uproar of bursting bombs and barking ack-ack guns, the rain of steel and fire upon the city. The way the British took it in their stride warmed de Gaulle to them. As for the Free French in London, they were almost glad of it. Not that they were happy to see their British friends suffer, but they were ashamed to be living in freedom and safety while their countrymen suffered at home. The bombing gave them a feeling of fighting, of risking their lives for France.

Maurice Schumann tells of how the BBC suffered a direct hit one night when they were broadcasting. Pierre Bourdan was wounded. When Schumann went to see him in the hospital, Bourdan received him laughing, "What a pity," he said, "that the French staff has missed a rendezvous with 'death on the field of honor.' But perhaps tomorrow evening . . ."

It sounds callous, but Schumann adds, "I shall never forget Bourdan weeping over the body of a young Frenchman who kept that rendezvous a few nights later."

The blitz was the least of de Gaulle's anxieties. Sometimes with Schumann or de Courcel he took off the mask of unconcern and confided his anguish at the difficulties and dangers of the darkening situation; the ravages of German U boats; the volcanic rumblings beneath the calm surface of the British Cabinet; and the harassments and intrigues which each day threatened the task of organizing his great enterprise.

The Free French, now installed in Carlton Gardens, were not immune to internal stresses. During de Gaulle's absence, Admiral Muselier "had fallen foul of the other services." De Gaulle had to assert all his moral force to restore order.

Infinitely more difficult was the task of maintaining the prestige and independence of France in the face of American disapproval and British absorption in their own war effort. Though he admired the British leaders immensely for their dedication and for their humor, which lightened the terrible pressures upon them, he had to fight them all the time to keep French independence. This was especially difficult, since they were financing the whole Free French operation.

"It is impossible to imagine," he said later, "what a concentration of effort, what a variety of procedures, what insistence, in turn gracious, pressing or threatening—the English were capable of deploying in order to get their way." Even de Gaulle's own people were frightened by the way he stood up to them.

But there were bright spots in the dark picture. One was of the success of his intelligence department, BRCA, *(Bureau Central de Renseignments et d'Action)* in establishing contact with the nascent Resistance Movement in Occupied France. "Passy," who headed it, though without experience, had a sort of cold passion for his job. Agents were successfully sent into France who not only brought back valuable information, but who also succeeded in establishing an embryo organization there which eventually brought the whole Resistance under the Cross of Lorraine.

Another bright moment came in the dusky dawn of March 9, 1941, when de Gaulle was staying with Churchill at Chequers. He was awakened at 4:00 A.M. by the Prime Minister of England bursting into his room and dancing around his bed like an exuberant bear. Churchill said excitedly, "The American Congress has passed the Lend-Lease Act. Now we'll get the tools!"

De Gaulle was delighted, not only because of the flow of materiel they could now expect, but because America had taken a giant step toward entering the war.

On March 14, de Gaulle flew again to Africa. He felt assured that his organization was now in good hands. Men of quality, like René Pleven, Gaston Palewski, who had been Reynaud's right hand man, Hervé Alphand, and the others, were running things in England. Free French delegations were planting themselves all over the world under the leadership of such brilliant young men as Ledroux, in South America, Garreau-Dombasle, in the United States, d'Argenlieu, in Canada, and Jacques Soustelle, in Central America.

The latter was a particularly devoted young fellow, stocky, vibrant and immensely energetic, leaning heavily toward the left, as ardent young men so often do. Neither he nor de Gaulle could foresee the ironic outcome of their long, intimate, association, with Soustelle playing a major role in making de Gaulle

President of France in 1958, and heading an ultra-conservative coalition against him in 1960.

De Gaulle remained away from England for nearly six months. During that time he again visited all of equatorial Africa and advised with Leclerc on the buildup of the Free French forces, giving precedence to the Sahara Task Force which was eventually to cross the vast desert and join the British in North Africa.

A much more important operation, which de Gaulle directed from Cairo, was the liberation of Syria. When the Vichy French there agreed to allow Nazi planes to use their airports, General Sir Archibald Wavell decided to act. De Gaulle, who had been urging such a course, sent General Legentilhomme with his Free French Brigade to assist the British. The Vichy French forces surrendered after a hard fight in which Legentilhomme was wounded.

It was the first significant success of a Free French and British expedition. But success was bitter to de Gaulle because of the French dead on both sides, who had killed each other. Sadly he said, "It made on me an impression of horrible waste."

After the battle the British naturally wanted to assume the dominant power in Syria. With Catroux at his side, de Gaulle opposed them vigorously. Syria had been a French mandate. De Gaulle proposed to offer it independence in association with France. So sharp was the conflict that de Gaulle, to the horror of some of his Defense Council in England, threatened to break the alliance and withdraw the French troops from British command. It was daring, it was intransigent (according to the British), and it was a dangerous bluff. But it worked. The British backed down.

Catroux, who understood the Levant so well, was invaluable in this affair. As de Gaulle wrote, "Possessing the sense of the greatness of France and a taste for authority, skillful in handling men, especially those of the Middle East, as sure of his own value as he was devoted to our great enterprise . . . General Catroux did France good service."

On September 1, de Gaulle came back to England. It was high time. Muselier had been stirring up trouble again in the Council. It was not enough to have to fight France's enemies and her allies to uphold her integrity, de Gaulle had to fight his own people as well. This was perhaps the period of his greatest appearance of arrogance. "I am too poor to bow," he once told Churchill.

Even to his faithful few, de Gaulle was sharp and inconsiderate. So engrossed was he in his problems, and so convinced that he must "encase himself in ice," that for a time he lost touch with his own people, forgetting Frenchmen in his concern for France. His aides served him no less devotedly for this. They cracked jokes about his crusty obliviousness. "There must be something wrong with him today," one of them said. "He asked how I was."

Even through all the clutter of intrigue, vexations, and small decisions, de Gaulle often sent his mind ranging far into the future, foreseeing improbable events. That was the year the Germans attacked Russia. Their armor had swept the Ukrainian plains to the gates of Moscow, which had nearly fallen to them. They held the most fertile and civilized portion of the country and were preparing to resume their conquest as soon as General January relaxed his icy guard.

But de Gaulle said reflectively to Maurice Schumann: "Since the Polish victory over the Teutonic knights in the fifteenth century, the Slavs have always been in retreat before the Germans. They were even beaten by Hindenburg in 1914. That state of affairs will have lasted for half a millenium. For next year the tide will turn. Where will the (Slavic) flood halt? That is the problem of tomorrow. Yes that is the real problem."

And he added, "The Russians are a sad people. They would make for us a funereal Europe. People say that their ideology is more apt to conquer than their military might. I strongly believe the contrary."

That winter another of de Gaulle's predictions was verified when the Japanese attack on Pearl Harbor brought the United States into the war. Now he could be certain of eventual victory. But because of President Roosevelt's distrust of him, it multiplied his immediate problems.

However, one tremendous success strengthened his hand. In May, 1942, German General Irwin Rommel broke the line of the British Eighth Army in Libya. But General Koenig, with 5,500 Free French, held the Oasis of Bir Hakeim. Rommel wanted to pursue the British, but he dared not leave the French in his rear. On June 1, he attacked Koenig with an Italian Division and the Ninetieth Division of his famous Afrika Corps, supported by hundreds of tanks and heavy guns. For eleven tremendous days Koenig held out against odds of six to one. On the eleventh day, following orders from de Gaulle, the remains of his division burst through the encircling German lines and rejoined the reorganized VIIIth Army.

That night a messenger from the British General Staff brought word to de Gaulle at his home in London that Koenig and 4,000 of his men were safe. The General received the message with an impassive face and, thanking the Englishman politely, carefully closed the door. As the latch clicked he burst into wild weeping—"sobs of pride and tears of joy."

Perhaps the sharpest personal blow de Gaulle received in the war years, and the most dangerous to his prestige and to the success of Fighting France—as it had now earned the right to be called—was the Allied invasion of North Africa in November, 1942. For Roosevelt, informed by his Consul General in Algiers, Robert Murphy, that "De Gaulle has a following of less than 10 per cent of the people of North Africa," not only rejected his leadership, but would not even allow Churchill to tell him about the plan until the attack was actually launched.

Of course the Deuxieme Bureau had penetrated the veil of secrecy. While de Gaulle did not know the exact day and hour of the North African landings, he did know that they were contemplated and that Roosevelt had selected his old commander at Metz, General Giraud, to rally the North African French to the Allied side.

Though de Gaulle admired Giraud as a soldier, the general was no diplomat. So the days of waiting, though an anxious time for him, were consoled by the thought that if Giraud made a mess of things they would have to call him in.

All day on November 7, 1942, American and British radio stations kept repeating "Robert Arriving! Robert Arriving!" It took no great acumen for de Gaulle to guess that this was the code signal to Algerian French sympathizers that the British-American landings were about to take place. "Robert" was obviously Robert Murphy. The morning papers of November 8 announced the landings.

Churchill asked de Gaulle to come and see him at noon that day. As de Gaulle entered the familiar door of 10 Downing Street, Churchill greeted him with uneasy affability. The Prime Minister was obviously terribly embarrassed. He described the operation and explained that, since the Americans were running the show, he had been forced to follow Roosevelt's wishes and leave de Gaulle out. Then with real emotion, he said, "You have been with us during the war's worst moments. We shall not abandon you now that the horizon is brightening."

De Gaulle was stiff as a newly starched shirt. He sympathized with Churchill's predicament, but he laid his own feelings on the line. "General Giraud is a great soldier," he said, "I wish him well. My hopes accompany him and the Allies. But if they had not prevented us from reaching an agreement I would have been able to get help for him."

Then he told Churchill and Eden how stupid he thought the Americans were not to seize Bizerte in Tunisia; as well as Algiers, Oran, and Casablanca. "The Germans will rush in," he said.

"The Americans want to play Vichy off against de Gaulle," de Gaulle added.

"What about the relations of Fighting France with the new authorities in North Africa?" Churchill asked nervously.

"We must achieve unity as soon as possible, but whatever the case, the thing that matters most today is to reach a cease fire."

That night de Gaulle showed that he could be flexible as well as stiff-necked when the interests of France required it. Speaking over the BBC to "the French chiefs, soldiers, sailors, airmen, officials, and French *colons* of North Africa," he said, "Rise up! Help our Allies! Join them without reservation! Do not worry about names or formulas. Only one thing counts. The welfare of our country!"

The French did not rise up. In Algiers, de Gaulle's old classmate from St. Cyr, General Alphonse Juin, was in command of the ground forces. Admiral Darlan also happened to be in Algiers. After intricate negotiations, a cease fire was arranged at Juin's insistence. But at Oran and Casablanca there were bloody battles. Giraud went over to rally the Algerians and the Army. He was greeted with tremendous indifference.

The senseless fighting continued for three days. It was a painful surprise to both the British and Americans. They did not understand the French career officers' passion for legitimacy, and did not expect them to put obedience to Pétain's Government above the real interests of France—they did not know when to disobey. General Juin was a magnificent exception.

Finally, the Americans made a deal with opportunistic Darlan, who was Commander in Chief of all the Armed Forces of Vichy France. He was to rule North Africa as High Commissioner under British-American authority. The fighting ceased; and French troops under Juin marched with the Americans to take the port and great airfield of Bizerte. They were too late. The Germans had rushed in.

These were desperately unhappy days for de Gaulle. Helplessly he watched French, Americans, and British killing each other in a foolish fight. Helplessly, he noted the ineptitude of American diplomacy. Furiously, he saw President Roosevelt give power over Frenchmen to Darlan, who had willingly collaborated with Hitler.

Yet he managed to retain a balanced judgment of the situation. However volcanic his feelings, the reins of discipline held his temper in check. René Pleven, in answer to a question as to how de Gaulle acted during those extremely trying weeks said: "Of course he was angry, very angry. But he did not show it as you or I would. For example, he did not curse. During the five tremendous years I was with him, through trials, reverses, calumnies, and plain stupidity, I never heard him swear. Nor was he inclined to judge individuals hastily. Even Roosevelt. During that dark time when the President of the United States was evidently doing all in his power—even to collaborating with collaborationists—to stop de Gaulle, he refused to criticize him. He never said, 'Roosevelt is a fool.' He would say, 'Roosevelt is blinded by Murphy's reports.' He judged the high caliber of Roosevelt, even though the President was turned against him."

In spite of Pleven's words, de Gaulle did not lack bitterness. He merely controlled it for the sake of France.

Meanwhile, the public reaction to the Darlan deal was violent. The English were furious as was the American press, feeling that the ideals for which so many men were dying had been betrayed. De Gaulle exacerbated public feeling with radio speeches, while from deep within enslaved France the voice of the Resistance made itself heard.

The situation became highly embarrassing to Roosevelt, who felt Darlan hanging around his neck like a decaying albatross. It was resolved by a young man named Fernand Bonnier de la Chapelle, who killed the Admiral on Christmas Eve, 1942.

De la Chapelle was secretly executed. De Gaulle felt deep sympathy for "this young man, this child overwhelmed by the spectacle of odious events (who) thought his action would be a service to his lacerated country."

Nor was he without compassion for the Admiral whom he regarded as a fine naval officer who had missed his chance because he lacked the greatness to resist the decay of the State. Nevertheless, for once he shared an emotion with Roosevelt, immense relief at the removal of the Admiral from the obfuscated African scene.

Two days after Darlan's assassination, General Giraud

was given his powers and what de Gaulle describes as "the rather astonishing title of Civil and Military Commander in Chief." Feeling that here was an opportunity to unify the French Empire and secure the independence of French sovereignty, de Gaulle cabled him, proposing a meeting. Giraud answered evasively.

De Gaulle was still firmly convinced that Giraud's reluctance was due to pressure from the Americans who, he believed were doing everything possible to oppose French unity while paying it lip service. He suspected that President Roosevelt wanted to control the French Army and French policy. He wrote, "That is why he had bet on both de Gaulle and Pétain at the start, then shoved Giraud into the track when a rupture with the Marshal became inevitable . . . Now the President found it convenient to keep Fighting France and the system at Algiers separate until the time came when he could impose on both parties the solution of his choice . . ."

Certainly de Gaulle's suspicions of Roosevelt's intentions were accurate, but not of the President's motives. For Roosevelt was motivated less by a desire to manage French affairs than by a profound distrust of de Gaulle, whom he still regarded as a charlatan with dictatorial leanings. However, he, too, wanted to unite the French and the moment of his choice was at hand.

On January 17, 1943, de Gaulle got a message from Winston Churchill, inviting him to Casablanca to confer with him, President Roosevelt, and Giraud, who were already there. Apparently the Deuxieme Bureau slipped up, for it was the first de Gaulle had heard of the Casablanca Conference. The message only confirmed de Gaulle's suspicions of Roosevelt and he refused haughtily, at the same time cabling Giraud that he was ready to meet with him "On French territory as one Frenchman to another."

In Casablanca Roosevelt with humorous impatience said to Churchill, "I have the groom. You produce the bride."

Churchill sent another message to de Gaulle, which stated

that Roosevelt joined him in the invitation. It was a virtual ultimatum—come, or else the British Government will break with you. De Gaulle knew the moment had come to bend rather than break.

Accompanied by Catroux, d'Argenlieu and Palewski, de Gaulle arrived at Fedala Airbase on January 22, in a very bad humor. He was madder still at his reception. No honors were paid him, no troops saluted. American General William Wilbur sneaked him quickly out of the plane into a staff car. Then Wilbur actually dipped a rag in the mud and smeared it on the windows of the car so that no one could see in. The object, said de Gaulle, was "to conceal the presence of General de Gaulle from his colleagues in Morocco." He was cold with fury.

It hardly seemed possible that the General's rage could tower higher, but it did. The staff car drove directly to Anfa, a rich suburb outside of Casablanca, where pretty white villas were set on a green hill on top of which was the modern Hotel Panaramique. As the car mounted the spiraling road, de Gaulle, peering through the mud-daubed panes, could see that the whole place had been cleared of its residents and surrounded by barbed wire and guarded by American troops in battle gear.

"This is captivity," he exploded to poor Wilbur. "I have no objection to the Anglo-Saxons imposing it on themselves, but applying it to me, and on French territory at that, is a flagrant insult."

When shown the villa, staffed by American soldiers, which was assigned to him, he demanded by what right foreigners took over a Frenchman's house for him. Someone hastily explained that it belonged to a Swede who was getting a good rent.

Somewhat mollified, de Gaulle consented to enter it. Then he went to see Churchill, who records that it was "A very stony interview. (De Gaulle) was very formal and stalked out of the villa and down the little garden with his head high in the air."

However, de Gaulle was persuaded, or bullied, into accepting the "Civil and Military Commander in Chief's" invitation to lunch. Under the Moorish arches and mosaic ceiling of his villa, Giraud, slight of figure, thin-faced, full-mustached, like a Second Empire marshal, received his former colonel. They had not met since Metz. *"Bonjour, Gaulle,"* he said (five stars addressing two stars).

"Bonjour, mon Général," said de Gaulle politely.

Then he lashed out, "And what's this?" he demanded. "Four times I asked you to meet with me, and now it is in a barbed wire enclosure in the midst of foreigners that I must encounter you. Don't you realize how odious this is from a purely national point of view?"

Startled and shamefaced, Giraud lamely excused himself saying, "I could not do otherwise. I think only of the battle, not of politics. I don't read the papers or even listen to the radio . . ."

They had a pleasant luncheon after all, talking of old times.

Late in the evening de Gaulle met Roosevelt in his big white villa. They sat together for an hour on a sofa. All the time de Gaulle was conscious of listeners beyond the curtains, and once caught a glimpse of Harry Hopkins' head.

Using all his blandishments, Roosevelt tried to persuade de Gaulle to accept the American proposals, which were to establish in Algiers a Council of Overseas Territories. It would be headed by Giraud and include de Gaulle and the governors general and other commissioners. As Commander in Chief of the Army, Giraud would be subordinate to the inter-Allied Command. The Council would have no political power. It would be as though France no longer existed as a state.

De Gaulle saw at once that this would make Giraud in effect First Consul. But he was no Napoleon. "Where are his victories?" he asked.

In fact the famous Roosevelt charm had all the impact of a butter ball on de Gaulle's steely determination. "Only Frenchmen can decide the government of French territory," he told the President icily.

However the meeting did some good. De Gaulle was ready to acknowledge that "Franklin Roosevelt was governed by the loftiest ambitions. He was now fulfilling his destiny, impelled as he was by the secret admonition of death . . . But Roosevelt meant the peace to be an American peace . . . France as a sovereign independent nation thwarted his intention . . . In short, beneath his patrician mask of courtesy, Roosevelt regarded me without benevolence."

But Roosevelt's impression of de Gaulle was softened somewhat. "I like the spiritual look in his eyes," he said to Churchill.

There were more meetings and reproaches. Churchill was furious, fuming, and threatening; Harold Macmillan delivered a tirade. De Gaulle was adamant.

At a final meeting, Roosevelt, acting kind and sorrowful, asked only for a face-saver, "In human affairs you need a bit of drama," he said. "Will you at least consent to be photographed with the British Prime Minister, myself, and General Giraud?"

"Willingly," de Gaulle answered, "for I have a high esteem for that great soldier."

Pushing his luck with winsome charm Roosevelt asked, "Will you shake hands with him before the cameras?"

With a flash of humor too quick for a camera's eye, de Gaulle said in English, "I shall do that for you."

It was not until May 30, 1943, that an arrangement was finally made with Giraud that enabled de Gaulle to go to Algiers. In theory they shared political power in the new French Committee for National Liberation. In practice de Gaulle, by his moral force and popular backing, soon assumed leadership, though Giraud for a time continued to command the Army.

De Gaulle said his farewell in London to dapper Anthony Eden, for Churchill was away.

"What do you think of us?" Eden asked.

"Nothing is more amiable than your people," de Gaulle said. "I don't think as much of your politics."

"Do you realize that you have caused us more trouble than all our Allies in Europe?" Eden said.

"I don't doubt it," said de Gaulle. "France is a great power."

The settlement in Algiers was not made without some threatened violence. At one point Giraud had the streets full of tanks while de Gaulle was in the white Villa Les Glycines guarded by only ten Spahis. But the streets of Algiers were roaring "Vive de Gaulle!" And the cry was echoed throughout North Africa. Giraud was not the man to challenge an Algerian mob. The Committee was announced on June 3, 1943, as "the central French power . . . which directs the French war effort . . . (And) exercises French *sovereignty.*"

Meanwhile, the Nazi armies in Africa had been broken and eliminated by the American and British armies supported by the French forces. On July 2, Giraud went to Washington, where he concluded an agreement with Roosevelt to supply American arms for a French Army of 300,000 men. This much longer had grown the Sword of France.

Bastille Day, July 14, thus, was something to celebrate in Algiers, which had become the capital of the Empire and Fighting France. The traditional parade contained all the elements of a reunited French Army. As he reviewed Berbers and black Cameroons, fierce Senagalese and the Spahi Cavalry, the swaggering Foreign Legion and Fighting French troops who had fought their way up half a continent through deserts and snow-capped mountains, de Gaulle's aquiline profile was as sternly impassive as ever, but behind it he was aflame with exaltation.

"It was a kind of resurrection," he wrote. "I saw rising toward me like a wall of flame their tremendous desire to take part in the coming battles."

Later he spoke in the Forum to an enormous crowd that spilled over all its walls and stretched for nearly a mile down the broad avenue. "France is not the sleeping beauty whom the Prince of Liberation will waken gently," he said. "France is a tortured captive, who beneath the blows that afflict her in the cell where she lies . . . has measured the causes of her misfortunes as well as the infamy of her tyrants. France has already chosen a new road . . .

"Frenchmen! For fifteen hundred years our country has remained alive in her griefs and in her glories . . . Let us lift up our heads. Let us close ranks as brothers and march together in the struggle beyond victory to our new destinies. *Vive la France!"*

Like the crash of thunder, earthquakes, and tempestuous seas, the crowd answered him, *"Vive la France! Vive de Gaulle!"*

As the sound rolled on and on, Robert Murphy, cadaverous but smiling, came up to offer his congratulations. "What a tremendous crowd," he added.

With a spark of malice in his blue eyes de Gaulle said, "Yes. Those are the 10 per cent Gaullists that you counted in Algiers."

That night there was a gala performance at the Opera House. Spahis lined the grand stairway like the Garde Republicaine in Paris. Josephine Baker, her brown skin shining in a white silk gown, was singing *J'ai Deux Amours.* Suddenly her voice died in her throat. "I can't go on," she almost whispered, pointing to the flag-draped center box. *"He* is there!"

The audience turned its back to the stage, and shook the house with acclaim to de Gaulle, the Chief of Fighting France.

✻ ⚜ ✻

THE CAPITAL OF FIGHTING FRANCE

T HE VILLA LES GLYCINES, which became the Algerian
White House, was in fact dazzling white. Draped in
wisteria, it stood in a big tropical garden at the beginning of the Mustapha Superieur. Passing the sentry post at
the elaborate wrought-iron gates, you mounted the hill toward
the long ornate façade. Prowling on the terrace was apt to be
Lieutenant of Spahis Libine, a fierce, broken-nosed, ex-boxer
who was de Gaulle's personal bodyguard. He had a thankless
job, for his General liked to slip out of the park and go for
solitary walks.

Entering *les Glycines,* you found yourself in a dark, neo-
Gothic antechamber furnished with heavy oak furniture. On
a carved console the General's two-starred kepi rested upside
down. Beyond a hideously decorated salon was de Gaulle's
businesslike office. Gaston Palewski occupied another room
close by.

At this epoch, Palewski was thought to be closest of the
entourage to de Gaulle and aroused a good deal of jealousy
by his supposed influence. The Conservative Algerian *colons*
considered him a bright red Republican and distrusted him
profoundly. His power over de Gaulle was as grossly exag-

gerated as his redness. He was a good and trusted watch dog. Though officers on duty and soldiers of the guard lounged at familiar ease while de Gaulle was safely in his office, the announcement, *"Le Général!"* produced a panic. Officers jumped for their kepis, dropping telephones in mid-talk. Guards hastily seized their rifles and came to rigid attention, and Libine, grabbing his sub-machine gun, literally dove into the escort car.

General Giraud lived in far greater state in the former Summer Palace of the Bey of Algiers about fifty yards up the hill. Eisenhower's headquarters were at the Hotel St. George still higher up.

The French Committee of National Liberation (C.F.L.N.), of which de Gaulle and Giraud were alternate presidents, met twice a week in idyllic surroundings at the *Lycée Eugène Fromentin,* a former girls' school, on top of the Mustapha Superieur. It consisted of a red brick main building and a dozen pleasant villas set among pines and eucalyptus trees in a park overlooking the city and the harbor. The villas had names oddly inappropriate to their present purpose like "The Nest," and "The Hive."

In fact, once the C.F.L.N. moved in, the only idyllic thing about the place was its setting, for the meetings were a series of Gallic Donnybrooks. Reporters waiting outside could hear the babble of angry voices as the Giraud and de Gaulle factions went at each other furiously. The one voice they never heard was de Gaulle's, for the louder others shouted, the more softly he spoke. It was very effective.

The arguments between the factions were not, as many Americans thought, a squabble between jealous generals. It was a clash of political philosophies—between the authoritarian leanings of Giraud and the republican principles of de Gaulle, and between a materialistic, "practical" approach on the one hand, and the romantic, idealistic policy of independence and grandeur on the other. "Never settle for mediocrity," was de Gaulle's favorite aphorism.

In Algiers, as a matter of policy, he insisted on as great a formality of dress and dignity in his personal staff as he does now at the Elysée. Once, Committee Member André Philip got back from the beach just in time for a Council meeting. He rushed in wearing white shorts and an open-neck shirt. De Gaulle regarded him coldly and said, "Voilà, Philip, you have forgotten something."

"What can that be?" Philip asked nervously.

"Your hoop," said de Gaulle.

As soon as possible de Gaulle asked Yvonne to join him in Algiers. He was never happy away from his family. She came, bringing only Anne, for Elizabeth was finishing college and Phillipe was now a junior officer on a French destroyer.

Quite typically, de Gaulle did not install them at *les Glycines* but rented *des Oliviers*, a smaller, more secluded villa outside the city. Every afternoon on the dot of seven he left his office to join them for one of the quiet country evenings he loved so well.

As usual, the society of the place interested the de Gaulles not at all, in spite of the fact that Algiers had become a regular little Paris. Drawn to it by the taste of freedom were many men of high intellectual and moral value. André Gide, with his air of an aging Buddhist monk and his young mischievous eyes, was teaching at the university. Massive Antoine de Saint Exupéry, whom everybody called Saint Ex, promenaded the streets in his beribboned uniform and his enormous ego. André Maurois arrived from America, and, of course, Maurice Schumann, scholar and historian, now made his eloquent appeals for heroism and glory over Radio Algiers.

A rather astonishing figure among the warriors was Eve Curie, wearing the bars of a second lieutenant, on the staff of General Jean de Lattre de Tassigny.

There were also a great crowd of frustrated emigrés, whose croaking over the hardships of exile gave Algiers the nickname of "The Frog Pond." In addition there were no less than 110 generals of the Pétain regime who, with other very conservative senior officers, were called "The Mustaches."

[137]

Other relics of Vichy days occasionally turned up. One day de Gaulle inspected two fine French cruisers in the harbor. Aboard the *Georges Leygues* he noted with approval a bronze plaque which read: *Narvick, April 1940.* Aboard the *Émil Bertin* was a similar plaque, but his face turned quince-sour as he read, *To the Victorious Repulse of the Enemy at Dakar 23 September, 1940.*

~ On September 8, 1943, word reached de Gaulle that the Italian Government of Marshal Badoglio, which had replaced Mussolini, had signed an armistice with the Allies. Naturally, de Gaulle was in a fine fury at not having been informed of what was brewing. It was a deliberate slight to Fighting France. Giraud was irritatingly smug, since Robert Murphy had secretly told him in advance.

The meeting of the Committee the next day was a terrible tempest. De Gaulle, in a cold rage, threatened to resign. Five-star General Georges, who had been field commander of the beaten French Army in 1940, dared to rebuke the two-star President of the Council. "You always want to slam doors," he said to de Gaulle. "That is not a policy."

Angrily de Gaulle snapped, "Perhaps. But at least I've said often enough what I think of defeatists, not to have to sit next to one."

In the end, of course, things were once more smoothed over, and France was given a place on the Italian Armistice Commission.

A short time later Corsica, which had been garrisoned by Italian troops, fell to the Fighting French with no Allied assistance. Giraud had prepared the attack very cleverly, but had not informed de Gaulle until quite late in the day. On V-Day for Corsica, de Gaulle congratulated Giraud, and then rebuked him for his attitude toward the Committee.

"Now you're talking politics," said Giraud.

"Yes," de Gaulle answered, "because we are fighting a war. And war is one kind of politics."

He privately decided that Giraud had to go.

Then he flew over to Corsica. When he arrived Crosses of Lorraine suddenly blossomed everywhere, and de Gaulle was enthusiastically acclaimed. So Corsica, the first area of Metropolitan France to be liberated, was brought under the Government of the C.F.L.N.

Meanwhile, in France itself the Resistance Movement had swelled into a great underground Army, which at its peak was over 300,000 strong. They fought as guerrillas in her rugged hills and, perhaps more dangerously, as saboteurs in her factories and mines and vulnerable railways. But even guerrillas cannot fight without some supplies. These were sent them by parachute drops organized by the C.F.L.N., though mainly carried out by the British and American Air Forces.

At first the Resistance consisted of many little organizations fighting and working on their own. De Gaulle, through emissaries parachuted into France, had reached out to bring almost all the different elements into unity under his leadership. By the autumn of 1943, these men and women of all parties from Communist to Royalist were joined in a single purpose, to drive the enemy out of France. Their symbol was the Cross of Lorraine.

Now, de Gaulle made a move designed at once to give them a part in the Government of Fighting France and also to give that Government a republican form in the eyes of the world. He created the Consultative Assembly. It was a brilliant strategic conception, for it was not only a forum for all different points of view but also a splendid sounding board before which he could make his pronouncement without the appearance of dictatorial decisions. It was also an earnest expression of his real intent to re-establish the Republic in liberated France.

The delegates were a very mixed bag indeed. There were the old politicians like Félix Gouin, who was elected its first president; Vincent Auriol, Marcel d'Astier, Marc Rucart, and Paul Giacobbi, all delighted to be able to make speeches again. But the main body of the delegates represented Resistance organizations.

These delegates came from France by all sorts of hazardous routes—in fishing boats and by clandestine airplane pickups; through that wild and rugged brush country along the Spanish border of France; and then across the Pyrenees and, in disguise, through neutral but hostile Spain. They came acknowledging de Gaulle as their Chief. But they, too, were of many different political views.

As is the way of French parliaments, the delegates immediately formed into splinter parties. These included the Metropolitan Resistance, the Exterior Resistance, and the Independent Resistance. The former politicians preserved the names of their old parties—Socialist, Radical, and so forth.

The most powerful and disciplined party was, of course, the Communists, led by Russian-trained André Marty. If there is wonder that de Gaulle permitted this group to function, remember that the Russians were not then enemies, but allies in the midst of their heroic defense of Stalingrad. Likewise, the Communist members of the Resistance were its finest and fiercest fighters. And finally, de Gaulle was determined that the Consultative Assembly must represent all of France; and in those days the Communists were a full third of France—even today they poll at least 25 per cent of the vote.

But, though the Assembly splintered into small parties, just as it had under the Third Republic, the cohesive force of a united war effort brought considerable unity to its deliberations. And, as de Gaulle himself wrote, "There was also the attachment they felt for Charles de Gaulle because he had protested against conformism; because he had been condemned to death; and because throughout the nation his words, however remote and blurred, defied discretion . . ."

In short, the Assembly rendered good services by giving the Resistance a feeling of having a voice in the future Government of France liberated, and in planning the organization of that liberation.

Nor did its disputes cause any trouble. For it had no real power.

That was in the hands of de Gaulle and his staff. Giraud was quietly eased out of politics and more forcefully ejected from military command. The Committee itself was reorganized by de Gaulle on the basis of government departments. They were headed by a brilliant group of commissioners whose names still stand high in the leadership of France. They included Pierre Mendès-France, Commissioner of Finance; Pierre Louis Jacquinot, Navy; René Pleven, Colonies; General Catroux, Moslem Affairs; Henri Bonnet, Information; René Mayer, Communications; Henri Queuille, State; André Le Troquer, War and Air Force; and Jean Monnet, Special Commissioner to the United States.

Meanwhile, the Allies had breached "Fortress Europa" and were fighting their way up the Italian peninsula under American General Mark Clark. His forces consisted of the American Fifth Army and the famous British Eighth Army. The latter now consisted of a British army corps and a Fighting French army under General Juin. When the matter of naming Juin's command came up, de Gaulle said, "We'll call it the Army of Italy. That has a fine ring in French ears."

With the Army of Italy performing heroic service in the desperate battles on the Peninsula and the French Committee of National Liberation so strongly and soundly organized, de Gaulle had reason to expect that President Roosevelt would adopt a more cooperative attitude toward his Government. The contrary proved to be the case.

By April, 1944, the preparations for the great Allied landings in France were well under way. De Gaulle had been informed that General Eisenhower would govern France by means of an American anomaly called Allied Military Government of Occupied Territory—AMGOT, for short. He heard that the Americans had printed Occupation Francs which were to be declared legal currency. Naturally he did not take kindly to this proposed infringement of the sovereignty of France— his sovereignty. On April 21, the British announced that they would no longer permit the Fighting French Mission in London to transmit code messages to Algiers—for "security reasons."

De Gaulle regarded this as a final insult and promptly instructed Ambassador Pierre Viénot and General Koenig in London to make no further agreements with the Allies until it was rescinded. As he expected, this greatly embarrassed Eisenhower and his staff, who were depending on French officers to establish liaison with the Resistance forces within France.

It surprised no one, least of all de Gaulle, when Alfred Duff-Cooper came to Algiers with a message inviting him to England to confer with Churchill. However, it appeared that Roosevelt was willing to recognize de Gaulle only as "the leader of a group of Frenchmen."

Just returned from a visit to the Army of Italy where he had watched their desperate assault across the Garigliano River, de Gaulle was in no mood for trifling. He countered Roosevelt bruskly by having the French Committee for National Liberation vote itself "The Provisional Government of the French Republic."

On June 2, Churchill's private York airplane arrived in Algiers with an urgent message:

"My dear General de Gaulle,
"Please come now, as quickly as possible with the greatest secrecy. I give you my personal assurance that it is in the interest of France. I am sending you my York."

De Gaulle realized that this meant that the invasion was imminent, but he was not inclined to accept. For once the more flexible members of his Council prevailed over his rigidity. He took off the next day in Churchill's plane, accompanied by a small staff including de Courcel. For these two it was another of those flights to London upon which great events hinged; and though it was far different from the desperate journey of June 18, 1940, they were faced by yet another crisis in their long pilgrimage.

❦ ⚜ ❦

THE SOIL OF FRANCE

WINSTON CHURCHILL, with his desire to be in the thick of things and his flair for the dramatic, received de Gaulle in his private train in the Portsmouth staging area of the great invasion. It was on a siding deep in the English countryside, green with spring and white with blossoms.

With Churchill were Eden and Ernest Bevin, General Ismay and the great South African, Marshal Jan Smuts. De Gaulle was accompanied by Palewski, de Courcel and Ambassador Viénot. As he and Churchill sat side by side at luncheon, two men very much alike in their very different ways, the warm friendship which underlay their political quarrels enveloped them.

Said Churchill, "I shall never forget that you, alone, were the first who came to share our hardships."

And de Gaulle, deeply moved, told the Prime Minister of his abiding affection and admiration.

Then Churchill vividly described the enormous military preparations for the great enterprise; the thousands of ships and planes, the hundred of thousands of men who were poised for the grand attack. Proudly he said, "The Royal Navy is to play the crucial role in the transport and protection of the landings."

De Gaulle responded by saying that Great Britain's ability to stage this great attack after the ordeals she had so valiantly endured was the signal justification of "the courageous policy you have personified since the darkest days of the war."

"Whatever coming events may still cost France," he went on, "she is proud to be in the line of attack, in spite of everything, by the side of the Allies for the liberation of Europe."

With typical understatement de Gaulle writes, "At this moment an identical flood of esteem and friendship carried away everyone present, Frenchmen and Englishmen alike." They were in fact almost in tears. Then he added, "But afterward we got down to business."

The business was not so pleasant.

Skillfully taking advantage of that emotional moment, Churchill proposed, "Let us make an arrangement for our cooperation in France. You can then go to America and propose it to Roosevelt. And perhaps he will grow less adamant and recognize your Government in one form or another."

De Gaulle encased himself in ice; you could almost see the frost forming. "Why do you think I have to submit to the authority of Roosevelt?" he said. "The French Government exists. I have nothing to ask of the United States or Great Britain in that area."

Then he went on to say that he knew about the plan for occupation francs and for Eisenhower to take France under his authority and that he would not agree.

At that the old bulldog roared, "We are going to liberate Europe, but only because the Americans are with us. There is something you ought to know! When we have to choose between Europe and the open sea, we'll choose the open sea. Every time I have to choose between you and Roosevelt, I'll choose Roosevelt."

Eden looked startled. Bevin looked shocked. The Laborite said loudly, "I want you to know that the Prime Minister is speaking on his own initiative and not in the name of the British Cabinet."

Everybody calmed down and Churchill took his guest to Eisenhower's command post in a Neissen hut in a woods nearby. All the walls were covered with tremendous maps. Ike, at his most charming, briefed de Gaulle in great detail about the plans. The ships, the planes, the troops, the whole vast machinery of invasion was cocked and triggered for the signal. But the weather reports were terrible. The moon and the tides commanded that the invasion must take place before June 7, or be postponed for a month. With his genuine humility Eisenhower asked de Gaulle, "What do you think I should do?"

"The decision is inevitably yours," de Gaulle said. "Whatever you do, I approve it in advance without reservation. This only will I tell you. In your place I would not delay. The danger of bad weather seems to me less than that of delay which would prolong the nervous tension for several weeks and endanger secrecy."

As de Gaulle prepared to leave, Eisenhower handed him the proclamation he was to make to the peoples of Europe, especially France. "It's only a draft," he said. "I am ready to alter it at your suggestion."

On their way back to Churchill's train, de Gaulle read the proposed speech hastily. In it the peoples of Norway, Belgium, Holland and Luxembourg were not questioned as to their political destiny, but Eisenhower took another tone with France. He urged the nation to carry out orders and stated that once France was liberated "the French themselves will choose their representatives and their government." There was not a word about de Gaulle or the Provisional Government of France.

"This is unacceptable," de Gaulle said.

Churchill writes that he invited de Gaulle to have dinner and ride back to London on his train, "But he drew himself up and stated that he preferred to motor with his French officers separately."

It was painfully evident to de Gaulle that Roosevelt

was determined to exclude him from any power in France if possible. He was equally sure that Eisenhower, of whom he was genuinely fond, had written his D Day proclamation under the orders of the American State Department. When he had first been appointed Supreme Commander, Eisenhower had come to see him in Algiers and frankly said, "You were originally described to me very unfavorably. Now I realize that was an error. For the coming battle I must have your assistance and I have come to ask you for it."

Grasping his hand de Gaulle said, "Splendid! You are a man! For you know how to say 'I was wrong.'"

Later when they talked of establishing cooperation between the Allied armies and French authorities Eisenhower said, "Now I can assure you that whatever apparent attitudes are imposed on me, I will recognize no French power other than your own in the practical sphere."

It would appear to an unprejudiced observer that the American general was definitely exceeding his authority in making that semi-political commitment. However, even on the eve of D Day, de Gaulle did not for a moment doubt Eisenhower's sincerity.

When he reached London, de Gaulle installed himself once more at the Hotel Connaught, which had a nostalgic attraction for him. There he received word that his suggested amendments to Eisenhower's proclamation had been turned down "for lack of time to print them." It was what he had expected. Titting for tatting, he ordered the French liaison officers attached to the American and British general staffs not to accompany them to France. This would appear unnecessary for French prestige, and a good deal less than magnanimous.

The schedule for D-Day broadcasts was brought to him at five P.M. on June 5, by Charles Peake of the Foreign Office. Peake was plainly embarrassed, for it was another slap in the face for de Gaulle. The King of Norway, the Queen of Holland, the Grand Duchess of Luxembourg, and the Prime Minister of Belgium were to speak in that order. Then Eisenhower would make his proclamation. Lastly de Gaulle would address the French people.

De Gaulle instantly saw the trap. Using the language of the radio business he said, "For me, this script won't play!

"By speaking after Eisenhower I will seem to ratify his proclamation. Furthermore, my place in the succession is unsuitable to the dignity of France."

At two o'clock in the morning Viénot came pounding at de Gaulle's door in the Connaught. The Ambassador was shattered. He had spent the previous hour taking a terrible tongue-lashing from Churchill about de Gaulle's obduracy. A moment or two later, Peake came trotting in to plead a cause for which he had no heart. De Gaulle was as deaf to their arguments as Nelson on his pillar in Trafalgar Square. "If I make a speech at all," he said, "it will be at a different hour and entirely disjunct from the series."

So it was finally arranged. At 6 P.M. on D Day, while American and British troops were still fighting hard on the barely-won beaches of Normandy, de Gaulle spoke to France. As he always did, Maurice Schumann announced, "Honor and Country! Here is General de Gaulle!"

Then de Gaulle took the microphone saying:

"The supreme battle has been joined . . . It is of course the Battle of France, the battle for France. For the sons of France, wherever they are, whatever they are, the simple and sacred duty is to fight the enemy by every means in their power . . .

"The orders given by the Government of France and by the leaders it has recognized must be obeyed . . .

"From behind the clouds so heavily laden with our blood and tears, the sun of our greatness is now reappearing. *Vive la France!*"

The Allies held a finger-nail paring of the map of France. But they held it strongly. Naturally the one thing de Gaulle wanted to do was to set foot on that thin slice of liberated land. Naturally that was the last thing Roosevelt wanted him to do. The ensuing jockeying lasted a week. During that time the Governments in Exile of Norway, Czechoslovakia, Poland, Belgium, Yugoslavia, and Norway officially recognized the Provisional Government of the French Republic. Doubtless they thoroughly enjoyed asserting a little independence of their own.

In that week also, many of the leading American journalists were needling their own government about its attitude to de Gaulle, as, of course, were the British press. Finally popular pressure became too strong—Roosevelt also knew when to bend. On June 13, 1944, de Gaulle sailed in the French destroyer, *La Combattante,* for Normandy.

In the blue and orange dawn *La Combattante* came abreast of the Norman Coast. The sea was covered with ships and the shore was a forest of masts and a log jam of landing craft. There were wrecks in the shallows, and the beach was as ugly as a junk yard with the scrap-iron wreckage of war. But the offshore wind was apple-sweet with the lovely, authentic odor of France which de Gaulle's quivering nostrils could have mistaken for no other. It was four years less three days since he had last tasted it on just such a morning.

With de Gaulle were his most faithful—de Courcell, Palewski, d'Argenlieu, Pierre Billotte, Viénot, Colonel de Chevigné, Hettier de Boislambert, and Maurice Schumann. Observe that no member of his civil government was present—this would have made his mission political in the eyes of the Allies. But there was a civilian, a journalist named François Coulet, whose presence was no accident.

The party went over their destroyer's side by landing nets into a wallowing amphibious Duck. In the midst of a Canadian division they hit the beach and, clambering out, de Gaulle stood on hard, wet sand.

Look at him there in his first moment in France. Dressed in his familiar Brigadier's uniform and the two-starred kepi, he has changed a bit in four years. His tall frame has filled out becomingly and he has grown up to his nose. He is a handsome figure of a man and, though he is trying to keep his impassivity, he cannot quite conceal the deep surge of his emotion.

There, on the sand, de Gaulle, by clothing Coulet with the civil authority, a post for which he had been, so to speak, smuggled into the liberated France, assumed the power Roosevelt had tried to deny him. Then he sent Coulet and the others on to await him in Bayeux, while he and de Courcel went to pay their respects to General Sir Bernard Montgomery, Commander of the Allied Forces in the beachhead.

Their jeep ground and lurched over the dunes and through the fishing village of Courseulles-sur-Mer. Then, into a narrow Norman lane between high banks and hedgerows. If the beach was ugly, the countryside was verdant, carpeted with the delicate snow of apple blossoms.

De Gaulle found Monty in his trailer, working at his folding desk under the portrait of Rommel, whom he had had the honor of conquering at El Alamein, and whom he ardently admired. De Gaulle admired Montgomery. "In this great British leader," he wrote, "prudence and rigor went hand in hand with zeal and humor."

Montgomery briefed him on the satisfactory progress of the landings; and de Gaulle "graciously" congratulated him on his success. Then, as he wrote, "having expressed my confidence in him, I left Montgomery to his affairs and went on to mine in Bayeux."

On the way there he and de Courcel were startled by an anachronistic sound; amid the roaring motors and grinding caterpillar treads of mechanized war was the irregular beat of galloping hooves. Mounted bareback on a farm horse, black robes bouncing, came a fat, rosy-cheeked, country priest. He pulled up, and sliding to the ground, approached the jeep. "Ah there you are, *mon Général*," he said indignantly. "I listened to your appeal of the eighteenth of June; I helped the patriots and received the parachutists. I have been in league with the Maquis. And you! You were passing close to my village without even stopping to shake my hand! Oh well, if I had realized things would turn out like that!"

[149]

Laughing de Gaulle jumped out of his jeep and folded the priest in his arms. *"Monsieur le Curé,"* he said, "I will not shake your hand but I'll embrace you."

A little further along two gendarmes came pedaling down the road on their bicycles. De Gaulle stopped the car and hailed them. Seeing his stars, they dismounted and stood at attention. He presented himself, "I am General de Gaulle."

Flabbergasted is the only word to describe their condition. They began backing off and saluting rapidly; getting tangled up in their machines.

"My friends," de Gaulle said. "I have a small service to ask of you. I am going to Bayeux. Will you be so amiable as to turn around and tell them there that I am arriving? We won't budge from here for a quarter of an hour."

The policemen saluted again hastily and took off for Bayeux as though they were sprinting in the Tour de France. De Gaulle laughed and, watching their vanishing figures, said, "The reconnaissance is made."

He well knew that to the country people the gendarmes represented law, authority, the State. He wanted to show Bayeux that here was France herself come to recognize her chief. As Gaston Bonheur points out, "Against those two gendarmes Roosevelt could do nothing."

At the gates of Bayeux, Coulet was waiting with Mayor Dodman and the entire municipal council. The General greeted them, and the whole party went on foot from street to narrow street while the people pouring out of their houses stood in a kind of daze at the sight of de Gaulle, then burst into bravos or tears. De Gaulle walked ahead, followed by a growing emotional crowd, women weeping, men shyly stretching out their hands to touch him.

In the formal reception room of the town hall de Gaulle noted with amusement the clean spot on the wall where Marshal Pétain's picture had hung only an hour ago. There, Subprefect Rochat formally put himself under de Gaulle's authority and Monsignor Picaud, Bishop of Bayeux and Lisieux, came to pay his respects.

[150]

Acknowledged now by people, State, and Church, de Gaulle went to the Place du Chateau, where a great crowd had gathered. In tremendous tones Maurice Schumann shouted the words he had so often spoken into the microphone: *"Honneur et Patrie! Voici le Général de Gaulle!"*

As he stood in the misty French sunshine, while Frenchmen for the first time in four terrible years heard a French leader on French soil denounce the enemy and high-heartedly call on France victorious, de Gaulle was no longer impassive but impassioned. Those who were close to him saw the tears rain down his cheek, unnoticed by him, heard his voice break and soar again as emotions swept over him.

But at the very end his tone hardened to authority as he announced, "I have appointed Monsieur François Coulet as Commissioner of the French Republic for Normandy. You will obey him in all matters!"

American Brigadier General Lewis, in charge of civilian affairs for First Army, had hastily arrived to monitor the proceedings. At de Gaulle's words he turned turkey red and said furiously to Coulet "We will not tolerate this. We will not accept you!"

To which Coulet said softly, "It is not a question of accepting us. We are here. At home!"

After that de Gaulle drove on to the shattered town of Isigny, where the bodies of French men and women were still being carried from the smoking ruins. But all the bells in all the steeples that still stood were clanging madly. Every house that still had a wall was draped in tricolor bunting that had magically appeared from hiding places. Every man and woman and child who could still stand was pressing around him shouting, *"Vive la France! Vive de Gaulle!"*

And all the cables and air waves of the world were carrying the news of their acclamation.

A few hours before, de Gaulle had landed as "the leader of a group of Frenchmen." When he sailed away from Courseulles no one anywhere doubted that he was the President of the French Republic.

❦ ⚜ ❧

THE ROAD TO RAMBOUILLET

T HE IMMEDIATE RESULT of that day in Normandy was a sudden anxiety on the part of Roosevelt to meet with de Gaulle. Where before the President had indifferently said that he would receive the general if he cared to come to Washington, his ambassadors, and even his military men, like Eisenhower's Chief of Staff, General Walter Bedell Smith, came with pressing invitations from Roosevelt.

De Gaulle agreed that it was indeed high time, and past time, for a meeting if any sort of cooperation were to be arranged for liberated France. On July 6, 1944, the President's own plane brought him to Washington. On the columned portico of the White House, with the press out in full force, President Roosevelt, leaning on the arm of Secretary of State Cordell Hull, gave de Gaulle a warm and smiling welcome. The Americans treated him with all the courtesy, if not quite all the forms, due a head of state, and during his five days in Washington de Gaulle had an opportunity to talk with almost all the top men in Washington. His descriptions of them are bright flashes of insight.

For example, Cordell Hull had "great conscientiousness and distinction of spirit," but he was "hampered by his slight understanding of anything not American, and by Roosevelt's interference in his domain." In the latter remark de Gaulle showed his unfamiliarity with the Constitution of the United States, which directly charges the President with the conduct of foreign affairs.

Others whom he touched off accurately were Robert Patterson and James Forrestal (Secretaries of War and Navy), conducting their ministries with "the psychology of big business." General George C. Marshall was "a bold organizer but a reserved conversationalist, the animating spirit of the war effort." Admiral Ernest J. King was "zealous and imaginative, not concealing his pride that the scepter of the seas should pass into the hands of the American Navy." General H. H. Arnold was one to whose genius for organization de Gaulle paid tribute. And, a sour note, Admiral William D. Leahy, former United States Ambassador to Vichy, was "astonished by the events which had defied his counsels of conformity; surprised to see me there, but persisting in his prejudices" (against de Gaulle).

He shrewdly sums them all up as "a coherent assemblage which, because of their characters and of Roosevelt's own glittering personality, permitted itself only a restricted brilliance, but which was, without doubt, equal to its task."

But the important event of de Gaulle's visit took place in Roosevelt's office, where the President sat behind his great mahogany desk crowded with a boyish collection of memorabilia, political symbols, and gadgets. It was this intimate talk between a "glittering" Roosevelt and purposefully somber de Gaulle that counted.

Out to charm, bedazzle, and convince his guest, Roosevelt frankly described his vast idealistic plans for remaking the world nearer to his heart's desire. De Gaulle admits that, as the President lightly sketched in his Utopian prospectus for a union of nations to assure peace and freedom to the world, "it was difficult to contradict this artist, this seducer, in a categorical way."

Roosevelt envisioned his supranational community as consisting of all the nations of the world, basically controlled by the four great powers, America, Russia, Great Britain, and China. He was quite clearly ready to sacrifice some of the interests of Europe in order to secure Soviet approval.

It was at this point that de Gaulle categorically disagreed.

"It is the West," he told Roosevelt, "that must be restored. If it regains its balance the rest of the world will take it for an example. If it declines, barbarism will eventually sweep everything away. Now, Western Europe is essential to the West. Nothing can replace the value, the power, the shining examples of these ancient peoples. This is true of France above all, which of all the great nations of Europe is the only one which was, is, and always will be your ally."

"I know you are planning to help France materially," de Gaulle went on, "but it is in the political realm that she must recover her vigor, her self-reliance, and consequently her role. How can she do this if she is excluded from the inner councils of the great world powers, if she loses her African and Asian territories, in short, if the settlement of the war definitely imposes on her the psychology of the vanquished?"

Roosevelt's reply showed that his "powerful mind" was sympathetic to these ideas. He also displayed a genuine love for France. And he told de Gaulle that it was because of this deep feeling that he, and most Americans, had been so terribly shocked by her physical and moral collapse in 1940.

Nor was he hopeful of her future. "For the moment you are there," he said with all his winning warmth. "But will you still be there at the end of the tragedy?"

Sadly de Gaulle replied that Roosevelt's remarks showed that in foreign affairs logic and sentiment do not weigh heavily in comparison with the realities of power.

With his slightest smile he added, "What really counts is what we can take and hold on to. It is evident that if she is to regain her place in the world France must count on no one but herself."

Smiling warmly Roosevelt agreed. "We will do what we can

to help," he said. "But it is true that no one but the French people can help France."

So they ended in agreement on the facts of life for France, if not on the best way to help her. As Roosevelt in his wheel chair accompanied de Gaulle to the entrance, he pointed out the big, heated pool he had installed in the White House. "That's where I swim," he said with what de Gaulle thought was "defiance of his infirmity"; but which, in view of Roosevelt's exuberant personality, was more likely boyish pride in its white-tiled splendor.

Catching something of this youthful quality of the President, de Gaulle sent him a wonderful toy submarine, made by workers in the French Naval Base at Bizerte, which could perform amazing aquabatics. In return Roosevelt sent his picture inscribed, "To General de Gaulle who is my friend."

This was not quite accurate, for the relations between them were never to be friendly. De Gaulle respected and in some degree understood Roosevelt. But his private judgment was that, "As was only human, his will to power cloaked itself in idealism."

And Roosevelt wrote of de Gaulle to Congressman Joseph C. Baldwin, "In relation to future problems he seems quite tractable as long as France is dealt with as a world power. He is very touchy in matters concerning the honor of France. But I suspect that he is essentially an egoist."

De Gaulle says that he was never sure whether Franklin Roosevelt thought that "Charles de Gaulle was an egoist for France or for himself."

Many others have wondered.

After a tremendous reception in New York, headed by its enthusiastic little mayor, Fiorello La Guardia, and even greater acclaim in Canada, de Gaulle returned to Algiers. There he found waiting for him the first fruits of his Washington visit. A communication from the American Government stated, "The United States recognizes that the French Committee of National Liberation is qualified to exercise the administration of France." As Félix Garas says in his book, *De Gaulle Against the Powers,* "They still recoiled from the term 'Provisional Government of France,' while inclining before accomplished fact."

France by now was no mean ally. In fact her rearmament was little short of a miracle. Her regular military establishment included an army of 150,000 men, a navy of 320,000 tons manned by 50,000 sailors and comprising every sort of ship from battle cruisers to submarines, and an air force of 500 fighter planes manned by 30,000 men. In addition there were over 300,000 men in the French Forces of the Interior (F.F.I.), consisting of the Maquis or guerrillas fighting in the mountainous forests of France from the Alps to the Pyrenees and small secret bands of *Franc Tireurs* and Partisans who, armed with false papers, operated in the cultivated plains and great cities. Most valuable of all, perhaps, was de Gaulle's intelligence network, consisting of no less than 30,000 men and women.

Though these figures are impressive considering the beginnings of Free France with two men in a London hotel, they were, of course, merely a fraction of the Great Allied effort which included on the Western Front and in Russia at least twenty million men in arms. However, so concentrated was de Gaulle's attention on the French that if the other records of World War II were lost and a future historian had only de Gaulle's memoirs to go by, he might almost suppose that the Second Battle of France was won mainly by French troops, assisted, like Caesar's legions, by groups of barbarian auxiliaries.

All through June and July the tremendous allied build-up had been going on in the Normandy bridgehead. On July 25, Eisenhower touched off the great offensive that never stopped rolling until it had cleared virtually all France of the enemy. By mid-August, the broken German armies were falling back fast, harassed on flank and rear by the French Forces of the Interior who made a shambles of supply lines and communications. Eisenhower reckoned their efforts were worth fifteen divisions.

On August 15, a second Allied invasion was launched against the Riviera coast of France. This force included the American Seventh Army and the First French Army under de Lattre. They began fighting their way north toward a junction with Eisenhower's forces. Everywhere the Germans were on the run. It was clearly only a matter of days before Paris would be liberated.

In this situation a number of people had ideas of seizing the civil power before de Gaulle could arrive—"Who holds Paris holds France." Desperate Pierre Laval thought of convoking the old National Assembly of 1940. Though he is supposed to have had some assistance from the Americans, he never had a chance. A more serious possibility was that the National Council of the Resistance might be able to seize power, according to de Gaulle, "as a kind of commune, which would proclaim the Republic . . . On my arrival they would bind my brows with laurel, invite me to assume the place they would assign me, and thenceforth pull all the strings themselves."

This seemed perfectly natural to de Gaulle, but very undesirable. He proposed to frustrate it. For this purpose he slipped his own men into Paris. Charles Luizet of Corsica, whom he had appointed prefect of police, sneaked through the German lines on August 17. General Hary secretly took over the Garde Republicaine, the Gendarmerie, the Garde Mobile and the firemen. Jacques Chaban-Delmas, de Gaulle's delegate to the F.F.I., arrived to keep the Council itself in hand. At the political summit was Alexander Parodi, who spoke in de Gaulle's name. It was a very neat political operation, though not as yet decisive.

On August 18, de Gaulle left Algiers for France. First he flew to Casablanca in his personal Lockheed, followed by General Juin and other colleagues in an American Flying Fortress. The next afternoon they landed in Gibraltar.

There was a rather weird dinner party in the great Renaissance dining hall of the Governor's palace, with de Gaulle so stiff and silent—he was annoyed at having been delayed at Casablanca—that the Governor's lady hardly knew what to say. "Have you noticed, General, that your name is the ancient name of France?" she babbled foolishly.

"Yes," said de Gaulle, dead-pan.

Abashed, she studied him in silence, so elongated in figure with his long medieval face wearing an expression of abstract dedication—like a crusader painted by El Greco, she decided.

Then an American officer came in to say that there was something wrong with the Fortress, there would be a delay. De Gaulle was icily furious; there had been too many delays. He suspected the Americans were trying to keep him from reaching France in time—in time for Paris.

An hour was wasted. Then the officer returned. "The Fortress cannot be repaired for take off tonight, Sir," he said.

"I doubt it," de Gaulle remarked acidly, while the Governor turned as red as the ribbon of his DSO. De Gaulle said, "In any case, I shall leave immediately in my own plane. Unescorted."

His French pilot said, "We'll have to fly very low and take the long way by sea, *mon Général,* to avoid enemy planes—if possible."

"We will do that," said de Gaulle.

So they took off for France under the blazing searchlights and silent cannon of the Rock. Strangely, the Fortress found itself able to follow almost immediately.

On Sunday, August 20, they landed at Maupertuis in Normandy, where they were joined by Koenig and Coulet, who briefed de Gaulle on the latest news from Paris. The city had risen against the Nazis. The F.F.I. and the Partisans, even the Police, were fighting from house to house and had seized most of the *mairies* or "town halls." Barricades were up in the streets and most of the old part of the city was in their hands. Oddly enough the Germans had not reacted very strongly. They seemed content to hold what in tourist times was the

American sector—from the Étoile down the Champs-Elysées to the Louvre, the Palais Bourbon and the Luxembourg across the river, and the area around the Place Vendôme and the Place de l'Opéra including the American Express Company. From there they held open the line of retreat northeast to Le Bourget.

De Gaulle went first to Eisenhower's field headquarters in an apple orchard. The Supreme Commander greeted him cordially and took him to see the operations maps which showed Patton's Third Army racing to throw two long arms around Paris, embracing the city but not taking it.

De Gaulle showed his disappointment. "I don't see why you plan to cross the Seine at Melun, at Mantes, and at Rouen, in short, everywhere but Paris," he said. "You need Paris, which is a great communications center. If it were not also the capital of France I would not presume to offer you advice. But the fate of Paris is of fundamental concern to the Government of France. That is why I must intervene and ask you to send French troops there immediately. Leclerc's Second Armored Division is, of course, the obvious choice."

Eisenhower agreed that this was logical from a military point of view, but that he was by-passing Paris because he feared that a battle in the city would risk irreparable damage and great loss of civilian life. De Gaulle pointed out that there was already fighting in Paris and said stiffly, "If the Allied Command delays too long I'll order the Second Armored to take Paris myself."

De Gaulle says that Eisenhower, who was usually so frank and open, seemed embarrassed; and he records his belief that Allied strategy was dictated by the American State Department's desire to keep de Gaulle out of Paris until some other French group established a government there. However, this can be discounted somewhat because of de Gaulle's intense suspicion of the American Government, which was equaled only by Roosevelt's distrust of de Gaulle. Considering the fact that General Eisenhower's humane nature revolted against unnecessary bloodshed, in fact he loathed *any* bloodshed, the reason he gave de Gaulle for his decision to by-pass Paris may well have been the real one.

Leaving Supreme Headquarters, de Gaulle and his generals started on the battle-scarred road toward Paris. Though the towns were in ruins, the countryside was green and gentle beneath the August sun. Everywhere they drove between lines of fluttering flags and wildly cheering people.

And everywhere were immensely touching sights—at Coutances a white sheet hanging from a broken window on which with childish crayon had been drawn the Cross of Lorraine; at Quettreville some boys and girls in tricolor sashes proudly saluting from a burned-out tank; at Breal the shell holes in the road filled with summer flowers and the curé swinging madly on the bell rope.

They spent the night at Rennes, ancient capital of Brittany. There administrative life was invincibly recovering. From the balcony of the Hotel de Ville, de Gaulle talked to the crowd standing under a gentle summer rain. As in all the shattered cities where he spoke, he did not dwell on past heroism or past sorrows, but talked of the future, of the greatness of France, and of the difficulties still to be faced and the sacred duty to overcome them. "The future is in our hands," he said.

Then he went off alone with a driver to visit his mother's grave at Paimpont. It, too, was bright with flowers and the tricolor flags of France.

On that same day the life of Paris hung by a hair. It happened that General Dietrich von Choltitz, the German military governor, was a connoisseur of beauty and a man of sentiment, and as such inevitably a lover of Paris. That was the luck of the city—and the world. To him, on August 22, an order came from his crazed Feuhrer that drained the blood from his head and the strength from his bowels. It directed him to blow up every one of Paris' sixty-two bridges and destroy as much of the city as possible; and to shoot all civilians who offered resistance.

In his headquarters at the Hotel Meurice on the Rue de

Rivoli von Choltitz sought desperately for a way out. Certainly he had the means to carry out the order—there were still 80 tanks, 60 pieces of artillery, 60 planes and 20,000 men under his command, whom he had been holding in check. But he had not the will or the stomach for it. He thought of the glowing, medieval stained-glass walls of the Sainte Chapelle, the incredibly intricate stone-work of Notre Dame and the Pont Neuf—the New Bridge that was over half a millennium old— of Sacre Coeur, gleaming white and rose at sunrise on the Mount. And a thousand irreplaceable bits of beauty in the Louvre, and he saw himself relegated through the ages to the lowest pit of the hell of human obloquy as the man who had blown up Paris. "If I execute that order," he is reported to have said, "nothing will remain for me than to kill myself on the sixty-second bridge as a monument to the dead."

He decided to defy Hitler—briefly.

So he sent for his friend, Swedish Consul General Raoul Nordling, and explained the Feuhrer's orders to him. "I can hold off for two days," he said. "But that is the limit. After that I would be relieved of command and shot. My wife and children in Germany would be shot as well. Even as it is I am risking my life and theirs. Will you help me to get a message to American General Bradley that he must not by-pass the city? He must take Paris in two days."

Nordling thought that his friend Count Alexandre de Saint Phalle, of the Paris banking house of that name, would be the best person to carry the message. Saint Phalle's mother was an American. He was well known in both countries and spoke English as well as he did French. The Americans would listen to him, Nordling hoped.

Saint Phalle tells of how he was summoned to von Choltitz's office at the Meurice. The situation was explained to him. Of course he volunteered to go. Passes were procured from both the Germans and the Resistance leaders, and the little party set off on the night of August 22. It consisted of Saint Phalle, Jean Laurent, who was a director of the Bank of Indo-China; Rolf Nordling, the Swedish Consul General's brother; and von Choltitz's aide-de-camp, Austrian Baron Poch-Pastor, who was both a German officer and an Allied agent.

At the German command post outside the city on the road to Versailles it was touch and go. The officer in charge examined their passes and did not like the look of things. Surely these were strange traveling companions. They were placed under a guard of suspicious Nazi troopers, while the officer held interminable telephone conversations with headquarters. Finally he came back and said, "It's all right. They can go through."

The troopers evidently did not think it was all right. Saint Phalle heard them mutter "Treason," as they handled their automatic weapons with itchy fingers. But they obeyed.

In the golden light of early morning they started on. Sitting in front of the car was a Nazi sergeant who guided them on a crooked course through the mine fields. At length he said, "It's clear from here on," saluted grudgingly and started walking back.

From that point, Saint Phalle says, they drove for at least ten miles without seeing a sign of war. The French peasants were plowing or reaping in the fields without even knowing that they were between the armies. So fluid had war become compared to 1914, when the front lines of trenches were frequently only a hundred yards apart.

Finally they found an American G.I. who dubiously called his commanding officer. Rapidly, then, they were passed up the echelons of command—to Chartres to see Patton, and then by plane to the city of Laval, where General Omar Bradley received them. He told them that Leclerc had already been given orders to take Paris.

From Laval, Saint Phalle went back toward Paris to seek de Gaulle. In another dawn, August 24, he found the General at the Presidential Chateau of Rambouillet, and his description of their meeting is so typical of de Gaulle that it is worth recording.

Saint Phalle went up the broad steps past two fierce-looking Senagalese troopers and was shown into one of the great salons.

There he waited interminably while the sun rose over the lovely park and dried the dew-wet lawns. At last he was taken into a smaller room where the General sat stiffly at a Louis XV table desk whose inlaid top was bare of papers. De Gaulle looked at him coldly and said, *"Alors,* Saint Phalle, what are you doing here?"

Saint Phalle explained his mission, aware of mounting rigidity. When he had finished de Gaulle asked with icy anger, "Why did you go to the Americans first."

"Because, *mon Général,* those were my orders and what my passes permitted."

"How are things in Paris?"

Saint Phalle described the chaotic conditions in the isolated capital; with fighting flaring and dying; all public utilities cut off, and the food supply running frighteningly low. The political situation among the French was very dangerous, with different factions grasping for power. "I respectfully suggest, *mon Général,"* he said, "that as soon as you make your entry you summon the National Assembly to confirm your government."

De Gaulle had seen enough, and more than enough, of the National Assembly of 1940 which had confirmed Pétain. "I shall not do so," he said. "I am the Government of France and need no one to confirm that fact."

Then Saint Phalle made another suggestion. "If you will send me to General Leclerc, I think I can guide his tanks through the mine fields. I took careful observations as I came through them."

"You stay here!" de Gaulle said harshly. "Nobody is going to Paris before I do."

It was clear to Saint Phalle that a few tanks—and their men —mattered nothing beside the necessity of establishing the State. He was on his way to the door when de Gaulle said, "A moment, Saint Phalle! What relation are you to Mother Saint Phalle of Sacre Coeur?"

"She is my aunt, *mon Général."*

"Fine! Goodbye, Saint Phalle."

De Gaulle had arrived at Rambouillet only twenty odd miles from Paris, the evening of August 23. All the way from Rennes, through the fairest country in France, he had driven amid emotional scenes of high enthusiasm and tears of joy. At Chartres he heard mass in the superb Gothic Cathedral with sunlight pouring through the empty windows from which the glorious glass had been removed for safe keeping. Just beyond Chartres he caught up with elements of Leclerc's Second Armored pounding along toward Paris as fast as the tanks could travel.

In the evening he walked with Leclerc and Juin on the terrace of Rambouillet, whose pointed towers rose behind them like the castle of a princess in a fairy tale, which indeed it was —*his* princess, France.

The generals were planning "Operation Étoile." Various brigades of the Second Armored were assigned to break through the German lines still ringing the city. One group was to enter it by the Pont de Neuilly and march down the Avenue de la Grande Armée to the Étoile. Another would go by the Auteuil viaduct and along the Seine. Leclerc himself planned to enter the city by the Porte d'Orleans and move up the Boulevard Montparnasse to the Palais Bourbon and the Invalides, while still another took the Louvre and the Hotel Meurice. These detachments were all to connect at the Place de la Concorde. This was scheduled for August 25. De Gaulle himself would enter Paris that afternoon by the Port d'Orleans.

"Where shall we rendezvous?" asked Leclerc.

Smiling nostalgically at Alphonse Juin, his fellow cadet from St. Cyr, de Gaulle replied, "At the Gare Montparnasse, of course."

Leclerc then started to leave. As he shook hands with the young general, who was already concentrating on the demands of the battle, de Gaulle said softly, "How lucky you are!"

And he thought, "In war, the luck of generals is the honor of governments."

❦ ⚜ ❧

DAY OF GLORY

THAT NIGHT de Gaulle slept in the presidential chamber at Rambouillet between sheets that were monogrammed R. F. (République Française). All the next day he walked the terrace while receiving reports of the hard fighting as Leclerc cracked the stubborn German resistance. Everything went on schedule. De Gaulle thought of the tribulations an army of only seven divisions like Leclerc's would have spared France, and of the impotence which had deprived her of them. It hardened his resolution never to permit such an insolvency of governmental power to impair his own administration.

At three o'clock the next afternoon, August 25, de Gaulle left Rambouillet in a small motorcade of three black sedans, guarded by two jeeps mounting machine guns. In the car with him rode his old comrade General Juin. The familiar, ugly suburbs of the workingmen's districts were brightened with flags and bunting, gay with cheering crowds. As they passed through the Port d'Orleans they heard a burst of firing speeding the parting Nazis.

What a reunion that was at the Gare Montparnasse, better even than in the days of St. Cyr! Leclerc was already there with the news that General von Choltitz had just signed the surren-

[165]

der. De Gaulle congratulated him saying, "What a stage on the road to glory!"

With Leclerc was a young German major and an ensign of the Second Armored Regiment of French Naval Rifles. The young French officer saluted stiffly and de Gaulle formally returned it, smiling into the eyes of his son. Then Philippe de Gaulle left with the German major to receive the surrender of the garrison of the Palais Bourbon.

De Gaulle did not continue to smile after he read the surrender document. It was signed for France by Leclerc *and* Colonel Rol-Tanguy of the Resistance.

"I disapprove of this," he said to Leclerc. "First of all it's not exactly true that the German Command surrendered to the Resistance as well as to you. Secondly, as the highest ranking officer present you were the only person responsible; more important, Rol-Tanguy's insistence on signing proceeds from an unacceptable tendency."

He then showed Leclerc a proclamation published that morning by the Council of National Resistance on behalf of "The French Nation," which made no mention of the Provisional Government or General de Gaulle.

Leclerc understood the political significance of this immediately and said, "I was wrong."

And de Gaulle writes, "With all my heart I embraced this noble colleague."

All the Resistance leaders and a vast crowd were waiting for de Gaulle at the Hôtel de Ville, but he had no intention of going there first. To his subtle political mind this would be to accept power from them. Instead he had planned all along to establish himself in the Ministry of War, the seat of government and command, and *then* go to the Hôtel de Ville.

He left the Gare Montparnasse in a small cortege of four cars, de Gaulle's, Juin's, Le Troquer's and an armed jeep. They drove through the Left Bank boulevards familiar to de Gaulle's childhood. At the beloved square of St. François Xavier, almost under the iron balcony where he had played as a little boy, a burst of machine gun fire from nearby houses made them veer suddenly into the rue Vaneau and take a roundabout route to the rue St. Dominique.

At five o'clock, his car drew up in the courtyard of the Ministry of War. As he stepped out, de Gaulle felt like a man walking backward into time. A platoon of the Garde Républicaine presented arms just as they had four years ago. A familiar looking porter swung the great doors back. Inside it was as though the clock had stopped the night the Government fled from Paris. De Gaulle reflected that in the years between the world had been turned inside out; the proud French Army had been shattered; France reduced to impotence; and civilization itself had trembled on a hair balance. Nothing on this earth would ever be the same again; but the Ministry of War seemed immutable.

As de Gaulle walked through the vestibule and up the stairway, he saw the same military trophies hanging on the walls. The very same stewards and ushers greeted him as he strode along. He writes:

"I entered the Minister's Office, which M. Reynaud and I had left together on the night of June 10, 1940. Not a piece of furniture, not a rug, not a curtain had been disturbed. On the desk the telephone was in the same place, and on the call buttons were exactly the same names. Soon I was to learn that this was the case in all the other buildings in which the Republic had housed itself. Nothing was missing except the State. It was my duty to restore it.

"I installed my staff at once and got to work."

Luizet and Parodi came to make their reports and tell him of the anger of the National Council of the Resistance and the Parisian Committee of Liberation at his non-appearance at the Hôtel de Ville. He agreed to go there a little later. Then a message came from General Koenig that he would not be present for the celebration planned for the morrow as Eisenhower had sent for him to sign an agreement settling the relations between the Provisional Government and the Allied

Command. De Gaulle noted, "Done at last. And better late than never!"

After going first to the Prefecture to inspect the police of Paris, who had revenged themselves for their years of service under the Occupation by taking an heroic part in the final battle to throw the rascals out, de Gaulle walked through surging, cheering crowds to the Hôtel de Ville. Resistance troops in civilian clothes and F.F.I. brassards presented arms with military precision. In the great hall Georges Bidault, André Tollet and Maurice Flouret received de Gaulle. As they escorted him up the grand staircase in a tumult of cheering that echoed deafeningly in the marble halls, Resistance soldiers stood rigidly at attention with tears running down their cheeks.

In the large salon on the second floor members of the Council of National Resistance and the Parisian Committee of Liberation surged around him in enthusiastic, vibrant greeting. Everyone of them wore the Cross of Lorraine. De Gaulle knew now that they and he were joined as fighters in the same great battle. To a noble speech by George Bidault, de Gaulle replied by expressing the "sacred emotion of all of us, men and women alike, in these moments which transcend each of our poor private lives." He saluted Paris "liberated by her people with the help of the Army and all France."

Finally, as he always did, he spoke of the future: "The Nation will not permit her unity to be broken. All her children must be strong. All the sons and all the daughters of France will march forward hand in hand. War, Unity, and Greatness. That is my program."

Then, as he was about to leave, came a moment of politics. Bidault cried out anxiously, "General! Here around you are the National Council of the Resistance and the Parisian Council of Liberation. We ask you formally to proclaim the Republic before the people who have gathered here."

In an authoritative tone that was also informed with passionate conviction de Gaulle said, "The Republic has never ceased to exist. Free France, Fighting France, and the French Committee of National Liberation have successively embodied it. Vichy always was, and still remains, null and void. I myself am the President of the Government of the Republic. Why should I proclaim it now?"

Then he stepped quickly through the tall windows onto the balcony. The thunderous crash of cheers from the French people outside answered his rhetorical question, as it answered those who might challenge his authority.

The next morning, the radio kept repeating "At three o'clock on the Champs-Élysées! At three o'clock on the Champs-Élysées!" All Paris was afoot, gathering from the remotest suburbs. There was no public transportation. In the War Ministry de Gaulle was working out the final arrangements. To him there came an officer from General Leonard Gerow, commanding the American Fifth Army Corps, with orders that Leclerc's Division should not take part in the celebration. De Gaulle said coldly, "On this day in this place such an order indicates a remarkable lack of comprehension. I lent you General Leclerc. I am taking him back for today."

Other than this the Americans were very tactful. Their regiments, which had supported the Second Armored and reached the Place d'Italie, were withdrawn. No American general officers appeared. They felt it should be an all French occasion.

The risks of holding this celebration were very grave. The Germans were still fighting hard at Le Bourget and St. Denis —in the very fields where Henry de Gaulle had been wounded in 1870. Their armor was making tentative thrusts into Paris and might break through in flame and death. The Luftwaffe in crazy vengeance might stage a raid that could be a massacre. But de Gaulle said, "That afternoon I believed in the fortune of France."

At three o'clock that Saturday, August 26, de Gaulle, with Juin and Leclerc and Koenig, who had come after all, arrived at the Arc de Triomphe. Before them the Champs-Élysées sloped down toward the distant Place de la Concorde. De Gaulle

[169]

wrote, "Oh it is the sea. An immense crowd fills it from side-walk to sidewalk. As far as my eyes can see there is nothing but billowing life under the sunshine and the tricolor . . ."

Around the Arc the guard of honor was the black-skinned regiment from the Tchad which had fought all the way up the ladder of Africa and the slope of France. De Gaulle greeted them gaily.

Then he mounted the temporary platform crowded with his old faithful friends and his new comrades. For the last time Maurice Schumann said resonantly into the microphone *"Honneur et patrie! Voici le Général de Gaulle!"*

After a few emotional words de Gaulle left the platform. In a tremendous silence he relit the flame on the Tomb of the Unknown Soldier. Then he started down the Champs-Élysées. He wrote in the passionate present tense,

"I go on foot. This is no day to pass in review with the brilliance of arms and ringing fanfares. It is a time to give myself, in the spectacle of their joy and the evidence of their liberty, to a people who yesterday were crushed by defeat and dispersed in slavery. Since almost all of those who are there had in their hearts chosen Charles de Gaulle as the recourse of their sufferings and the symbol of their hopes, they shall see him, familiar and fraternal, in order that the sight shall restore to splendor the national unity."

As he strode along, de Gaulle was guarded only by two soldiers on motorcycles who were totally overwhelmed by that immense crowd. They pressed around him happy if they could even glimpse the two-starred kepi, ecstatic if they could touch his clothing. The authorities had feared that the pressure of the crowds would crush him, but he had trusted them to discipline themselves. He had no security except the love and respect of the people of Paris.

And as he marched down "the most illustrious avenue in the world," the whole history of France marched with him. Beneath the Arc de Triomphe the flame of honor was burning bright. He hailed Clemenceau on his pedestal and thought he looked as though he would "spring off it to march beside us." The chestnut trees of the Champs-Élysées, bending beneath swarms of joyful people, reminded him of L'Aiglon dreaming in his Austrian prison. Ahead of him was the Place de la Concorde, which had seen the ecstatic fury of the Revolution and the sinister flash of the Guillotine. To the right, the golden dome of the Invalides, still sparkling with the splendor of the Sun King, guarded the tombs of France's greatest soldiers—Turenne, Napoleon, Foch. . . .

Still far ahead loomed the gray majesty of the Louvre, the ancient palace of the kings of France where through the centuries Saint Louis and Henry IV, the great Louis and all the other royal personifications of the State had reigned and ruled.

He thought of the bad things, too, of Saint Bartholomew's Massacre, the assassination of beloved Henry IV, the bloody civil wars of the Fronde; royal heads beneath the guillotine; the disastrous confusion of the National Assembly in the Palais Bourbon across the Seine; and the tramp of steel-soled German boots on this same avenue.

But this afternoon, Paris "gleamed with all the greatness of France." And Charles de Gaulle was lifted by such spiritual exaltation as seldom comes to men or saints. There is a photograph of him looking upward as he walked among a million friends. Even the camera's dull eye caught the ambience of his eyes. So must Saint Joan have looked as she watched her Dauphin crowned at Rheims.

Rapture ended with a loud report. As de Gaulle's car drove up before the splendid portals of Notre Dame, there was a shot and then the strident chatter of automatic weapons. Like a gigantic string of firecrackers the reports rippled around the square as the Resistance people began firing wildly. Even the disciplined troops of the Second Armored caught the fever, shooting at non-existant enemies on the twin towers of the cathedral. Panic-stricken people were diving under automobiles.

De Gaulle instantly assessed it as one of those nerve-triggered shooting matches that sometimes sweep over excited troops. He got out of his car and, expressionless, walked slowly through the great arched portal of the cathedral.

As he made his way up the long dim nave between a crowd of worshippers who murmured subdued salutations, a machine gun suddenly shattered the religious hush. Bullets ricocheted high in the vaulted ceiling, ripping fragments and shards of stone from the forest-like arches. Escorted by Monseigneur Brot, de Gaulle and his party moved steadily up the aisle under the falling flakes of stone. As they approached the altar, Le Trocquer said "Play the organ!"

"There is no electricity."

"Then make them sing."

The opening notes of the *Magnificat,* hesitant at first, then swelling in glorious volume as everyone joined in, rang through the ancient church, punctuated still by desultory bursts of fire, and shouts of "God save de Gaulle!" from the faithful. Singing as though he had no thought of anything but his devotion and gratitude to God, de Gaulle led the chant of praise.

Late that evening Maurice Schumann came to the Ministry of War to congratulate his cherished chief. He found de Gaulle working at his desk, his strong profile highlighted and darkly shadowed by candles burning in silver candelabra. Through the open windows came the bruit of occasional fanfares which must have sounded in the General's ears like echoes of the endless acclamations and senseless bursts of shooting that had heralded his passage through the city.

Behind the flaring candles, de Gaulle's face, impassive and more stern than ever, seemed to Schumann infinitely remote in time. In that scene, designed for history, the central figure seemed to wish to withdraw into himself.

As Schumann started to offer his congratulations the General stepped from the shadows to grasp his colleague's hand. "Let's not go all over that again," he said, speaking not in the tones of a conqueror bored with glory, but as though he wished to release his guest of the burden of giving conventional praise.

De Gaulle had, in fact, already moved out of the splendid

tableau of his triumph and was thinking ahead, beyond victory, beyond probability. For at that time, when President Roosevelt's honeymoon with Stalin was in its rosy bloom, de Gaulle, pursuing aloud the thoughts that Schumann had interrupted, told him: "I think that in the years ahead, perhaps not so long from now, Russia and America will become rivals for the domination of the world. This may be dangerous for France, and it may be a great opportunity. We must begin to think what we can do to avert the danger so that France can profit by the opportunity. . . ."

🙦 ⚜ 🙤

PARIS, STRASBOURG, AND MOSCOW

THE LIBERATION OF PARIS was a tremendous emotional splurge in which the French people saw the culmination of all their hopes. De Gaulle knew that it was only the beginning of his most difficult task, to unify the country and restore the State.

He appraised the situation realistically. There were more than 300,000 armed irregulars in the French Forces of the Interior and the Partisan militia. Almost half of them were Communists. Though they accepted him as their symbolic chief and wore the badge of the Cross of Lorraine, they were by the very circumstances of their clandestine role a lawless lot whose immediate loyalties were to their local chieftains or to Moscow. The first time he reviewed the self-organized Resistance Army old soldier de Gaulle said, "My, what a lot of colonels!"

With the memory of the Black, Brown, and Silver Shirts of the 1930s fresh in his mind, he had no intention of letting these private armies fight each other for power or challenge the authority of the State.

But even here in Paris the challenge was evident. He had a strong suspicion that the shootings at Notre Dame, which had been repeated simultaneously in other parts of the city, had not been due either to enemy snipers or accident. He thought that they might well have been planned to give an appearance of dangerous disorder as an excuse for the F.F.I. and the militia to remain under arms. This may have been true; but it seems rather farfetched. De Gaulle had a suspicious mind.

True or not, there were certainly members of the National Council of the Resistance who still proposed to turn the Council into a permanent organization controlling the Government by behind-the-scenes power politics, backed up by their paramilitary formations. Since the Parisian public was practically unanimously back of de Gaulle, this was the right moment to assert the power of his Government. He says, "The iron was hot. I struck."

On Monday morning, August 28, two days after the Liberation, de Gaulle summoned the Bureau of the National Council of the Resistance to the Ministry of War. He writes that first he acknowledged, "quite loftily," their share in the battle of Paris. If de Gaulle himself describes his attitude as lofty, it must indeed have resembled the icy pinnacle of Everest.

He then informed these ambitious gentlemen that since his Government was now installed in Paris, the National Council of the Resistance had become "part of the glorious history of the Resistance." In other words, they were out of business. Certain of its members, he said, would be invited to join his Government, but they must sever all connections with the Council.

As they digested this statement, he gave them the rest of the bad news. The French Forces of the Interior would be absorbed by the French Army. Public order would be maintained by the police and the Gendarmerie with an assist from the regular Army if necessary. The militia would be disarmed and disbanded.

The tone, completeness, and authority of that declaration threw the Resistance leaders into such a state of shock that they could only babble their objections almost incoherently.

[175]

For a few moments de Gaulle listened to them courteously. Then he "put an end to the audience."

Now de Gaulle held Paris, but in the chaotic condition of communications and lines of authority throughout the country—telephone lines cut, railways disrupted, 3,000 bridges blown up—he did not yet hold France. In each isolated department, city, and town the Resistance leaders had set up personal governments and were proceeding to dispense the high, low, and middle justice, which consisted of taking revenge on any French man or woman who was suspected of collaborating with the Nazis, and quite a few who were innocent. In addition they were running their domains to suit themselves with slight regard for the policies and orders of the Provisional Government.

In this situation de Gaulle's first move was a personal appearance tour of all liberated France. In each city and town he courteously greeted the Resistance leader, who had usually made it his personal fief, and promptly replaced him by an official appointed by the Government.

In one provincial town the mayor met him accompanied by a small army of officials and Resistance officers. *"Mon Général,* may I present my staff?" he asked.

Pointing to his single aide, Captain Claude Guy, de Gaulle said with an amused glint in his eye, "This is *my* staff."

It would have been easier to cope with disorganized local governments had not organized Communism deliberately fomented chaos. In Toulouse, near the Spanish border, Colonel Asher, who had taken the dashing *nom de guerre* of Ravanel, had set up a sort of military soviet with his Resistance chieftains. De Gaulle received word that if he went there he would be repudiated or arrested. So of course he went.

Toulouse is in that wild and rugged kind of wilderness from which the fiercest of guerrilla fighters took their name. On September 17, with "calculated solemnity," de Gaulle reviewed the "Maquisards." By making direct contact with them he

[176]

hoped to arouse in each man the soldier he wished in his heart to be.

Under the orders of Colonel Ravanel, all their elements defiled before de Gaulle. It was a wildly picturesque sight. At their head, with bayonettes fixed, came a battalion of Russians who had been forced into service by the Germans and deserted to join the Resistance. They were followed by a small army of Spanish refugees from Franco's dictatorship, led by their generals. Then came the French Forces of the Interior, at once pathetic and heroic.

As their different elements marched past with their home-made battle flags and pennants inclined at the salute, de Gaulle, noting their touching efforts to give their ragged clothing a semblance of military uniform, was deeply moved. They in turn marched by with "eyes right," which filled with tears at the sight of him. Then he knew that, whatever their chieftains did, he could count on them. It was a sort of plebescite.

From one end of France to the other, from Marseilles to Bordeaux and from newly liberated Lyons to Lens in the North, similar scenes were enacted. Thus de Gaulle, traveling alone except for a single aide, restored the authority of the State by his moral grandeur and the power of the legend he had made of himself.

Meanwhile, on September 9, 1944, de Gaulle had set up his new Government. Many of the ministers were comrades who had been with him from the time of Free France. Others were brought in from the Resistance. Jules Jeanneney and General Catroux were the Ministers of State. Others in the most important ministries were Minister of Justice, François Menthon; War, André Diethelm; Colonies, René Pleven; Foreign Affairs, Georges Bidault; Finance, André Lepercq; Interior, Andrien Tixier; and Economics, Pierre Mendès-France.

Because of the utter ruin of French industry and transportation, Mendès (as everyone called him) had perhaps the most important post of all. Three thousand kilometers of railroads were out of business and only 2,500 locomotives remained out of 12,000. The great ports were in ruins. Dwellings totaling 452,000 had been demolished and 1,500,000 badly damaged. Over two million Frenchmen were still prisoners in Germany, and the Budget was a bottomless pit with 137 billion francs of income and 437 billion of expenditures, leaving a deficit of 300 billion.

Mendès also had the freest hand of all the ministers. For de Gaulle, absorbed in restoring order, in directing the enormously enlarged military effort and the consolidation of the F.F.I. into the Army, and in his compulsive efforts in the field of diplomacy to restore France to the position of a great power, had little time left for economics. Nor, to tell the truth, did he, at this epoch, understand them very well.

Mendès was—and is—an extraordinarily brilliant economist, with a strong left-wing bias. He plunged into the business of picking up the shattered bits of French industry and putting them together with ardor, courage, and intelligence. Almost before de Gaulle knew it, he had given France a semi-socialistic economy.

The great Renault automobile works was nationalized on the grounds that it had collaborated with the Nazis. Mendès then saw to it that the State took over the Paris Gas Company. Other industries followed. Had it not been for the individualistic peasant farmers and the equally intractible small businessmen, France might have become a true socialist state which, considering the feeble governments of the following fourteen years, is horrifying to contemplate.

Meanwhile, the treasury was also functioning as an almost independent wheel in the governmental machine. With goods scarce or totally unobtainable, a colossal deficit, and banking disorganized, inflation was inevitable. To meet the situation, Finance Minister Lepercq attempted a huge perpetual loan of 164 billion francs. In the prostrate condition of the country, it was a daring expedient, but due to the inspired patriotism of the time, it succeeded.

In November, in the final days of the loan drive, Lepercq was killed in an automobile accident. De Gaulle desperately called on René Pleven to take over. He was unhappy about accepting this but patriotically agreed. So hastily was the appointment made that when Pleven walked into his new office in the Ministry of Finance he was horrified to find it occupied by a handsome coffin containing the remains of his predecessor. He says, "I believe I was the only French Minister of Finance ever to be received like that."

The Hotel Matignon is the official residence of the Premiers of France. De Gaulle lived there throughout the entire period of the Provisional Government. As soon as Paris had settled down he sent for his wife and daughter to come from Algiers and join him.

The de Gaulles liked the Matignon because of its secluded environment. The fine old palace, famous for having been the home of Prince de Talleyrand, is situated in park-like grounds surrounded by a high wall. Strolling in that bit of country in the city, de Gaulle could find a facsimile of the solitude he always needed to think things out and refresh his spirit.

Yvonne was happy there, also, except for one thing that shadowed both their lives—little Anne's failing health. Every rare moment that de Gaulle could spare from his tremendous tasks was spent with his daughter.

He had very little time for affection or contemplation in the autumn of 1944. The days were filled with action and quick, vital decisions, with plans and improvisations. There was, as de Gaulle never forgot, still a war going on; and he was determined that France should play the greatest possible part in it to re-establish her position as a great power and entitle her to a voice in making the peace. In this he was not altogether successful.

For one thing, though France had the men (despite her losses and those two million French prisoners in Germany, she could have fielded an army of at least 500,000) she did not have the means to equip them. The soldiers of the F.F.I. who had managed to arm themselves gladly joined the French Armies fighting, now, almost on the borders of Germany. But a great many others had to be returned to civilian life for lack of arms.

Naturally de Gaulle blamed the United States for not providing more munitions of war for the French Army. Equally naturally, the Americans, hard-pressed for transport to supply their own enormous war efforts in the Pacific as well as the Atlantic, were able to meet his requirements only partially. Though short of equipment, de Gaulle, enthusiastically supported by the French Army, determined to make up in derring-do what they lacked in supplies.

An example of this is a dramatic scene in General de Lattre's camp at Valdahon on November 13, the eve of the offensive against the Germans entrenched in the Vosges Mountains. Snow was falling in huge flakes, clogging roads already slick with ice. A council of war was being held to consider the situation, when it was announced that a special train, bringing de Gaulle and Winston Churchill, had arrived at Besançon. The official motorcade struggled over the tortuous roads to Valdahon, where de Gaulle got out, followed by Winston Churchill and his daughter Mary, very trim in her uniform.

As the little group stood shivering in the whirling snow, Churchill said to de Lattre, "You can't possibly attack in weather like this, can you?"

"It is not in question," the French general declared enigmatically.

Then, despite the danger of pneumonia, Churchill drove with de Gaulle and de Lattre to several of the advanced positions. All the troops were in tremendous spirits, marching past in the swirling snow, singing the old French battle songs. "Can you imagine them in such high feather at a time like this?" de Lattre asked de Gaulle.

The latter smiled fondly at his young general, whom he has characterized as "so ardent and as sensitive as he was brilliant."

"It is because you and I are here together," he said.

At dinner that evening in the cozy warmth of the private train they were all as optimistic as the troops. Churchill notes, "I was struck by the awe and even apprehension which half a dozen high generals showed to de Gaulle in spite of the fact that he had only one star (sic) on his uniform and they had lots."

The next day, while the snow fell more heavily than ever, the offensive was unleashed. Three days later the First French Army, augmented now by 50,000 men of the Resistance, had broken the enemy line. By November 21, the fortress of Belfort was encircled, and the troops pressed on to the banks of the Rhine, liberating Mulhouse, Thann, and Strasbourg, the capital of Alsace.

Thereby hung another clash of wills between de Gaulle and SHAEF.

A month later, on December 16, the Germans hurled their last great offensive against the Allies. Known as the Battle of the Bulge, it pierced a thinly held portion of the American line in the Ardennes and threatened to erupt into the French valleys of invasion across the Meuse River at Dinant and also to capture the great American supply dumps at Antwerp. To bolster his shattered lines, Eisenhower was forced to send Patton's Third Army roaring to the rescue, thereby weakening all the rest of the front. On January 1, in order to shorten their lines and avoid a possible disaster in Alsace, Eisenhower ordered General Jacob L. Dever's Army Group, which included the First French Army, to retreat to the Vosges Mountains. This meant giving Strasbourg up to the enemy again.

When General Juin, who was now Chief of Staff, brought him the news, de Gaulle was both shocked and determined, though not surprised. He recognized the logic of Eisenhower's strategy, but his emotions and his concept of honor refused to accept it.

Give up Strasbourg, the sad lady of the Place de la Concorde, without a fight? Give up the capital of Alsace to German troops who would be followed by Himmler and his Gestapo? That would be a frightful wound to the honor of the nation and her soldiers; and a terrible cause for despair to the Alsatians. "It was time for me to intervene," he says.

This he did in no uncertain terms. That same day, January

[181]

1, he sent de Lattre this order: "The French Army must not consent to abandon Strasbourg. . . . In the event that the Allied Forces retire from their positions to the north . . . I order you to make arrangements to assure the defense of Strasbourg."

It was an order to be insubordinate. It was endangering the whole Allied strategy, which he admitted was logical, for a point of honor. It was de Gaulle!

Even de Lattre was shocked. He wrote to de Gaulle that the order for the retreat had been given by the Allied High Command and, in view of the pivotal position of the French Army, he thought that this order might supercede de Gaulle's command to defend Strasbourg. De Gaulle sent his general a telegram that chilled the wires: "I have little appreciation of your last communication. . . . The First Army and yourself are at the disposition of the Allies for the unique reason that the French Government has ordered it and only until the moment when they decide otherwise. . . . If you find it necessary to evacuate Alsace, the Government cannot admit that it should be done without a great battle, no matter—and I repeat—no matter whether your left is covered or finds itself uncovered by the retreat of your neighbors."

De Gaulle, not unnaturally, was anxious that Eisenhower should agree with his views. He had sent him a letter reaffirming his order to de Lattre and giving his political and personal reasons for holding Strasbourg. Copies went to Franklin Roosevelt and Winston Churchill.

Under the burden of the Cross of Lorraine, Churchill hurried across the Channel to patch things up. Accompanied by General Juin, de Gaulle met with Eisenhower and Churchill at SHAEF Headquarters in the gay little Hotel Trianon at Versailles. Surrounded by the great war maps, Eisenhower patiently explained the dangerous nature of the German offensive backed up as it was by new Panther tanks, and the first appearance of German jet fighters.

"If we were playing war games I'd say you were right," de Gaulle answered. "But giving up French territory is not merely a military maneuver. For France it would be a national disaster because Alsace is sacred to us. The Germans claim it, and will therefore revenge themselves on the inhabitants for their patriotism. . . . I have given the First French Army orders to defend Strasbourg. Dispersion of the Allied Forces and a possible rupture of the system of command would be deplorable. Therefore I ask you to reconsider your plan and order Devers to hold firm in Alsace."

Eisenhower seemed impressed. "You are asking me to change military orders for political reasons," he said slowly.

"Armies are made to serve the politics of states," said de Gaulle. "For the people and soldiers of France, Strasbourg has an extreme moral importance."

Churchill spoke for the first time. "All my life I have seen what a great place Alsace holds in French sentiment," he said. "I agree with General de Gaulle that this fact should enter into your decision."

Eisenhower was above all a politic man; de Gaulle himself has called him greater as a statesman than a general. The unity of the Allies was to him the most important consideration. After a rather hot discussion he yielded with the frankness which de Gaulle found "one of the best traits of his sympathetic character." With de Gaulle and Churchill standing by, he telephoned Devers that the retreat was off.

After the hot argument the four of them had hot tea and friendly talk. Eisenhower spoke confidentially of the headaches of trying to keep peace in the Allied coalition, in which not only the different nations, but the different services of each, armies, navies, and air, were all jealous of each other. De Gaulle, without seeming to realize that he was one of Ike's thorniest problems, gravely sympathized with him. "Glory costs dear," he said. "But you will be victorious."

So on the threshold of the Hotel Trianon they parted good friends.

Strasbourg held out.

To backtrack a little. On November 24, 1944, having checked Communism in France, de Gaulle flew to Moscow to make a treaty of alliance with the arch-Communist, Josef Stalin. This sort of thing has been looked upon as evidence of de Gaulle's inconsistency. It is nothing of the sort. Communism at home was bad for France. Communists in Russia might help her escape from dependence on America and Britain, whom de Gaulle always referred to with wild inaccuracy as "the Anglo-Saxons," and about whom he worried almost as much as he did over the growing power of Russia.

Accompanied by General Juin, Gaston Palewski, and Foreign Minister Bidault, de Gaulle took a roundabout route to Moscow, pausing to call on King Farouk of Egypt and the Shah of Iran. The party landed in Bakou on November 26, and went on to Moscow via Stalingrad in the late Grand Duke Nicholas' luxurious special train.

In an icy fog, they toured Stalingrad, which might be called the Verdun of World War II. The great battle had left its marks in every shell-holed street, in blind, boarded-up windows of half-ruined houses, in burnt-out tanks, rusting at main crossings; and it was still apparent under the muddy surface of the Volga, on the bridge the Russian defenders had built laboriously under the ice, on which the decisive tank attack had crossed. De Gaulle insisted on seeing every part of the city-battlefield, and on that prematurely wintry day his respect for Russian soldiers became boundless.

In Moscow, Stalin staged one of those lavish Russian welcomes for the Provisional President of France. It was evident that he desired to make his guest feel wanted. De Gaulle was pleased but not seduced. During the eight days he spent in Moscow he shrewdly appraised Stalin's politics as "grandiose and disingenuous," and the man himself as, "Communist dressed as marshal, dictator cloaked in artifice, conqueror with an air of bonhommie . . . but not without a certain tenebrous charm."

Stalin had bursts of perfect frankness. Once he mentioned Maurice Thorez, the leader of the French Communist Party. At de Gaulle's frigid silence, Stalin said, "Don't be upset by my indiscretion. I only want to say that I know Thorez, and I think he is a good Frenchman." Then smiling broadly he added, "In your place I'd put him in prison."

In the interims of banquets and gala performances at the Opera, de Gaulle and his colleagues discussed a treaty of mutual aid and friendship with Stalin, Molotov and Bogomolov. Its rather general terms were easily worked out, but, as a precondition of signing it, Stalin demanded that the French Government recognize the new Communist Government of Poland. De Gaulle felt that to do so would be neither honorable nor honest. Much as he wanted the treaty, integrity was more important.

On the final night of de Gaulle's visit Stalin gave a banquet for him in a huge, brilliantly lighted salon in the Kremlin. The table set with massive silver, crystal and many triple-branched candelabra seemed unimaginably luxurious after French wartime austerity. De Gaulle noted, "We were served a stupefying repast."

The usual vodka toasts were drunk, for which the French had prepared by drinking olive oil. Stalin bounced up at least thirty times to clink glasses with his subservient ministers and generals. There was a toast to Poland, icily received by the French; at least ten toasts to the glories of France, and a toast to Danton of the French Revolution, "One of our own," said Stalin.

The tough old peasant was in great form, with his heavy mustache dripping with vodka; his face beaming with good fellowship, and his eyes hard and watchful.

After dinner the conference was resumed. Stalin sat doodling at the big table while the talk went around and around the same point; the Russians still insisting that the French give at least unofficial recognition to Communist Poland, and they as adamantly refusing.

At length, seeing the bored expression on his guest's long face, Stalin said, "These diplomats are all babblers. There is only one way to shut them up—with a machine gun. Bulganin, go get one!"

Then he added, "Let us go watch a cinema."

When the film was over at midnight and the diplomats still talking, de Gaulle rose. Towering over the stocky master of all the Russians, he courteously thanked him for his hospitality, adding, *"Au revoir, Monsieur le Maréchal."*

Stalin did not seem to understand. "They're going to show another film," he said weakly.

De Gaulle simply shook him firmly by the hand and walked to the door. There he turned, bowed to the stupefied Russian ministers, and started down the corridor with long strides. Little Molotov, his face livid, followed him at a run. The Communist Foreign Minister was so shaken up that he really babbled as he saw de Gaulle to his car.

At two o'clock, de Gaulle was in bed in the French Embassy. At about three-thirty, Bidault arrived to say the Russians had given up. They would sign the pact without any conditions about Poland.

De Gaulle dressed and went back to the Kremlin where the treaty was signed at 4:00 A.M. Stalin was a good loser. He said to de Gaulle, "You held out well. Good luck to you! Now we must celebrate."

By magic a long table appeared laden with another enormous Russian meal. At supper Stalin was quietly philosophical, almost dreamy. As they parted, he heaped de Gaulle with assurances of Russia's undying friendship and support. "You can count on me," he said warmly.

Accepting this pledge with graceful thanks, de Gaulle thought, "How different are the Russians' actions from their words."

At the doorway, he paused to look back. Stalin, sitting alone at the long table, was beginning to eat again. . . .

De Gaulle's diplomatic triumph in Russia, did not accomplish very much. Two months later the "Big Three" in English, "Les Grands" in French,—Roosevelt, Churchill, and Stalin—met at Yalta to settle the fate of Europe without consulting France. Roosevelt, on his way home, invited de Gaulle to meet with him on his battleship off Algiers. Still quivering from the insult to France of being left out of the Yalta Conference, de Gaulle refused, implying that Roosevelt should at the least come to see him. Had he known that the American President was a dying man, he might have been less concerned for protocol. Or he might not.

However, in spite of his many rebuffs at Roosevelt's hands, he could write in his memoirs, "When on April 12, death came to snatch (Roosevelt) from his gigantic task at the very moment when he might have seen its victorious conclusion, it was with a sincere heart that I tendered his memory my regret and my admiration."

❧ ⚜ ❧

"ONE MUST DISAPPEAR"

THE BELLS RINGING for victory in May, 1945, ironically signaled the decline of de Gaulle's power and prestige, and still greater difficulties in realizing his ideals for France. Relief from pressure quickened internal demoralization. The road to greatness lay open, but France had neither the material resources nor the will to take it.

In external affairs the "Greats" became more arrogant than ever.

Just before the end of the war, from Germany's final agony, Gestapo Chief Heinrich Himmler wrote de Gaulle an extraordinary letter. After bootlicking him with congratulations and praise of his greatness, Himmler wrote: "So you have won. Now what do you do? Join the Anglo-Saxons? They will treat you as a satellite and make you lose your honor. The Soviets? They will subjugate France and liquidate you. . . . In truth, the only road that can lead your people to greatness and independence is an entente with conquered Germany. If you dominate the spirit of vengeance and seize the occasion History offers you today, you will be the greatest man in history."

Even in the bitterness of war, de Gaulle could reflect, "Flattery aside . . . that message from the tomb had a certain truth. . . ."

Though the "Greats" had discussed the terms of peace at Yalta without France present, they at least agreed that she should have a zone of occupation in Germany and be represented at the formal signing of the surrender in Berlin. Since General Juin was with Foreign Minister Bidault representing France at the United Nations Conference in San Francisco, de Gaulle designated de Lattre to sign for France. The latter was very upset when he found that the preliminary armistice had been signed without him and telegraphed a furious message to de Gaulle, who replied with unexpected humor: "Better to be a victor than a signer."

The Russians made quite a fuss about protocol before de Lattre could take part in the surrender ceremonies. However, it was straightened out, and de Gaulle heard with some satisfaction that when Field Marshal Keitel came into the room where the victors awaited him to sign Germany's surrender, he started at the sight of de Lattre and cried, "What? The French here, too. It only needed that!"

When the Potsdam Conference met in July, 1945, France was again left out. The future of Europe was settled by Russia, America and Great Britain, three extra-European powers. However, Churchill and his successor as Prime Minister, Clement Atlee, loyally stood by France when the formation of the permanent Council of Ministers was proposed. "Our foreign ministers must decide whether the council will consist of four or five members," Churchill told Stalin.

"Three is plenty," Stalin said bruskly. "France is not a great power."

But the British felt that they might need France's help, especially if the Americans went home, as they had before. So they stood firm. And France was rather grudgingly elected to that exclusive club called "The Greats."

Nevertheless, that first summer of peace was anything but peaceful for de Gaulle. Instead of one enemy to contend with, the Armistice had produced a dragon's-teeth crop of them within France and without. In the field of foreign affairs he had a sharp skirmish with England, who was trying to muscle in on France's traditional sphere of influence in Syria. French and British troops came close to shooting each other up before de Gaulle's firm stand forced Britain to back down.

On August 21, de Gaulle flew to Washington at President Truman's invitation to try to improve Franco-American relations, which had never regained their pre-war cordiality. He got along far better with Truman than he had with Roosevelt, but his final judgment of the new American President was that he was honest and humane, but very naïve about Europe's problems.

Meanwhile in France the bitterness engendered by the Vichy regime and the Occupation culminated in the trials of the two most famous collaborationists, Marshal Pétain and Pierre Laval, before the High Court set up for that purpose.

The trials were a political charivari with everyone from the politicians to the press trying to prove how patriotic they were by throwing themselves into the political battle and settling old accounts with more enthusiasm than they had fought the enemy. De Gaulle was deeply distressed by this manner of procedure. To his mind, the crime of the Pétain Government was in surrendering France to her enemies. All their other errors, from Dakar to delivering political prisoners to the Germans, stemmed from that poisoned source. He would like to have seen them tried on that issue with dignity and justice.

Only Marshal Pétain preserved his decorum. Day after day he sat enclosed in silence while vituperative witnesses abused him. De Gaulle wrote admiringly, "His silence was in harmony with the military dignity in which his great services of other days had clothed him."

Despite the vindictive atmosphere of the trial, the witnesses only confirmed the fact that the Marshal's fault was that his great age had robbed him of the power to lead, and he had become the tool of unscrupulous men.

Inevitably, the court condemned him to death with a recommendation of mercy. De Gaulle promptly commuted the sentence to life imprisonment, and sent him to comfortable durance on the Ile d'Yeu off the Atlantic Coast of France.

Thus ended the long intimate, tragic association between these two men which might have been predestined by the irony-loving gods of Greek tragedy. De Gaulle closed the record with an apostrophe wrung from the heart: *"Monsieur le Maréchal! You who had always done such great honor to your arms, you who were once my leader and my inspiration, how had you come to this?"*

The trial of Pierre Laval followed that of the Marshal. At first he tried to excuse his deeds of collaboration by the theory of expediency. Then he turned as vicious as a cornered fox and out-cursed his accusers. The death sentence was automatic. Oddly enough, de Gaulle felt a certain sympathy for Laval, believing that he was, in fact, false to France because of his distorted thinking and not through a desire to injure her. Nevertheless, the man deserved to die.

Laval took poison in prison, but he was revived to face the firing squad. On a dismal autumn morning, wearing the same black suit and white necktie which had been his trademark when he ruled France, the strange little man, who had known power without glory and plumbed the depths of ignominy, marched bravely to his death.

As de Gaulle regretfully sent his oldest friend to life imprisonment, he had the good fortune to make a splendid new one. In the course of revamping his Council of Ministers for peacetime conditions and preparing for the elections, de Gaulle appointed André Malraux to be Minister of Information. This was one of the most important acts of his life, for Malraux has influenced his philosophy more than most of his other associates. Malraux says, "There is a charming legend that I met de Gaulle while I was fighting with the Resistance forces in Alsace. This is not true. I met him at the Matignon when he asked me to join the Council."

[191]

The new minister was, and is, a thin, delicate-looking man with burning eyes that betray the intensity of his inner fires. His words erupt like sparks of lava from a live volcano for there is never time enough to express all his thoughts and emotions.

Malraux is a mystic. And a realist, like de Gaulle. In the thirties, at the height of his career as a writer, he was, if not a card-carrying Communist, a very diligent fellow traveler. As he puts it, "For many years before the war I was interested, indeed I was devoted to the idea of the rescue and welfare of the proletariat through Marxist principles. Then, in the Resistance during the war, I married myself to France, which means that I now believe that the improvement and welfare of the proletariat can only be achieved through France herself."

By the time Malraux met de Gaulle, he had recognized the dangers of Communism for France, for the world, and for the very proletariat of which it professes to be the champion.

This ardent young man was not only in tune with de Gaulle's thinking, he amplified and clarified it. In *France et Son Armée*, de Gaulle said that every great leader of men has had a philosophical background—"Behind Alexander there is always Aristotle." As de Saint Phalle once remarked, "De Gaulle searched for his Aristotle for a long time. He found him in Malraux."

To which Malraux replied, "There is one objection. Aristotle came before Alexander and left him when the Conqueror was still very young. Later Aristotle's son took over his position as adviser. Alexander had *him* crucified."

In the Government, Malraux introduced modern methods to an organization so old-fashioned that it was slightly suspicious of typewriters and resolutely opposed to dictaphones. He organized the first public opinion polls in France at the time of the referendum of October, 1945, and predicted its outcome within a few percentage points. He says, "At that moment the General realized that I was a serious man."

Malraux also inaugurated the plan for strengthening the system of teaching by using aural and visual aids, radio and moving pictures—television came later. "I was attempting the transformation of French youth through modern methods," he says, "and I am still doing it.

"The General and I were completely in accord on the idea that France can only be brought into the full radiance of light through the youth of France. That is why I used these new methods in an attempt to make the youth of France fully aware of their country and so of their wonderful heritage.

"On one occasion de Gaulle said to me that the day when he felt certain that the young people of France were really aware of her, really loved and revered her as he did, would be a greater moment in his life than the Day of Liberation."

While the war lasted, French unity had been achieved through the leadership and the legend of de Gaulle, reinforced by the pressure of danger and the power of patriotism. As soon as pressures eased the political machine began to fly apart; legend and leadership were not enough. The same thing happened in Saint Joan's time.

The Consultative Assembly had been brought over from Algeria in 1944, and greatly enlarged by the addition of members of the Resistance and the old political parties. However, de Gaulle had not given it any more real power; and to mark the fact that it was *not* a national assembly he decreed that it sit in the Luxembourg Palace. The Palais Bourbon was reserved for the new National Assembly when it should be elected. As soon as the Armistice was signed, de Gaulle began preparations for a general election and referendum, as he had promised the French people. The elections were set for October 21, 1945.

Immediately this was done, in fact even before that, the Consultative Assembly tried to arrogate to itself powers it did not have. Its members, though not elected but only *appointed,* wanted to make it a real parliament. And while grasping for legislative and executive power they also split up into numerous jealous factions who, in the tradition of French parliaments, were in disagreement on every subject but one. They all feared and disliked de Gaulle and covertly hoped to ease him out of power.

He was completely aware of this, and became progressively less enthralled by the Consultative Assembly. "Your advice will be given due weight," he said to them, "according to how constructive it is."

Partly because of pride, but also because of shyness, de Gaulle could not even pretend to like the back-slapping, hail-fellow attitude of the Resistance politicians, and he considered their fondness for military rank and decorations undignified. He could not understand these new men who had no traditions. Even many of his ministers seemed to him lacking in dignity. "Ministers?" he once said. "They are more like a board of aldermen."

Naturally this incompatibility made many difficulties for him. Mendès-France had resigned in a huff because he felt he was not given sufficient economic power to stop inflation. The other ministers were in general disagreement, like the Assembly. The General's aloof attitude hardly improved the situation.

In short, the task of governing in a post-war period, which had been too much for Clemenceau and had escaped Winston Churchill, confronted de Gaulle. He set about it lucidly, but, unfortunately, coldly.

Preparing for the elections was his most controversial task. The points at issue were first, whether the Third Republic should be revived or a brand new constitution with a strong executive adopted. And, second, whether an all-powerful national assembly should be elected to write the new constitution or if it should be a constituent assembly of limited duration and powers.

The politicians of the Consultative Assembly were naturally for the former as were a majority of the Council of Ministers. De Gaulle was resolutely opposed. He had seen France brought to defeat and servitude by the bickerings of an all-powerful assembly. He pointed out that from 1875 to 1940 the United States had only 14 governments, Great Britain but 20, while France had *102*. This was not government, it was chaos.

What de Gaulle hoped for was a republic modeled on the American system with a strong executive and strict separation of the legislative and executive powers. Ignoring the vote of the Consultative Assembly and pressuring the Council into agreement, he presented two simple propositions to the voters for a yes or no vote.

1. Do you authorize the legislators to draft a new constitution?

2. Do you approve the proposals of the Provisional Government to limit the duration and powers of the legislature (to seven months duration and temporary legislative powers)?

In addition to the referendums, the voters were to elect the members of the new Assembly.

This marked the first time in nearly 100 years that the French voters had been allowed to express themselves directly on a national issue. The last time was the plebiscite that confirmed Napoleon III and the Second Empire. Ever since then French politicians of all shades of opinion, while prating of democracy, had so distrusted the people that they were frightened to let them vote on any national proposal. De Gaulle thought contrarily. He profoundly distrusted politicians and put his faith in the French people. He was profoundly right.

With all his heart he urged the people to vote Yes-Yes on the two propositions. They did so with a roar. A No vote on the first question would have meant restoring the Third Republic. Nobody wanted France to wear that shoddy political garment again. The vote was 96 per cent in favor of a new constitution (17,957,868 to 670,672). On limiting the powers of the new Assembly it was 67 per cent in favor (12,317,882 to 6,271,882).

Though the vote was a splendid victory for common sense (and de Gaulle), the result of the election of deputies was a disaster. By winning 5,005,000 votes and 168 seats in the new Assembly, the Communists became the largest party in France. Next in strength were the Socialists followed by the M.R.P. *(Mouvement Républicain Populaire.* This was the new party of the Catholic Left, born just before election, whose slogan was "Revolution through the Law." Thus all major parties were left wing. The conservatives, discredited by their association with Vichy, poled only 15 per cent of the vote.

The National Constituent Assembly (the "Constituent," for short) met on November 9, 1945, at the Palais Bourbon. It was a pitiful spectacle. There was disorder on the floor and intrigue in corridors, as in the darkest days of the Third Republic. De Gaulle attended to hear the resignation of his Government's powers to the Assembly. Sitting at the foot of the hemicycle of red plush seats that rose high around him, he records that "I felt converging upon me the veiled eyes of six hundred parliamentarians, and experienced, almost physically, the weight of the general malaise."

Although he was the obvious choice for Premier, he neither announced his candidacy nor his program. "They will take me as I am or not at all," he said proudly.

On November 11, after laying a wreath on the Tomb under the Arc, de Gaulle called for "Frenchmen to unite as brothers to heal the wounds of France. Fraternally we must try to silence the noise of our absurd quarrels."

There was a great deal of liberty and equality in the Palais Bourbon but a minute amount of fraternity. The Communists were intriguing with the Socialists to throw de Gaulle out. Only when the Socialists would not play did the deputies decide to make one final gesture of unity.

On November 13, the "Constituent" unanimously elected de Gaulle Premier. Round little Jacques Duclos, speaking for the Communists, announced, "We will vote with the others." Then they all stood with tears in their eyes and sang the "Marseillaise."

Winston Churchill, who had dined with de Gaulle at the Matignon that night, offered enthusiastic congratulations. "Plutarch wrote that ingratitude toward great men is the mark of strong people," he said. "Plutarch lied."

But de Gaulle noted that the vote was a reverence addressed to his past deeds, not a promise for the future. Plutarch had not lied.

General and Mme. de Gaulle at home "La Boisserie," Colombey-les-deux-Églises. © *Paris-Match. Courtesy, French Embassy Information Div.*

General de (corting his church where *French Emb*

De Gau investit: © *A.F.*

Charles, Yves and Jean, the three children of Genera Philippe. © *Elle A Cerf. Courtesy, French Embassy I*

Crowd *Match.*

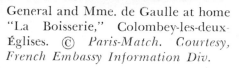

...le on the Government bench, in the National Assembly, the day of his ...re as the last Premier of the IVth French Republic (June 1, 1958). ... *Courtesy, French Embassy Information Div.*

...t Tamatave, Madagascar, welcomes de Gaulle in July, 1960. © *Paris-*
...Courtesy, French Embassy Information Div.

De Gaulle's first premiership lasted just three days. He never succeeded in forming a Cabinet. The Communists demanded that, as the largest party, they be accorded one of the great ministries—Foreign Affairs, Defense or Interior. De Gaulle replied that he could not in conscience give to a party that owed allegiance to a foreign power "one of the three levers which command foreign policy, diplomacy, which expresses it, the Army which upholds it, or the police who protect it."

The Socialists backed the Communists' demands. At the end of three days, de Gaulle returned his powers to the Assembly.

Another parliamentary wrangle followed. The Communists happily announced they would assume responsibility for forming a government. However, the Socialists and the M.R.P. made a deal that they would support neither de Gaulle nor the Communists, but would force them to compromise. So on November 19, the Assembly voted to return the mandate to de Gaulle at the same time appealing to him to compromise with the Communists.

The compromise was a typically French face-saver, a sort of Judgment of Solomon in reverse. The Ministry of Defense was split into two unhappy twins, The Ministry of the Armed Forces and the Ministry of Armaments. The first was given to Catholic Edmond Michelet, the second to Communist Charles Tillon. The Communists' headman, Maurice Thorez, became Vice Premier.

All parties to the transaction knew it could not last long. Most of all, Charles de Gaulle knew it. His mission and his dream had become impossible. He waited only for the right moment to end it.

For a few weeks more the new Government and the new Parliament functioned, with intriguers boring like termites behind a façade of unity. The straw—and it was a mere wisp—that broke the camel's sagging back was a sudden Socialist proposal to cut the military budget by a flat 20 per cent. The Communists gleefully announced that they would support it. De Gaulle stormed down to the Palais Bourbon.

[199]

Mounting the tribune, grim-faced and rigid, he said, "If the credits are not voted this very evening, the Government will not function for one hour more. . . ."

Then he went on, "Now one more word. This word is not for the present but for the future . . . we have begun to reconstruct the Republic. After I go you will continue this work. So I say to you in all conscience—*and this is without doubt the last time I shall speak in this place*—I say that . . . if you do not take account of the absolute necessity for authority, for dignity, for responsibility of the Government, you will put yourselves in a situation where one day or another you will bitterly regret the course you have taken."

In dead silence he left the chamber. That evening the credits were voted; but de Gaulle had made up his mind.

On Sunday, January 20, 1946, the Council of Ministers was summoned to meet at noon in the Ministry of National Defense on the Rue St. Dominique. Always before they had met at Matignon and, save for two or three who had been told the secret, they wondered uneasily why they were not there. With his dramatic sense of history de Gaulle had chosen the place. Here he had re-established the State; here let his mission end.

At noon precisely de Gaulle entered the large somber Salle des Armures. His ministers noted that he was wearing his old uniform with the brigadier's stars on his shoulders. As they all stood anxiously constrained, he made the full circle of the group, shaking each man's hand, and saying a few courteous words to each.

Then, before they could sit down, he said in his clear soft voice, "The regime of parties has reappeared. I disapprove of it. But, unless I establish a dictatorship by force, which I do not wish to do and which would doubtless turn out badly, I cannot prevent this happening. Therefore I must retire. Today I have sent the President of the National Assembly a letter telling him of the resignation of the Government.

"I sincerely thank each of you here for the assistance you have given me and I beg that you will remain at your posts to assure the expediting of business until your successors are chosen."

As the General stopped speaking there was a deathly silence in the room. Every face looked inexpressively sad. No man moved. No man spoke either in remonstrance or regret. They seemed stunned.

After pausing just long enough to give an opportunity for words that did not come, de Gaulle bowed stiffly. *"Au revoir, messieurs,"* he said.

Then clapping the two-starred kepi on his head, he wheeled smartly as though on parade and left them.

It was Maurice Thorez, Communist, who pronounced the requiem, saying in awe, "That departure does not lack grandeur."

Ever since that historic five minutes at the Rue St. Dominique, men have been asking, "Why?" Why did de Gaulle suddenly give up the fight he had fought so well. True the situation was difficult, but it was not hopeless. And he had never despaired even when there seemed no hope. Some blamed him bitterly, saying that had he remained he might have given the Fourth Republic a more viable constitution; saying that it was sheer egotism that made him quit.

Nor does de Gaulle's letter of resignation to the Assembly shed a clear light. In it he said that he had only remained this long to assure an orderly transmission of power, that his work was now done. And he cited the great progress France had made since her liberation: "The life of France is now assured. . . . The economy revives. Our territories overseas are in our hands. . . . We hold the Rhine. . . . We participate in the international organization of the world as a power of the first rank. . . ."

All this does not explain his departure satisfactorily. The situation was simply not that good. France was not yet either secure or stable. And he knew it.

The real explanation lies in de Gaulle's knowledge that if he mixed in partisan politics, win or lose, his fame would be tarnished, his honor defiled, and his value to France destroyed.

Back in September 1944 he had a pre-vision of this, and he said, "I shall retire. It is necessary to disappear. Some day France may have need of a pure image. One must leave that image for her."

Then he added, with that whimsical, little quarter-smile of his that lightly mocked, without denying, his words, "If Joan of Arc had married, she would no longer have been Joan of Arc. Yes, one must disappear. . . ."

CHAPTER NINETEEN

❧   ⚜   ❧

THE SQUIRE OF COLOMBEY

THE DE GAULLES WERE, so to speak, on the street. From
the time of the Liberation they had lived at the Matignon. Now it belonged to the new Premier, Félix Gouin,
who was named three days after de Gaulle's resignation by a
coalition of the M.R.P., Socialists, and Communists, while
Mendès-France led the small Radical opposition.

Colombey-les-Deux-Eglises had been right in the path of the
advancing Germans and La Boisserie was half ruined by their
attentions. De Gaulle had no time during the intense months
of his government to see to its restoration. The business would
take many weeks to complete. Where to go?

Neither the General nor his wife could envisage living in a
Paris hotel. The stares of the curious whom his fame would
attract would make a semi-public existence unbearable. De
Gaulle had enough of cities and longed for the serenity of
the country. For six years he had carried an intolerable burden
with hardly a moment's rest; he was very tired. In addition,
Anne's health was failing fast.

However, so great was the invective launched against him
for his retirement, which his revilers had devoutly hoped for,
that he did not want to go far from Paris lest he give the

impression of running away. In this situation he had a happy inspiration. He rented from the Service des Beaux Arts the Pavillon of Marly in a park outside Paris. There, on state-owned property, he could enjoy the peace and privacy he needed while the work on La Boisserie went forward.

It was a successful compromise. There were a great many visitors at Marly, and also in the bare, spartan office he rented on the Rue de Solférino. Most of the politicians were delighted to be rid of de Gaulle. "There is one great man who is impossible," observed one of them, "but there are many middling men who will do well enough." But the most faithful of his friends were shattered. Malraux and Michelet could not conceal their emotion, nor Maurice Schumann his state of despair. They were accused of being more Gaullist than de Gaulle. Also, many people who had no connection with politics wanted to see him to testify to their loyalty and the hope he would not forsake them.

Their comings and goings threw the new Government into a state of panic. It envisaged some sort of Bonapartist coup in the works and fairly mobbed Marly with security agents "for the protection of the General," but really to spy on him.

In spite of these attentions de Gaulle managed to relax wonderfully. His splendid constitution rebounded in health and vigor. He laughed as he had not done for seven years and even began to play practical jokes again.

In the park and its environs he resumed his solitary walks, solitary that is except for the security men skulking behind. One of de Gaulle's favorite tricks was to walk very fast for a while, then suddenly about face and charge in the opposite direction, often colliding with his security tail. Then he'd roar with laughter at the blushing agent.

At Marly in April, de Gaulle received a letter from Michelet, who was still Minister of the Armies, stating that Premier Gouin wanted "to regularize" his position in the Army by making him a marshal of France. De Gaulle replied: "Since 18 June, 1940, the day I left the corps to enter into an exceptional career, events of such a nature and such dimensions have occurred that it is impossible to 'regularize' a situation absolutely without precedent. . . . Any administrative solution would be both strange and ridiculous.

"The only measure that is in order is to leave things as they are. Some day death will charge itself with smoothing over the difficulty, if there really is one."

Sometimes two stars are better than five.

La Boisserie was ready in May. So in the enchanting French spring the de Gaulles returned at last to the home they loved so much. Yvonne went hard to work in her neglected garden. Her first project was a formal flower bed in front of the manor house in the form of the Cross of Lorraine. Showing it to Louis Terrenoire after it was finished, de Gaulle said, "Some day when I die I will be buried here, and perhaps on this hill the Government will see fit to raise a tall marble Cross of Lorraine, which is all the memorial I want."

It was apparent that he expected La Boisserie to become the Mount Vernon of France.

However, the de Gaulles' joy in being home at last was soon shattered by Anne's death in her twentieth year. She was buried in a marble vault in the small churchyard at Colombey. How deep the grief de Gaulle felt was known only to Yvonne and his remaining daughter and son. For the General goes by the Spartan rule that the private sorrows of a public man are very private indeed. His appearance at that time was more monolithic than ever; his profile might have been carved from the same marble as Anne's tomb; and his only acknowledgment of the depth of his feeling was the setting up of a foundation for retarded children in Anne's memory to which all the revenues from the world-wide serialization of his books are paid by his publishers.

Meanwhile, the way France was going also caused de Gaulle great unhappiness, and this he voiced in loud lamentations and bitter phrases.

The triple alliance of Socialists, Communists and *Mouve-*

ment Républicaine Populaire in the Constituent Assembly proceeded then to write a new constitution which, if that were possible, was even worse than the Third Republic. Like the Bourbons, the politicians had learned nothing and forgotten nothing. Based on "the necessary dependence of the executive on the legislative," the proposed constitution provided a single-chamber, all-powerful assembly. This body would elect a President of the Republic who had no powers whatever, and, according to Léon Blum, should be nothing but "a decoration and a symbol"; and a Premier whom it could unseat at the drop of a vote. Reverting to a favorite phrase of his youth, de Gaulle called it "Absurd!" At his urging the new constitution was turned down by the French people on May 5, 1946, by over one million votes.

So a new Assembly had to be elected on June 2. The M.R.P. which called itself, "The Party faithful to de Gaulle," was the greatest winner. It became the largest party in France and Georges Bidault, who had been de Gaulle's Foreign Minister, became Premier.

While the new Assembly was organizing itself de Gaulle made an immensely moving speech at Bayeux on the second anniversary of his landing there. "It was here," he said, "that the efforts of those who would never surrender . . . found at last their decisive justification. And it was here, on this ancestral soil, that the State reappeared, the legitimate State because it was founded on the interest and sentiments of the Nation . . . . Now the Nation and the French Union await a constitution."

Then he sketched in his ideal constitution which would provide a popularly elected Assembly, a Senate elected by municipal and township councils, and a Chief of State above party with real power to assure "the continuity of the Nation." In brief the separation of executive and legislative powers.

"All our history," he said, "is an alternation between immense sorrows brought about by a divided people, and the fertile grandeurs of a free nation grouped together under the aegis of a strong State."

The people cheered, but the Assembly shouted "Bonapart-ism! Dictatorship!"

Assured of the balance of power in the Assembly, the M.R.P. became a good deal less faithful. They had second thoughts about creating a strong executive. So they led the way in draft-ing a constitution which made but a faint bow to the popular demand for reform. There were to be two houses—a sort of Senate called the Council of the Republic, which had only the power to give advice—that naturally no one was ever known to take—and an *almost* omnipotent Assembly. The President of the Republic would be elected by both houses, and have the shadow of a shadow of power, merely that of proposing a premier to the Assembly.

Maurice Schumann and Paul Henry Teitgen made the pil-grimage to Colombey to beg de Gaulle not to raise his voice against this new constitution. He said mordantly, "It's as like the other one as a sister." And when the time came he de-nounced it bitterly.

But the French people were bored by all these elections. A third of them stayed away from the polls. The constitution was approved by a little more than half of those who bothered to vote.

The two houses of the Parliament met at Versailles to elect a President of the Republic. It was a dreary day in January 1947. The old palace was freezing cold; its splendid halls and marble corridors were grimy with the accumulated dirt of the war years. The parliamentarians, wearing overcoats or storm jackets, looked as dingy as the faded glories of the Sun King's palace.

The deliberations were hastened by the frigidity. Vincent Auriol was elected President of the French Republic. Thus, without dignity or ceremony, the Fourth Republic was born in magnificent squalor typical of its whole history.

De Gaulle had honestly intended to withdraw from the political scene and live a life of philosophical contemplation at Colombey. But the course of events drew him out again against his better judgment. For, as the Fourth Republic went into effect, the ritual dance of the Premiers began. Bidault was succeeded by Léon Blum, the grand old man of the Socialist Party, for whom de Gaulle had a great deal of respect. But in a few weeks Blum was followed by Paul Ramadier, who at least had the strength and the courage to throw the Communists out of the Cabinet. They never got back. However, it seemed that the only object on which all parties were united was to diminish the authority and prestige of the State. It was more than de Gaulle could sit still and watch.

He determined to re-enter politics, to stake his great personal prestige on an all-out effort to unify the French people. Despite his reputation for caring only for the power and greatness of France, national unity has always been his primary object, perhaps because he feels that if he could accomplish this miracle, the material advance of the nation would inevitably follow.

Let it be admitted that de Gaulle was led astray by romantic dreams, that in his comparative ignorance of practical politics he exaggerated his own influence with the French people. That they loved, respected and trusted him beyond any other man was certainly true. That they would give up their selfish interests to follow his lead at any time but that of dire emergency was not.

His wife was more clear-sighted than he. Yvonne begged him not to re-enter politics, not for selfish reasons—though she had looked forward to, oh how she had anticipated, the peace of Colombey!—but because she feared that he would compromise his historical position, would muddy the clear image. So did his remaining brothers and his few close friends who had no political axes to grind.

De Gaulle himself was more than half convinced that they were right. In addition, he shrank from the mechanisms of vote-getting, the hand-shaking and backslapping; the campaigning and the innumerable committee meetings; the inevitable compromises, if not with principles (which he would never do) at least with men and means.

But all these were selfish reasons. As he watched the State

slide down the easy descent to impotence, he was impelled to one great effort to rally the people of France to save it.

On March 30, 1947, in Normandy, he broke his long silence, saying "The day will come when, rejecting this sterile game and reforming the badly built structure (of government) which misleads the Nation and disqualifies the State, the immense mass of Frenchmen will reassemble with France."

The wildly enthusiastic crowd shouted, "De Gaulle to power!"

Premier Ramadier, badly frightened by this popular demonstration, went to Colombey the next day. In a frigid interview, he informed de Gaulle that the Government had decided to deprive the General of his military honors (which was hardly possible since they had granted him none) and of his right to speak on the state-owned radio, which was more serious.

The following Sunday, at Strasbourg, which he had saved by his intransigence with Eisenhower, he spoke again. This time he criticized the parties but magnanimously praised their leaders, who, he said, "are worthy and very capable of directing public affairs except for the system which misleads and paralyzes them."

Then he said, "It is time for a reassemblement of the French people, which within the structure of the law . . . will triumph over the differences of opinion in a supreme effort for the public safety and the profound reform of the State."

The nervous Government breathed easier at the phrase, "within the law." The specter of Bonaparte receded to Elba. There would be no revolution; and they knew they could outwit a purely political movement.

The Rassemblement du Peuple Française (R.P.F.) was formally organized under de Gaulle's leadership in April 1947. It was meant to be, not a political party, but a movement above all parties. It attracted a tremendous following of idealistic leaders and patriotic citizens. In the municipal elections in October it polled 40 per cent of the vote, an almost unheard of figure for a single French Party. Had there been a national election then de Gaulle might well have won an absolute majority of the Assembly. And had he been able to run for President in an American-style popular election he would certainly have been elected.

But his timing was awfully bad. There were still four years to go before a general election. During that time the fine flame of enthusiasm for a rally of the French people died to a mere flicker. And all the other parties and special interests ganged up on R.P.F.

By 1951, when a general election was finally held under an electoral law especially rigged against the Gaullists, they could poll only 21.56 per cent of the vote. It was a very respectable showing for a new party which became the third largest in France after the Communists and Socialists. But it was far, very far, from the majority de Gaulle required to assume the premiership. He would not, he could not in consistency or honor, play the game of compromise and combination which would have enabled him to function in a coalition government. Though he continued half-heartedly to make the motions of a political leader, de Gaulle, the realist, knew he was licked. By 1953 the R.P.F. was finished as a Gaullist Party. De Gaulle released its members from allegiance to him and again retired from politics.

Though this great rally of the French people failed, it was an immensely valuable experience for de Gaulle. He learned a lot. In his intensive campaigning he learned how to go out and mingle with the people, if not to kiss babies at least to shake hands with warmth and a smile. He learned to speak intimately from the hustings instead of oracularly from on Olympian height. And he learned a great deal about what could be done and, more important, what could *not* be done, in practical politics.

Another thing he gained was association with many ardent and idealistic men of the R.P.F. who were of inestimable value to him when his moment came at last. There were, of course, always *"les fideles"*—the faithful—like Malraux, Soustelle, Michelet, Schumann, Palewski, de Courcel . . . though, even in their cases, fighting a political battle together renewed old comradeship. Of course, those who had broken with him, like Bidault and Pleven, opposed him most bitterly of all.

And then there were the new men, who became his devoted adherents, like the intellectual political tactician Michel Debré; foreign affairs expert Couve de Murville; enthusiastic, vigorous Louis Terrenoire, who had the common touch, political know-how and complete loyalty; boyish, idealistic Olivier Guichard; and young Georges Pompidou, a financial genius turned politician. There were, of course, dozens more; there is no space for catalogues of names. From these men, who were primarily interested in politics, de Gaulle also learned many things.

Most important of all, the necessity for proposing a program and explaining it to the people forced him to clarify his own thinking and, in association with his colleagues, develop the form and structure of the political philosophy known as Gaullism.

Incidentally, de Gaulle said one day at the Élysée, "I do not like that word, and I never use it. If I am forced to, I always put it in quotation marks."

So much was gained by this adventure in party politics which failed. Despite the apprehensions of Yvonne de Gaulle and the jeers of those who helped to cripple it, it did not damage the General's image. It failed to achieve power, as some say, because de Gaulle was a prisoner of his own historic personality, of the legend and the dream. But his eventual success came about because, while gaining political techniques and new flexibility, he remained true to himself.

With the diminishing and breakup of the R.P.F., de Gaulle really retired as much as he ever could, considering his passionate concern for France. He became for a while the good Squire of Colombey-les-Deux-Églises, living a country life with his dogs and his horses; his long walks in the forests or in the little park of which he says he has made the tour fifteen thousand times.

Elizabeth and Philippe were both married and often came

with their children to stay at La Boisserie. De Gaulle loved to play with his grandchildren with whom he was far more indulgent than he had been with his own, always excepting Anne.

Though family gatherings were, as always, his greatest pleasure, there were many guests at Colombey. Edmond Michelet, who was often among them, says, "The courtesy of that house was like that of olden days." But it was, at the same time, very simple. De Gaulle was the good host—making drinks for his friends, helping his wife serve after dinner coffee in the salon, and talking in his gentle musical voice with unaffected simplicity.

Every Sunday the de Gaulles went to Mass in the ancient village church, where they chose to sit, not in the front pew where protocol would have placed them, but midway between two stained glass windows depicting Saint Louis and Saint Joan of Arc. There they saw their neighbors who regarded the General with affectionate awe.

Retirement, however, did not mean idleness for de Gaulle. In 1952, in his tower study overlooking a wide sweep of the rough tilted fields of Champagne to the distant mountains, he began work on his memoirs of the war years. They were intended to be a record for future historians by a man to whom History was the most important guide to the future.

He wrote, as he said, "with great difficulty," which means with infinite care. The manuscript was written with a fine-pointed pen in nearly perpendicular handwriting. It was filled with corrections, emendations and inserts, for he spared no pains to polish his classical prose and find the one word that expressed his exact meaning. M. Orengo, his editor at Plon, says that even after the books were in galley proofs, de Gaulle practically rewrote them—a costly process—in his passion for precision.

In those years de Gaulle also made extended trips, always to visit countries of the French Union. The purpose of these trips was two-fold: first to remove himself from metropolitan politics and, secondly, to see for himself how the countries of the Union were doing. For he took a deep interest in these colonies, or former colonies, which by their loyalty had made it possible for him to re-establish France. He had always intended to offer them their freedom either in equal association in a French commonwealth, or complete independence if they so desired. For he said that after their services to France it was impossible to treat them as colonies. The Government of the Fourth Republic had frustrated this intention.

Though de Gaulle was in eclipse in Metropolitan France, his fame and popularity was undiminished in her possessions beyond the sea. Everywhere he went, enormous, enthusiastic crowds greeted him. They had not forgotten his promise; and hoped only for the day when he would have the power to implement it.

Yvonne de Gaulle, who loved to travel, always accompanied him on these trips as did Olivier Guichard who had become director of his small personal staff in 1953, when Georges Pompidou retired to enter the Rothschild Bank. The first trip, in 1953, took them to North Africa. In 1955, they visited Madagascar and Djibuti, and in 1956, they made the longest voyage of all, to the French Islands of the Pacific and back through the Panama Canal to Antigua and Martinique.

On the long slow voyage from Panama to Tahiti, Guichard says that the General became pretty restless. He had no one to talk to but Yvonne and his aide, for the other passengers were Australians "who did not concern themselves with politics or intellectual matters." For almost the only time on record de Gaulle was driven to attend the nightly movies, which were rather thin fare. Guichard recalls one night when a grade-B Western was running. De Gaulle watched it for a little while, then abruptly stood up. With a wry twinkle he said in a phony American accent, "I've had it, Guichard. I'm going bye-bye."

It was in this same ship that de Gaulle coined one of his famous phrases. He and Guichard were leaning over the rail watching ominous triangular fins above monstrous shadowy forms cutting the silky water alongside. The General said thoughtfully, "You see, Guichard, in the M.R.P. the sharks ate the apostles."

During the years when he remained at home, de Gaulle traveled in France a great deal. Louis Terrenoire tells of a visit he made with the General to the historic fortress of Alésia where the Roman Legions conquered the last and greatest of the ancient Gauls, Vercingétorix. Inspired by the sight of the Romain ruins, de Gaulle became the history teacher again.

"You can see that this place is very well situated to withstand a siege," he said. "The Romans had a lot of trouble taking it. Here they met the best army of Gaul. Caesar began by encircling the town and laying a formal siege. But other tribes of Gauls, the "Maquisards" of that time, came out of the hills to attack the Romans in the rear. It looked as though they were done for.

"But like many of us who lead the Gauls," he added bitterly, "Vercingétonix had his compromises, his Plevens and Bidaults, so victory was impossible."

It is easy to see from that, that de Gaulle was retired in body, but not in spirit. In fact, he still kept his office on the Rue de Solferino and spent two days every week in Paris, where he continued to keep in touch with those leaders of French opinion who still believed in him.

His small staff, headed by Guichard, Jacques Foccart, Palewski, and Colonel de Bonneval, were very active indeed, seeing to it that de Gaulle was not forgotten; and keeping him abreast of the political news and rumors, and briefing him on the actions and personalities of the emerging figures in the gladiatorial arena of the Assembly; as well as the latest shifts and dodges of the old masters of the tricky art.

Despite their efforts, de Gaulle's hopes of being able to rescue his Lady of France began to dim. People who knew him in 1957 and early 1958 speak of his "bitter serenity."

Well might he be bitter. The history of the Fourth Republic had been one prolonged disaster. Political and military bungling in Indo-China had resulted in the tragic defeat at Dien-Bien-Phu and the loss to France of her position in Southeast Asia. Because of the niggardly policy and vacillation of the Government, Tunisia and Morocco had broken away in complete independence. Now the hills of Algeria were aflame with revolt and half a million French soldiers seemed unable to subdue the Rebels.

In France itself the structure of government was becoming chaotic. Faster and faster wheeled the dance of the Premiers, it was a lucky Government that lasted two months, some survived only a few days. And the crises, when the Deputies could not agree and France had no government at all, became longer and longer.

This was not only terribly bad for the spirit of the country itself, but was seriously damaging to the position of France on the world stage. In fact, each day saw her prestige sink lower.

Ironically, this paralysis of the State was accompanied by a great economic boom. Aid furnished by the United States under the Marshall Plan and the enterprise of French industrialists were paying off in a big way. During the last four years of the Fourth Republic the gross national product increased a fantastic average of 10 per cent a year. Production in all areas was far above pre-war levels. Almost everybody was making money, and appeared satisfied with the status quo.

Speaking of this time André Malraux said, "I, myself, have seen nations dying, Far Eastern countries like China and Indo-China. In each case the peoples of those countries were mortally wounded. I could see the tragedy written in their faces, the gray look of despair. There was no joy in all those lands.

"This was not true of my country. France was dying, but the French people were having a high old time. There was only one man who could make them care."

But even that man was beginning to lose hope that he would be able to work a second miracle of rejuvenating France. The years had begun to lay their hands on him. Cataracts had narrowed his vision so that he was able to see only straight ahead. He had been forced to give up hunting and riding. His

[215]

habits became even more ascetic. Among other things, he gave up smoking.

The way this latter deprivation came about was typical. De Gaulle had been a heavy smoker, with the eccentricity that he hated to light a cigarette from a lighter but always used a match. One day at Colombey he and Malraux were discussing the tobacco habit. "It's not so hard to give up," Malraux said. "When the Nazis had me in jail I found it quite easy."

De Gaulle said, "Ho! ho! ho!"

"All right, I'll prove it," said Malraux, who is a chain-smoker. "I'll give it up for a month."

When Malraux came back to Colombey and reported that he had kept his tobacco fast, de Gaulle eyed him respectfully.

"If you can do it, I can," he said.

He has never smoked since.

Everyone who knew him well, says that the years at Colombey mellowed de Gaulle. He became far more gentle and affectionate—"doux" is the word they use. This mellowing process was, perhaps, the final assurance for the future of France.

In a sense de Gaulle enjoyed his loneliness. "In the tumult of men and events," he said, "solitude was my temptation. Now it is my friend."

Forgotten, de Gaulle never felt himself to be. But he did think his great days were past. During the last of what Terrenoire calls "the ungrateful years," for the first time in his life de Gaulle began to turn his eyes away from the future. He who had always looked ahead now began to talk, as old men do, of the past.

Something of this melancholy mood appears in the final page of his memoirs, written early in 1958. Speaking of winter at Colombey, he apostrophizes the Land, the Nation, and himself:

> Old Earth, eroded by the ages, polished by rain and tempests, stripped of vegetation, but forever ready to produce whatever is necessary for the new life that follows.
>
> Old France, overwhelmed by History, mortally wounded by wars and revolutions, going and coming without respite from

greatness to decline, but restored from century to century by her genius for renewal!

Old man, worn out by trials, detached from enterprises, sensing the coming of the eternal cold, but never failing to watch from the shadows for the light of hope!

The light was no further off than spring.

CHAPTER TWENTY

※ ❖ ※

"RESURRECTION"

CHARLES DE GAULLE did nothing to topple the Fourth Republic. It fell down like a house undermined by termites. The Squire of Colombey became the Sphinx of Colombey. He made no move, but all France was conscious of his presence—"the last recourse."

But if de Gaulle did nothing to undermine the State, plenty of other people were working at it. There is a book about the crisis by Merry and Serge Bromberger called, *The 13 Plots of the 13th of May*. The title is a gross understatement. There were as many plots as there were parties and factions of parties —at least forty-five or fifty. De Gaulle took no part in any of them. But the Gaullists were working with almost all of them. One of his young aides said, "By the time we got through, everyone thought that the General's ideas were not too far from their own."

Of course de Gaulle was aware of activity on his behalf, but he was skeptical of any result. He said, "Bad as it is, the present state of affairs may last for thirty, forty, or fifty years. By then I may be of more service to France dead, than I now am living."

The first crisis began on April 15, 1958, when the Government of Premier Félix Gaillard resigned. There had been twenty-three governments in twelve years, some of which lasted only a day. For four solid weeks the Assembly failed to agree on a new premier.

Algiers was in a state of turmoil and terror. The one million Algerian French, who are called *colons* (colonists), feared that whatever Government came in would make peace with the rebels and "abandon" them. So did a million loyal Moslems.

The French Army was uneasy. They had been defeated in Indo-China and expelled from Tunisia and Morocco because of lack of support from home. The successful Anglo-French attack on Suez in 1956, had been stopped by America and Russia—weird allies. The Army felt that if they were ordered to abandon Algeria, which was legally not a colony but an integral part of France, it would be the final stain on their honor. Since the disastrous days of the Dreyfus Case, sixty years before, the Army had kept out of French politics. But this was too much!

In April de Gaulle had a visitor from Algiers, Léon Delbecque, a technician of the Department of National Defense. He was a handsome athletic, open-hearted man with a fine war record, who become a leader of the *colons*. Though de Gaulle did not know it, Delbecque was part of a counterrevolutionary organization in Algiers called, "The Antenna." He told de Gaulle that the *colons* were on the verge of revolt against the French Government. "Algiers lives in a state of permanent conspiracy," he said. "I fear a coup aimed at dictatorship. They will call in a five-star general or Prince Napoleon (the Bonapartist pretender, who, it happened, was an ardent Gaullist).

De Gaulle pooh-poohed him.

"The Army is restless," Delbecque went on. "The loyal Moslems are frightened. France herself is boiling under a quiet surface. There is only one man who can save the Republic—de Gaulle."

"That is absurd," de Gaulle replied. "The Army does not love me and the *colons* never have. These are illusions, Delbecque."

[219]

"Nevertheless," Delbecque said, "if in very grave circumstances the Army and the people call on you, will you reply, yes?"

De Gaulle was silent for a moment, as he looked from his tower window over the lovely land of France. Then he said very seriously, "Delbecque, I have always had a habit of accepting my responsibilities."

After over three weeks of haggling in the Assembly, it began to look as though the deputies had agreed on a government headed by Pierre Pflimlin of the M.R.P. whom the *colons* considered an appeaser. He planned to go before the Assembly for investiture as Premier at three o'clock on Tuesday, May 13, 1958. It was the signal the *colons* had been waiting for.

At one o'clock that afternoon, the French in Algiers rose against the Government. The Monument of the Dead in the Forum was the rallying point into which poured an enormous crowd shouting *"Algérie Française!"* The *colons*, summoned by leaflets dropped from planes, poured in from the country villages. Students and high-school kids were out in force led by bearded, hot-eyed Pierre Lagaillarde, who looked like Lenin but thought like Franco. The crowd was estimated at over 100,000. Quite typically they began by sacking the United States Cultural Center.

But it was a joyous crowd. There was no hate in their faces, only exaltation, even while they shouted, "To the gallow with Pflimlin, Mitterrand, Mendès-France!" The Tricolor was everywhere, and they sang the "Marseillaise" every few minutes. *No one was killed.*

The Third Regiment of Parachutists under Colonel Bigeard, who were sent in to disperse the crowd, promptly joined them. At seven o'clock the crowd took the big, white Government Headquarters of the Governor Generalship. (Governor General Robert Lacoste was in Paris.) At seven-thirty, Parachute General Jacques Massu, eagle-nosed under a black beret, arrived and shouted in his hoarse voice, "The Army is with you!" General Raoul Salan, Army Commander in Algeria, made an effort to bring the crowd to reason, but his heart was not in it. By eight that evening a Committee of Public Safety, headed by General Massu, assumed power with the blessing of General Salan. They sent word to President René Coty of the French Republic that they wanted to see a Committee of Safety formed in Paris under General de Gaulle.

That night the National Assembly was in an uproar. No one knows if they would have agreed to the investiture of the Pflimlin Government if everything had remained peaceful. But revolt in Algiers made them frantic for action. Pflimlin was confirmed by a handsome majority. The Algerians howled with rage. They called the honest but unfortunate Premier of France, "The abominable Pflimlin!"

At peaceful Colombey, Yvonne's flowers were bowing to the rapacious bees and the still air was heavy with their lovely odor. It was hard to realize that men were fighting and sweating; hard to conceive that an old man might twice be called upon to perform miracles. De Gaulle did not believe a word of it. His young aides, with stars in their eyes, rushed down from Paris with reports of disaster and great opportunity, but the "eternal cold" retreated slowly.

To please them, more than because he thought it would do any good—"The French people are awfully tired"—de Gaulle issued a majestic statement on May 15:

"In other times my country in her extremity gave me her confidence. Today, in the face of heavy trials . . . let it be known that I hold myself ready to assume the powers of the Republic."

The tremor that shot through the Government exceeded that produced by the news of revolt in Algiers.

The next day M. Diebolt, Prefect of the Department of Haute-Marne, called on de Gaulle at Colombey. "In view of the troubled times, *Mon Général,*" he said, "I should like to put a guard outside La Boisserie to assure your safety."

"That is absurd," de Gaulle said. "No one wants to kill me."

[221]

"Perhaps not, *Mon Général,* but if they should, I would lose my job."

De Gaulle's eyes twinkled. "You have a point," he said. "Do what you think right, but keep them out of my sight."

On Thursday, May 16, an extraordinary thing happened in Algiers. The Moslems poured out of the Casbah to join the revolting *colons* in a scene of racial amity unprecedented in the whole history of colonialism. Hand in hand with the French they stood in the Forum singing French patriotic songs and shouting, *"Algérie Française! Vive la France! Vive de Gaulle!"*

When the news of this reached Colombey de Gaulle was deeply moved. Ever since the days of Free France he had felt a paternal love for the native peoples of the Empire. That the Moslems put their trust in him was a confirmation and a demand on his feelings for them. Afterward he said that this was the controlling factor in his decision to move actively toward "assuming the powers of the Republic."

De Gaulle's Paris Brain Trust, Guichard, Michelet, Debré, Pierre LeFranc, Malraux, Pompidou—on leave from the Rothschild Bank—and the others were fearful that the extremists in Algiers or the Army would stage a premature coup d'etat in Paris. De Gaulle absolutely refused to take power by force. The only way he would accept was to be legally invested by the Assembly. "If the Army thinks they are going to carry me to Paris in their baggage, they are badly mistaken," he said.

The Brain Trust was agreed that the key man to hold Algiers in line for de Gaulle was his trusted lieutenant of Free France, Jacques Soustelle. Soustelle, a stocky man, vibrant with energy and ambition, had been Governor General of Algiers under Premier Guy Mollet in 1956-57. The *colons* adored and trusted him. He, in turn, was dedicated to *"Algérie Française."* And to de Gaulle.

But Soustelle was in Paris, and the Government would not let him go to Algiers. As a deputy, he had Parliamentary immunity from arrest, but they kept him surrounded by Sureté agents. How to get him out?

The Brain Trust concocted a fine scheme. Soustelle lived in a handsome apartment at 85 Avenue Henri Martin. On the ground floor of the building lived Gaston Dufour and his wife, Monique, a beautiful Brazilian golf champion. Monique parked her little Renault Dauphine in the courtyard. Soustelle's friend, Geoffroy de la Tour du Pin, asked her to "enter the History of France" by hiding Soustelle in her car and running him through the Sureté guards outside. "Why should I?" asked Monique. "Your Monsieur Soustelle is most rude. He never even says, 'Good day,' to me."

"It is for France."

"I love France next to Brazil," said Monique. "I'll do it! But I am apt to land in jail, we must think of an appropriate costume. I have a smart little suit from Dior. Very practical. . . ."

"Excellent," said La Tour du Pin.

At the appointed hour Soustelle dashed out of his apartment and crouched in the small back seat of the Dauphine. They threw a couple of rugs over him. With La Tour du Pin beside her, Monique took the wheel and drove past the guards who were used to her comings and goings. A big Buick was waiting in the alley behind the Observatory. Soustelle jumped out and ran to it, and it took off for Switzerland with a clash of gears.

"What did I tell you!" Monique said bitterly. "He never even said, 'Good day!'"

Soustelle reached Algiers in a chartered plane on May 17. The crowd in the Forum received him with wild enthusiasm. By popular acclaim he became the leader of the Algerians—without portfolio—and stoutly held the line for de Gaulle.

With all Algeria now in open revolt, the Pflimlin Government apparently paralyzed, and a coup d'etat looming in Paris, de Gaulle decided it was time to hold a press conference. It was done with Government consent. Television cameras, microphones and 300 reporters gathered in a great hall of the Palais d'Orsay on May 19. So Frenchmen glued to their television sets saw him again for the first time since his retirement.

De Gaulle was wearing a beautifully cut, double-breasted gray suit and a pearl-gray necktie. He had grown a little stouter during the years at Colombey; his hair was turning gray; and his voice was deeper. He seemed less the man of iron, more human than the people remembered, but he gave the impression of a very big man—a giant among dwarfs.

In his set speech de Gaulle again announced his readiness to assume power. He praised the Army; but said nothing whatever about Soustelle or the Committee of Public Safety in Algiers. He called Minister Resident Lacoste his friend, and spoke in a friendly way of Guy Mollet and the Socialists, pointing out that his own Government of Liberation had put in effect many of their economic ideas.

Then came the questions. Did he condemn the mutinous generals? He answered that he had no public power to do so. Did he plan to attack the public liberties? That roused him. "I was a man, alone," he said. "The Republic at that time had been denied, betrayed. . . . Well, I, myself, restored its arms, its laws, its name. I re-established the public liberties. What would you then? That I would overthrow them; that at sixty-seven years of age I am about to begin a career as a dictator?"

Not a person believed he would, from the ministers of the Government watching anxiously in their offices to millions of Frenchmen watching and listening by television and radio. Instead, they felt his gentleness, his integrity and his wisdom. On that day be became, not the father of his country, which after all had existed for 1500 years, but the father of his countrymen.

More and more people became convinced that only de Gaulle could reunite France and save her from civil war. The Government was under heavy pressure to resign. At a council of ministers they discussed it. The consensus was "We have no right to create a vacancy of power."

René Pleven, big, florid, beautifully groomed, stood up. "A vacancy of power?" he said. "Messieurs, let's stop playing with words. Power we have no more. The Minister for Algeria dare not cross the Mediterranean. The Minister of National Defense has no more army. The Minister of the Interior has no more police. . . ."

It was true.

The Army in Metropolitan France was completely in sympathy with its colleagues in Algiers. Chief of Staff General Paul Ely, beloved by the whole officer crops had resigned, and from his apartment in the Invalides, a few steps from his office, was secretly trying to maintain the unity of the Army. His successor as Chief of Staff, General Henri Lorillot, was completely in sympathy with the generals in Algiers. They both told the Cabinet that if the paratroopers (the *Paras*) came over from Algiers, their troops would refuse to fire on them, and they would refuse to give the order.

As to the security forces, when they marched off duty their drummer beat three taps, then two—the rhythm of *Algérie Française!*

But the Government still clung to office. Not because of pride or power-hunger, but because conscientiously they could see no way out. Above all they wanted to avoid civil war. In Algiers the rebels were getting restless.

It was Soustelle and Massu who thought of the way to give the final push to the tottering Fourth Republic. On May 24, they sent a company of *Paras* to Corsica. The Corsicans received them as liberators. Not a shot was fired.

Meanwhile they planned "Operation Resurrection." This was nothing less than a coup d'etat. General Miquel commanded it in France. Parachute officers coming in disguise from Algiers organized it. "I'll need 150 trucks," said a colonel to a general. "If you don't give them to me, I'll take them. It's the same price." Stars taking orders from eagles!

The details were worked out with military efficiency. Four thousand paratroops from Algiers and southwest France would land at the Paris airports of Le Bourget and Villacoublay. Eighty Patton tanks at Rambouillet and St. Germain would roll in from the west. The police would join—after changing to military uniforms. The *Garde Républicaine* was with them to a man. The Security was also ready. In addition there was a group of private armies, secretly armed, ready to rise. These included Veterans of Indo-China, Veterans of Leclerc's Second Armored Division and various rightest activist groups. The Army planned to bring de Gaulle by helicopter from Colombey. He had no intention of allowing it. "Operation Resurrection" was set for the night of May 27-28.

No one knew better than de Gaulle that the balance between peaceful change and civil war was as delicate as a goldsmith's scale. When he saw his eager young staff in Paris, he took each in turn by the hand and looking steadfastly into their eyes said, "Now remember! Above all, no stupidities!"

On May 26, de Gaulle, sinking his pride sent word to Premier Pflimlin. "It is time we met."

"I agree," said the Premier, sinking his.

They also agreed that their meeting must be secret. De Gaulle drove out of La Boisserie in his black Citroen at seven o'clock that evening. The reporters, bivouacked between their campfires at the gates, scrambled for their cars and were neatly blocked off by Government cars and police.

At eleven o'clock Premier Pflimlin went down a service stairs of the Matignon and out the back door. They met at eleven-thirty in the park of the Château de Saint Cloud on the Terrasse de Brumaire, named for Napoleon's coup d'etat. "A curious place for such a meeting," muttered Pflimlin in his car. For once de Gaulle appears to have missed the historical connotations.

For over two hours the Premier and the General walked and talked together in the mild May evening. De Gaulle was affable and courteous like a sovereign to a subject. Pflimlin was as nervous and technical as a fledgling attorney. He was willing to resign in de Gaulle's favor, but first the General must publicly disavow the generals in Algiers and the Corsican coup. "What right have I to disavow them?" de Gaulle asked a little maliciously. "They are your agents not mine."

The General's conditions were that the Assembly invest him for a year with absolute power, the right to submit a new constitution to a referendum of the people of France, and power to reorganize Overseas France from an empire to a common-wealth. During that year the deputies were to be "put out to pasture."

Pflimlin said, truly, that it was constitutionally impossible. The talk went on until one-thirty. They agreed only that they would meet again to explore the situation further. And parted coldly.

On the way back to Colombey a dense fog enveloped de Gaulle's car. The driver pulled up at the side of the road, and he and the General slept in the car until morning. No one knew where de Gaulle had spent that strange night.

In the clear morning at Colombey, de Gaulle thought clearly. "Operation Resurrection" must be stopped before night. The only way to do it was to give the generals an impression of greater progress than had been made. At noon he issued an ambiguous communique:

"Yesterday I began the regular process necessary to establish a republican government. . . . I expect the land, sea, and air forces in Algiers to remain exemplary under the orders of their chiefs. . . ."

Then he wrote a cable to General Salan:

KINDLY SEND ME A LIAISON OFFICER AS SOON AS POSSIBLE STOP IT IS NECESSARY FOR ME TO BE INFORMED OF YOUR SITUATION AND THAT OF THE FORCES UNDER YOUR ORDERS STOP IT IS NECESSARY FOR YOU TO RECEIVE COMMUNICATIONS OF MY MANNER OF THINKING AND MY INTENTIONS IN THE PRESENT SITUATION OF THE COUNTRY STOP COMMUNICATE TO ADMIRAL AUBOYNEAU AND GENERAL JOU-HAUD THE TEXT OF THIS MESSAGE WHICH GOES FOR THEM AS FOR YOU STOP. . . . BE ASSURED OF MY CORDIAL CONFIDENCE.

GENERAL DE GAULLE

With his usual superb effrontery, de Gaulle sent the cable through the regular channels of the Defense Department as though he were already commander-in-chief. *"C'est formida-ble,"* said General Lorillot.

In Algiers the *Paras* deplaned. But "Resurrection" was not abandoned, it was merely postponed for forty-eight hours to May 29.

President René Coty of the French Republic was seventy-six years old. He was of small stature in the eyes of his countrymen—a typical bourgeois gentleman; but under the pressure of circumstances he became wise and strong. During the long, drawn-out crisis he was in the apt phrase of J. R. Tournoux, author of "Secrets of State," at the summit of anguish.

Coty was scrupulous in his respect for the constitutional limitations of his office, but within its frame he was staunchly ready with advice and help to all his harried ministers. Since May 13, he had hardly slept at all. "How do you stand it at your age," someone asked him.

The President smiled. "I could not have taken it at twenty-five," he said.

At three o'clock in the morning of May 28, Premier Pflimlin arrived at the Élysée. His face was white as a candle, eroded by fatigue, and desperately determined.

"Have you brought me your resignation?" President Coty asked.

The answer was yes and no. Pflimlin felt bound in honor not to leave a "vacancy of power." But he wrote out a conditional resignation, leaving it undated. "It's either de Gaulle or civil war," he said.

At five that morning Coty received Gaston Monnerville, President of the Senate. At six came André Le Trocquer, the President of the Assembly. Coty persuaded them to meet de Gaulle secretly that night.

The day was not for de Gaulle. The Communists and Socialists called a Popular Front demonstration and a general strike. The strike was ineffectual. The demonstration was fairly impressive. Over 100,000 people turned out, Socialist and Communist leaders marching arm in arm singing the "Marseillaise." It was an emotional crowd, but not a militant one. Even the slogans on their banners were witty rather than vicious. "DE GAULLE TO A MUSEUM!" "SEND THE GIRAFFE BACK TO THE ZOO!" The demonstration changed nothing.

Meanwhile de Gaulle was receiving an old friend at Colombey. Marshal Juin came to offer his help in keeping the Army unified and holding off the coup d'état.

That night there was another of those curious meetings in the Park at St. Cloud between de Gaulle and the Presidents of the Senate and the Assembly. They could not agree on terms. At de Gaulle's insistence that the Assembly take a year off, Le Troquer said, "That is illegal. The Assembly is constitutionally obliged to meet in October."

"They did not tell me that," said de Gaulle thoughtfully. "But I need a year."

"Six months," said Monnerville.

"Perhaps," de Gaulle said.

But his other conditions seemed impossible to Le Trocquer. The discussion was hot and angry for a while, but there was some progress. Monnerville knew how to touch the General. "One cannot speak to you of honor and patriotism and devotion to the Nation," he said. "All your life has been devoted to that. All I ask is that you take time for reflection. Do not answer tonight.

"I have a son overseas. Only you can bring about the changes necessary to hold the Union together. For the people beyond the seas you are the Man of Brazzaville. If you do not put over these reforms they will secede in a few years. You alone can construct the great Community."

There were tears in the General's eyes when Monnerville stopped speaking. Very slowly, as though the words were dropping from far off thoughts, de Gaulle said, "I will reflect. Is the return of de Gaulle possible? Is it impossible? After all, you know, France will bury us all. Our passions . . . She alone is eternal. If my return is not possible I will retire to my village with my sorrow."

In their car going to the Élysée Le Trocquer to Monnerville, "Don't worry. I know de Gaulle. He is a man who evolves."

The President of the Republic received the President of the Senate and the President of the Assembly in his pajamas at one-thirty that morning. They made their report and left.

All night long President Coty sat at his desk thinking. He also knew that "Operation Resurrection" was rescheduled for the next night. A little before dawn he reached a decision. It was up to him to save France from civil war, even if he had to go a little beyond the Constitution.

At eight o'clock he telephoned Colombey. A servant's voice said, "The General is asleep."

"How I envy him," said the President of France. "Ask him to call me when he wakes."

Then Coty sat down and wrote a historic letter to the Assembly. In it he said that he was going to call on the greatest man in France to form a government. If the Assembly would not agree to invest de Gaulle, the President said he would resign. Then he ordered his valet to pack his suitcase and engage a room for the night at the Hôtel Meurice (Shades of General von Choltitz).

When the Assembly met at 3:00 P.M. Le Trocquer mounted the Tribune. "The Republic is in danger," he said abruptly.

Then, in a harsh, furious voice, like a 20-mm gun spitting shells, he read the President's message. Rage, confusion and fear spread. It was a curious situation. Over 75 per cent of the people of France wanted de Gaulle. Nearly 75 per cent of their elected representatives did not. But the deputies knew the choice was de Gaulle or civil war.

In mid-afternoon a letter from de Gaulle to former President Vincent Auriol was made public. It was so moderate in tone, so reasonable and so *republican* that it turned the tide. The leaders of all but the Communist Party—and Mendès-France —agreed to consider his investiture.

That afternoon the eyes of France, Algiers and all the world were fixed on the Élysée Palace. It is a classically beautiful house, built by Louis XV's mistress, the Marquise de Pompadour, and inhabited by emperors, kings and all the presidents of the French republics. There Napoleon signed his abdication. France is so heavy with history that it is impossible to get away from its repetitions.

In answer to the President's summons de Gaulle arrived at seven o'clock. The entrance court of the Palace was jammed by practically all the reporters in France, so he came in the side gate off the Avenue de Marigny, and walked in the slanting

resident de Gaulle before a joint session of Congress, April 25, 1960, with Vice resident Nixon in background. © *Wide World Photos.*

President and Mme. de Gaulle pose with their dinner hosts, President and Mrs. Eisenhower in the White House. © *Wide World Photos.*

Prime Minister Khrushchev presenting President de Gaulle with a model of th "Lunik" on his visit to France in March, 1960. © *Wide World Photos.*

President de Gaulle with Prime Minister Macmillan and President Eisenhowe at the abortive Paris "summit" conference in May, 1960. © *Wide World Photos*

sunshine across the soft turf under the fine old trees. President Coty met him on the west terrace above the *parterre* of brilliant flowers that Empress Eugénie had loved.

Tears were running down the cheeks of the President of France as he grasped de Gaulle's hand. All he could say was, *"Mon Général!"*

De Gaulle was coldly formal, some say that he was shy. But Coty's genuine warmth and goodwill gradually melted the ice. As the guardian of the Constitution, the President insisted that he was honor-bound to observe its forms. De Gaulle was in accord. He yielded every constitutional point. His tenure of power need last only six months. The Assembly would remain in session and would simply adjourn. He would meet with the Parliamentary leaders. Finally, subduing his pride and forgetting his words that he would never speak in the Palais Bourbon again, de Gaulle agreed to read his program in person to the Assembly from the Tribune.

In return de Gaulle would be given all the *essential* powers he had demanded. On that basis he agreed to form a Government.

Arm in arm, the President and the General walked out onto the stately Portico of Pompadour under white klieg lights and flash bulbs winking like fireflies on a summer night to give the news to the city and the world. Then de Gaulle went home to Colombey.

As the news was flashed through Paris the city went wild with joy. The Champs Élysée seethed with cheering, singing people, and waving Tricolors. All the automobiles raced around tooting forbidden horns—three long, two short—*Algérie Française!*

President Coty happily unpacked and put the picture of Madame Coty back on his bureau. In Algiers the *Paras* deplaned again.

Press Secretary of the Élysée, Georges Raynal, said, "Ouf! Next time we'll have to stop them on the way down."

❧ ⚜ ❧

NEITHER KING, EMPEROR, NOR DICTATOR

THE OPPOSING POLITICIANS who made the pilgrimage to Colombey had a pleasant surprise. They had known the stern soldier of the Liberation. They met a charming gentleman who had mellowed through the years. He was gentle, reasonable and willing to compromise on everything—*that did not matter.*

After going to La Boisserie, Vincent Auriol said, "That man is passionately devoted to France and the national unity. He is for the Republic, though his conception of it is different from ours."

"The greatest honor of my life!" exclaimed Socialist Leader Guy Mollet, who became Vice-Premier in the de Gaulle Government.

The Premier Designate offered cabinet posts to the leaders of all the major parties except the Communists. With his passionate desire to assemble all the people of France around him, de Gaulle would probably have offered them a ministry if he had thought they would accept.

On the afternoon of June 1, 1958, de Gaulle mounted the

tribune of the Assembly and presented the list of his ministers
and his program to the hostile eyes staring down at him from
the towering tiers of the famous hemicycle. It was, in sum,
contained in the last words of his speech, "Unity, Integrity,
Independence!"

"*Vive la France!*"

Then he gathered up his papers and stalked out with his
most monarchical mien.

The Assembly accepted de Gaulle by 329 votes to 224. No
one shouted "*Vive de Gaulle!*" One Communist yelled, "*Vive
la République!*"

The next day the empowering bill was presented. There
was still a question whether the deputies could bring themselves to swallow that bitter pill. De Gaulle dropped in unexpectedly. He was the perfect politician, charming them all.
The bill was passed. His Brain Trust called it "Operation
Seduction."

The generals and the men of the right, who had helped
de Gaulle to power, were also surprised—unpleasantly. He had
every intention of re-establishing the State and getting the
Army in hand. So he thanked them profusely and eased them
out of power.

Jacques Soustelle, who expected the Ministry of the Interior
was given Information and, later, the Sahara with the title of
Minister Delegate. Someone cracked, "That should be Minister
Relegate." Salan, who hoped to be Chief-of-Staff and a Marshal
of France, was made Inspector General of the Army—like
Giraud in 1944—honor without power. Miquel, who had
headed "Operation Resurrection" in France, got the Grand
Cross of the Legion of Honor and was retired. In fact, Legions
of Honor were distributed quite lavishly—salve for wounded
feelings.

At one meeting of the Council, de Gaulle proposed the name
of François Mauriac for the Grand Cross. Someone objected
on the grounds of Mauriac's political views. De Gaulle said
stiffly, "But he is the greatest writer in France." Then with a

little half smile and bow to his new Minister of Culture and friend, André Malraux, de Gaulle added, "Among others."

Of course he received the Labor leaders too. One of them, continuing to press for a previous program began, *"Mon Général,* as I was saying to your predecessor . . ."

"General de Gaulle has no predecessor," said General de Gaulle.

That stopped all conversation. With a faint twinkle, de Gaulle said courteously, "But continue, Monsieur, if you please."

The day after de Gaulle's investiture, Léon Delbecque arrived unexpectedly from Algiers. De Gaulle received him at the Matignon. "Bravo, Delbecque!" he said. "I congratulate you. You avoided civil war. You were magnificent. Not a drop of blood! France owes a great deal to you and Massu."

Then de Gaulle's lips ruffled with a breeze of humor as he said, "But admit, I played well, too."

However the Algerians and the Army were not altogether happy. They would have preferred a coup d'état that would have expunged "The System" and wiped the slate clean. De Gaulle's appointment of political ministers like Guy Mollet, Pinay, and Jacquinot worried them. Delbecque suggested that he bring a "pure" delegation with him when he came to Algiers.

"I am the arbiter," de Gaulle said loftily. "I am bringing Mollet, Debré and Michelet to Algiers."

"That will risk an incident."

"Oh well, you convert the recalcitrants before I get there. As to the Army, it must obey! They wanted de Gaulle. They've got de Gaulle. Now let them get back to work."

Two days later de Gaulle arrived in Algiers. The crowds were delirious. They accorded him a wild reception ("style Broadway") with a snow storm of ticker tape. Their leaders, whom he met at the airport, were less enthusiastic. "Well, are you content?" he asked them.

"Yes, *Mon Général,* but . . ."

"But what?"

"But you are surrounded by bums."

And over the radio Delbecque said, "We did not cross the Rubicon to go fishing."

With cold, controlled fury de Gaulle said, "What does that mean? I do not permit anyone in a public speech to address de Gaulle in that fashion."

With the Army he was equally severe. Colonel Bigeard of the *Paras* was presented to him. The Colonel expected thanks. De Gaulle said, "Bigeard, be ambitious, but don't be presumptuous!"

As he traveled through Algeria, de Gaulle visited in the *casernes*—the barracks—with the young officers, talking to them about France and their responsibilities as officers and heirs of the great traditions of the French Army. Of one of these speeches Guy Mollet said, "It was so moving I had to leave, or I would have made a fool of myself before those young men by crying out loud."

And once de Gaulle was sitting with some captains and lieutenants in a French-Arab cafe discussing integration. With a gesture that took in the crowd of Arabs in their sheet-like robes and curtained headgear an officer said, "But, *mon Général,* how can we integrate with people who dress like that?"

With his slight smile de Gaulle answered, "They can change their clothes—or you can."

His greatest reception of all was among the Moslems in their casbahs, cities and villages. They received him as a hero come to save them from a civil war in which they were caught between the Colons and their own fanatical co-religionists. As he walked among them, alone and fatherly, the men gave him the courteous Moslem benedictory greeting, and barefoot women in loose dresses and veils held out their babies. One Moslem mother said, "Now my children will be Frenchmen!"

Back in France, de Gaulle went hard at work on his program. Getting the new constitution ready for a referendum in September was no easy matter. Michel Debré, who was Minister of Justice, did the actual drafting, but all the cabinet were consulted as well as the special commission appointed by the Assembly.

However, de Gaulle had the final say, and it conformed largely to his ideas of a presidential republic with a strong executive. In order to placate the French politicians who believe that parliamentary government is essential to democracy —they do not consider the American Constitition democratic —a premier, responsible to the Assembly, was provided. There was also a Senate, with real power. But control of the Army, foreign affairs and relations with France Beyond the Sea was reserved to the President; as was the right to dissolve the Assembly. The former colonies were given their choice of joining a commonwealth, called the French Community, or of complete independence.

Thus the President of the French Republic was elevated from a mere symbol to greater power than that of the President of the United States, who, after all, cannot send Congress home. A man with such power should have a popular mandate according to American thinking. But the French people are terrified of popular elections; they are afraid of themselves. As Malraux says, "Do not forget *le gout français pour la guerre civile."* So it was provided that the President should be elected by a special college of electors numbering 81,761. It consisted of the Assembly and the Senate—who, however, represented less than 1 per cent of the total vote. It also included representatives of metropolitan and overseas departments, and of overseas territorial assemblies and the assemblies of the member States of the Community. But the greatest membership, 72,500, consisted of the members and delegates of the township and municipal councils of France and her overseas departments. Thus hardly any of the electors would be chosen for the *purpose of electing* the President of the Republic. It was as far from a popular choice as possible while keeping the forms of democracy.

This was in accordance with de Gaulle's own thinking. His ideal of the President was a sort of republican monarch, an arbiter above party, unifying all the different elements of France.

Another objection to electing the President by popular vote was that he would also be President of the French Community. That would mean that all the Africans, Tahitians, Madagascans, etc., far outnumbering the population France, would elect the President of the French Republic. This was unthinkable.

According to René Pleven, de Gaulle did not at first envision so powerful a president. "The way things go in France, it is too apt to become a dictatorship," de Gaulle said.

He would like to have seen two great parties in France as in England. But as he later said to Guy Mollet, "What will you? In France we must resign ourselves to having a number of parties." Since the thing he disliked most, and to which he attributed all the ills of the State, was the fractional parties in the Assembly—"They make me want to vomit," he once said to his cousin Louis Chevallier—he became convinced that a powerful President was the only solution.

The new Constitution was published on July 29, awfully fast work, and the referendum set for September 28. Then de Gaulle took off for Madagascar and a swing around the French African States that took him 13,000 miles in less than a month.

When the constitution was published, what a howl went up from Communists and the extreme liberals! There were also mutterings on the extreme right. A hot campaign ensued.

During September everyone in France was asking everyone else, "Are you going to vote Yes or No?"

In her salon in Paris, over which the widow of Marshal Pétain presided like a queen in exile, the question came up. "I shall vote Yes," said Madame Pétain.

"You wouldn't?" gasped an outraged lady of her court.

"I will," Madame Pétain said firmly. "But if I encounter that little de Gaulle who put the Marshal and me in prison, I'll give him a piece of my mind!"

Few Frenchmen were able to distinguish like that between de Gaulle and the constitution. In fact most of them did not bother to read the long legalistic document. In the election they were voting either for de Gaulle or against him.

On September 4, de Gaulle made his great appeal to the people of France:

> What is henceforth of the greatest importance to the Government is its effectiveness and stability. We live in a time when gigantic forces are transforming the world. Unless we would risk becoming an obsolete and scorned people, we must develop rapidly in the scientific, economic, and social domains. . . . Thus it is for us, for the people we are, for the century and the world in which we live, that the new Constitution has been created, so that the country will be efficiently led by those whom it chooses and to whom it gives the confidence which alone generates legitimacy . . . And so that there should exist, above political battles a national arbiter. . . .
>
> This, then, Frenchmen and Frenchwomen, is what inspires the constitution that will be submitted for your approval on September 28. With all my heart in the name of France I ask you to vote *Yes!*
>
> If you do not we will return to the troubled days you have known. If you approve, the result will be to make the Republic strong and effective . . . and there will also be in that positive declaration of the national will the proof that our country has recovered its unity and thereby its chance for greatness. . . .
>
> *Vive la République!*
> *Vive la France!*

The great day came and more French people voted than ever before in history. Nearly 85 per cent of eligible voters went to the polls, which makes the 50 per cent turnout of Americans look pretty shameful. When the votes were counted 79.5 per cent were for the new constitution—or de Gaulle.

The following day Overseas France gave it an equally enthusiastic approval. And in Algeria the vote was 96 per cent *Yes.*

At Colombey-les-Deux-Églises, Yvonne de Gaulle, who was not very happy over her husband's return to politics, watched the returns with mingled sorrow and pride. In that little village the vote was: *Yes, 239. No, 1.*

Since the ballot was truly and honestly secret, no one knew who had cast that lone *No* vote. But the neighbors strongly suspected that it was *"Tante* Yvonne."

As soon as the Constitution was approved, a general election was called for November 30 to elect the new Assembly. A great many people wanted to hop on the de Gaulle bandwagon. As Georges Bidault bitterly remarked, "Everyone wants a piece of the true Cross of Lorraine."

A new Party was formed, the *Union for the New Republic* (U.N.R.), which advertised itself as "the Gaullist Party." This dismayed the General, who had said, "Above all there must never be *one* party in France."

In setting up the electoral machinery he deliberately tried to make it easier for deputies representing other parties to be elected. In spite of this attempt to rig the vote against himself the U.N.R. polled so great a majority that one wit called it "The Massacre of the Innocents."

De Gaulle, true to his picture of himself as an arbiter above party, said, "Have all these people of the U.N.R. suddenly become wise? They were elected in my shadow. Obviously, I should have preferred more Socialists."

Then came the matter of electing the First President of the Fifth Republic. It was quite evident to everyone who he should be, but de Gaulle was troubled by a question of gratitude. He went to the Élysée to call on President Coty, whose term of office under the old Constitution would still have had several years to run. Sitting in two great armchairs in a splendid salon overlooking the gardens and through the winter-swept trees of the Champs Élysée toward the "temporary" Tower that has become the symbol of Paris to all the world, the President and his Prime Minister talked things over.

"I have come to ask counsel of you," de Gaulle said. "What should I do?"

"The success of your friends is your own success," said Coty.

"Public opinion expects you to go to the Élysée. It must not be disappointed."

"Nevertheless, we must consider carefully," de Gaulle replied, "for we are forging a tradition."

Coty smiled. "What would I do as President of the Republic with a Premier of your stature?" he asked. "If you remain at the Matignon, I could not say to you all the things I might like to say. There is no conflict between us now, but a situation might arise that would embarrass one or the other of us."

"Besides," he added frankly, "I don't want to remain here. If I were convinced that it was for the safety of the Nation and the national interest, of course I would bow to that. But that is not the case. So I leave."

De Gaulle arose and stood looking down at the man who was his titular chief. "In any case, *Monsieur le Président,*" he said emotionally, "you have earned the respect and gratitude of the Nation."

The presidential elections were a foregone conclusion. As a matter of form the Communists put up a candidate and Mendès-France's Union of Democratic Forces ran Albert Châtelet. De Gaulle won 78.5 per cent of all the votes polled.

On January 8, 1959, Charles de Gaulle, wearing the dress uniform of a brigadier general and the famous two-starred kepi, and surrounded by the *Garde Républicaine* in all their antique splendor of clanking breastplates and plumed Roman helmets, drove down the Avenue Gabrielle and through tall, grilled Gate of the Cock (reserved for Chiefs of State) into the Élysée Palace. President Coty received him joyfully.

The ceremony of the Inauguration was impressive, but brief. As it ended the President of the Fourth Republic gave his accolade to the President of the Fifth Republic, saying, "The French people have recovered their unity through the leadership of General de Gaulle. For the first time in History a revolution has been carried out calmly and with full respect for the laws that its main purpose was to change."—"The most civilized of revolutions," someone else called it.

Then President Coty departed. It is said that never did an evicted tenant go so gladly.

The invited guests and the voracious press left more reluctantly, but at last they, too, were gone. De Gaulle was alone with the hardest task he had ever attempted.

And for the first time in her history France had a ruler who was neither a king, an emperor, nor a dictator.

❧ ⚜ ❧

NEW DEAL Á LA FRANÇAISE

T HINGS HAPPENED FAST at the Palais de l'Élyée when de Gaulle moved in. The sloppy ways of politician presidents disappeared overnight. All the functionaries of the Palace, from the footmen who swarmed in the marble corridors and stately reception rooms to the officers on duty now wore sparkling dress uniforms almost all the time. On the great portico, at the foot and head of the grand staircase, and at the double doors of the presidential suite, soldiers of the *Garde Républicaine* in the dark blue and red uniforms of the Third Empire, with fresh white gloves and plumed helmets, stood rigidly with rifles at parade rest.

When the President himself appeared, one could almost hear invisible trumpets blowing. This was the de Gaulle, who embodied the greatness of France.

But almost every week end he and Yvonne dashed down to Colombey in his black Citroën, tearing over the narrow country roads at eighty or ninety miles an hour. There were only two motorcycle guards to clear the way—a situation that would give the American Secret Service nightmares.

In La Boisserie, de Gaulle became again the simple country gentleman. The house was loosely guarded by a company of gendarmes who were ordered to keep out of the way, while de Gaulle enjoyed his solitary walks in the forests, accompanied by his *corgi*, King of Cardiff, and occasionally by Yvonne.

When guests came to Colombey, he received them with his customary unaffected courtesy and helped to serve them drinks as he always had. Even in the Élysée he could not bring himself to accept the protocol that the President is served first. De Gaulle was served last like any other good French host.

The trips to Colombey were made so frequently because de Gaulle did not like living at the Élysée. When word of this got out some cynic said, "Isn't it grand enough for him? Perhaps the Louvre. . . ."

Grandeur had nothing to do with it. De Gaulle disliked the Élysée because of its fancy decorative motifs, and, most of all, because of its lack of privacy. He would have enjoyed strolling in its splendid gardens under the great trees, but the many window-eyes of towering apartment houses ruined the feeling of solitude which he needed, now, more than ever.

Nor did Yvonne de Gaulle like the Élysée. The General's niece, Madame Anthonioz, said, "It is a real privation for Tante Yvonne. The functions are not amusing to her, for, like my uncle, she loves family life. Also, she is a very good housekeeper, and likes to oversee her kitchen. Not to be able to run her own house is irritating to her. And she misses the garden she adores at Colombey. . . .

"But, like a good soldier's wife, she has adapted herself to her present life. She finds many interests, and smiles at her difficulties."

The de Gaulles soon settled down to a schedule of life at the Élysée. The General is a great man for regularity and promptness. If his wife is even a minute late he is apt to say reproachfully, "Yvonne, I have been waiting." At which she just smiles amiably.

De Gaulle got up every morning at seven-thirty, and read the papers while he ate the usual light French breakfast. At nine o'clock, wearing a dark, double-breasted business suit that fitted him as though it were tailored on Saville Row—though, of course, it was made in France—he was in his office.

It was a beautifully proportioned room on the second floor of the Palace lighted by long windows overlooking the gardens. His desk, under a superb crystal chandlelier, was an antique inlaid table with no drawers.

Colonel Gaston de Bonneval, assisted by aides from the other armed services, occupied an anteroom equipped with a rather elaborate telephone system, which in spite of its modernity, often broke down. Even in the Élysée!

The rest of de Gaulle's personal staff, headed by his ever-faithful young aides—Pompidou, Guichard, Lefranc, and, of course, de Courcel, were housed in almost equally splendid—and inconvenient—salons-become-offices throughout the Élysée. Now that the presidency had become the real executive power of France, there was not room for all the staff even in that big, rambling palace, and the lower echelons of the different sections were scattered in government buildings all over Paris.

At one o'clock de Gaulle took the usual French two-hour recess for lunch. Being decidedly frugal in appetite he spent most of it in solitary thought. At three o'clock he was back at his desk where he remained until seven-thirty. Then he went to his private apartment to watch the eight o'clock news on television and dine alone with his wife.

The de Gaulles seldom went out at night unless an official function required it. As often as possible they spent the evening together, reading or watching television of which the General, surprisingly, is very fond. Other nights de Gaulle played solitaire to relax after tensions of the day, while Yvonne sat knitting and watching, occasionally pointing out a play her husband had missed.

Quite often, of course, de Gaulle had to work late into the night catching up on the multitudinous papers which he was required to approve, disapprove, or entirely rewrite. There was a tremendous amount of work to be done, for France was being given a whole "new order" that involved more revolutionary changes than Franklin Roosevelt's New Deal brought about in America. In addition, the affairs of the whole world were never more tangled, and de Gaulle was passionately determined that his country should play a leading role in straightening them out, if that were possible.

This sudden work-load falling on the shoulders of a man nearly seventy years old who had been living in semi-retirement might have been expected to have disastrous consequences. The contrary occurred. Each day de Gaulle appeared younger and more vigorous. His skin was ruddy with health, his blue eyes flashed with excitement or humor, even his hair became crisp and the golden brown of youth showed beneath the gray.

He still spoke regretfully of his age. When someone answered that all the great foreign statesmen were older than he, de Gaulle answered, "They are too old. No one should accept certain responsibilities when over fifty."

But this was more a theory than a reality. In actual fact, he seemed to say, *"Adieu tristes!"* For the melancholy which had prevaded his being vanished completely. There was no more talk of the past or "the eternal cold," but only of the future and the high prospects it held for France. In short, de Gaulle regained his real self as he led his country to regain hers.

The great business at hand was turning Gaullism from theory into fact. This was complicated by the fact that the word had almost as many meanings as there were Gaullists. To Antoine Pinay, Minister of Finance, it meant hard money and conservative economics; to Edmond Michelet, Minister of Justice, it meant almost the exact opposite government-financed social welfare programs, workers committees on the boards of directors of the great corporations, in short, a socialistic approach to Government.

To Jacques Soustelle, Gaullism was *Algérie Française* and authoritarian government, while to Prime Minister Debré it was simply a more stable form of Parliamentarianism.

To André Malraux, Minister of Culture and "Philosopher Extraordinary," it was a *mystique* capable of world-wide emulation.

"To my mind," he said, "Gaullism is not just a movement

[247]

for the greater glory of France. It is a movement to serve democracy. The democratic ideas of the nineteenth century became outmoded with the advent of Marxist Communism. It was all right when everyone played the game according to the rules, but once a player kicked over the table other ways had to be found.

"Gaullism is a way of preserving democratic freedoms and counteracting Communism without lapsing into Fascism. It implies a more authoritative State that can act swiftly against totalitarian regimes while still preserving the popular basis and freedom.

"At the same time it is modern democracy that brings the people social benefits, (which *laissez-faire* can no longer provide) without lapsing into socialistic rigidity."

Malraux sees Gaullism as a philosophy of government which can be adopted by other nations according to their needs and customs. "On my recent visit to Brazil," he said, "when I explained the principles of Gaullism to the President, he thought of them as applying to Brazil, not France.

"We also discussed the unification and renaissance, in a philosophical sense, of the Latin peoples—a *rassemblement*. France desires less to be the leader of such a movement, than its midwife.

"And above all, in France itself, Gaullism means the unification and spiritual renaissance of her people."

To the man whose name became the word, it has a no less noble, though more local, application. Looking through his windows with far seeing eyes at the green heart of the city which is the heart of France, de Gaulle said, " 'Gaullism,' in its essence, is France; and the movement toward restoring her to greatness. Because if she is not great she is nothing—not France." Then realistically he added, "She is rising now, *Elle monte*. How far she can go I do not know, but slowly, she rises.

"Of course we need help to do this, but the mainspring must come from within France herself. She must not rely on foreign money or foreign companies to develop her resources. Her own people must do it. In the beginning, of course, it was different. There was no one to do this thing but me. I did it because I had to. *Il me faut.*

"But never forget," de Gaulle said, "that the French people are not France. For a thousand years it has been like this. France is the State. And the State leads the people to greatness."

Despite the different views of Gaullism and the different politics of the Gaullists, the new government moved steadily forward. The differences were resolved by arbitration from above. De Gaulle both reigned and governed. The Government of Premier Debré administered and acted as liaison with the Assembly. One deputy said, "The Assembly has become a shadow play."

But de Gaulle was no man to concern himself with petty details of administration. He delegated power. When Pinay said to him in exasperation, *"Mon Général,* what is your fiscal policy?" De Gaulle answered, "My dear Pinay, *you* tell me. You are my Minister of Finance."

This, of course, was an extreme case. De Gaulle does not enjoy economics. And Pinay did an excellent job. The franc was strengthened on foreign exchange. Taxes were reformed; subsidies cut, and the budget brought nearer into balance than at any time since the war.

However, in the matters which he felt deeply concerned the greatness of France, de Gaulle ran the show himself. He ordered an atomic bomb tested, so that France might take her rightful place in the councils of the Great Powers—it went off on schedule in Febraury 1960. He pushed the Sahara oil development so that she need not depend on foreigners for the black blood of her industrial life. And, with his able Foreign Minister, Couve de Murville, at his elbow, he pushed boldly forward in foreign policy, moving ever closer to West Germany.

When Chancellor Adenauer of the West German Republic came to Paris in March 1959, de Gaulle said to him. "It is true that Germany is the very core of Europe. What magnificent things we can do working together."

However, de Gaulle definitely disapproved of the way NATO

was set up, and he abruptly moved to change it—unilaterally. The NATO forces had been deliberately organized as an *integrated* allied army, in order to allay French fears of German rearmament, and also because such an organization promised greater coherence, efficiency and discipline than the loose confederation of national armies, navies and air forces of World War II. To de Gaulle, the idea of French divisions lost in a mongrel army was completely abhorrent.

His first action was to pull part of the French fleet out from under the NATO Commander in the Mediterranean. His second was to announce that no further French forces would be integrated in the NATO Army under General Lauris Norstad's command. Then he withheld permission to stock atomic warheads on French soil, which forced the American bombers to abandon their expensive bases in France, for more exposed ones in Germany. Finally, he barred NATO ballistic missiles from France.

The whole Atlantic Alliance shivered under the shock. "De Gaulle is an enigma," the generals said. But de Gaulle was not the least bit of an enigma. He was following his own logical theory of the best interests of France—and therefore, as he sees it, of civilization.

He explained his position one wintry day at the Élysée. It was perfectly natural, he said, for the United States, with its great power and its drive and its anxieties, to want an integrated military force led and directed by itself. He also admitted there were certain military advantages to be gained by such a setup.

But it would not work for France. She would be submerged in such a force with virtually, or absolutely, no control over its use.

He pointed out that NATO was, after all, only an European alliance, but France had other commitments—in the Pacific, in Africa, especially in Africa. Therefore she could not tie up her power.

Then he spoke as a strategist: there were two possible kinds of war to consider. The first was a total missile war, in which case Europe would not be involved. "The rockets will fly from continent to continent arcing over the countries of Europe. What we do will not matter."

However, in the event of a conventional war it would be necessary to have an Allied army. In such a war there would be one battle—the Battle of Germany. If we won it—fine. All would be well.

But what if it were lost? Then there would be no more NATO. It would disintegrate, leaving a vacuum. "In such a case," the General said very solemnly to his listener, "France must have control of her own power so that she can withdraw it to defend herself. So that I,"—and now he was France—"can defend her *even under occupation.*"

There spoke the Man of June 18, 1940, the leader of the Resistance, the General who never surrendered.

De Gaulle was almost as deeply concerned with the nations of the Community as he was with France herself. His full and free offer to them of the choice of complete independence or membership in the Community was applauded throughout the world as a gesture of magnificent magnanimity. Its terms surprised even the French Communists and Socialists. One left wing deputy said, "He is so liberal that it frightens me. He wants to be the Bolivar of Africa." The Conservatives were shocked. Was this the man they had backed on May 13?

The response of the overseas peoples was beyond even de Gaulle's expectations. All but one of the native states, in referendums whose honesty was unquestioned, voted to join the Community. Eleven African states and the Republic of Madagascar were joined in partnership with France, who retained control of their foreign affairs, defense, and finance.

"What if we want independence later," one of their leaders inquired.

"You have only to ask," said de Gaulle.

A year later some of them began to have second thoughts. The States of Senegal and the French Sudan joined together in the Federation of Mali. In November 1959, they asked for further independence. They wanted to have complete control of their destiny though they still desired to be "confederated" with France. De Gaulle called the leaders of Mali to Paris and in answer to their request said a little sadly, "It is your right."

Then he christened the new arrangement "Organized Friendship." All the nations of the community adopted it in the end.

A little later de Gaulle and Yvonne went to Saint Louis, the Capital of Senegal. The General got a great reception from frantic crowds, while women in calico mother hubbards beat tom-toms of liberty and native lancers in picturesque uniforms rode by with their color guard proudly carrying the red, yellow, and green flag of Mali beside the Tricolor of France.

To the Moslem President of Mali de Gaulle spoke earnestly of the Communist peril. Then he said with his exquisite courtesy, "Forgive me if I quote to you from our Gospel, *Abide with us; for it is toward evening and the day is far spent.*"

So the Community was off to a fine start. But Algeria was different. It was no ordinary colonial problem. There was no right or wrong, no black and white. It had been French for over one hundred years. More than a million Frenchmen lived there, as had their fathers and grandfathers before them. Billions of French capital had been invested there. Another million Moslems had thrown in their lot with France and relied on her for protection—they would be the first to be slaughtered if they were abandoned. Alphonse Juin, the only living Marshal of France, was born there.

Algeria was *French*. Yet it was not. For there were eight million Moslems who either wanted independence or were fatalistically neutral. While up in the hills and deserts and country farms, and down in the dark alleys of the Casbah, and even in the broad bright streets and brilliantly lighted cafés of Algeria, the rebels of the F.L.N. fought a merciless, murderous war.

There was no just solution.

The peculiar thing about de Gaulle, the "arrogant," "proud," "authoritarian" man who was the uncrowned monarch of

France, was that he could never conceive of governing people against their will—any people anywhere—no matter what their creed or color.)

(So on September 16, 1959, de Gaulle publicly offered the Algerians their free choice of integration with France, association with her, or complete independence.) His only condition was that the F.L.N. cease their terrorism and accept "a peace of the brave."

That did it. The *colons* were aghast; the Army furious. And the ultraconservatives of Metropolitan France saw their opportunity to get rid of the man who had disappointed them by turning out to be too democratic. The conspiracies burgeoned and exfoliated. In white, vine-embowered villas in Algeria and modernistic apartments in Paris men whispered, "The hour of the *Sixth* Republic is at hand." Young officers in barracks and old ones in their command posts avoided each other's eyes. And in the twisted, narrow streets of the ancient city of Paris the small, secret armies of the Right, the Ultras, and the neo-Cagoulards, who wore hoods and masks like the Ku Klux Klan, were arming.

❧ ⚜ ❧

THE TEST

THE PRESTIGE OF General de Gaulle's Government fell to
its lowest ebb in December-January 1959-60. Those were
dismal months in Paris with fog and sleet, and snow
like rain, and rain as cold as snow. All the discontents and
divisive forces that had been welded together by his prestige
seemed to be coming unstuck. There were three political crises
in three weeks—and a rebellion in Algeria.

In the course of these crises three eminent political cabinet
ministers resigned, among them the conservative Minister of
Finance, Antoine Pinay. French politicians and intellectuals,
wedded to the theory of Parliamentary Government, were
deeply concerned. "The Cabinet is now composed almost entirely of technicians," they mourned. "There is hardly a politician in it. They are just aides-de-camp for de Gaulle."

An American, accustomed to the presidential system asked,
"What of it? We only worry when the politicians are running
the ministries."

"The Government is losing touch with the people," was the
answer. "It will become dictatorial."

The truth is that the Government was losing touch only with
the politicians, not with the people. De Gaulle was deliberately

moving toward the American system. However, a strong undercurrent of opposition was rising against him among his conservative supporters in the Assembly. The Algerian speech and
Pinay's resignation gave it impetus. De Gaulle was thoroughly
aware of it, and also of the fact that both Pinay and Soustelle
were ambitious to succeed eventually him in the presidency.

In fact, he liked to tease Soustelle a little about it. On a
trip to Algeria in the summer of 1959, they both appeared on
the same platform. The crowd was yelling *"Vive de Gaulle!"*
Then in a sudden silence a single voice shouted, *"Vive Soustelle!"*

With a flash of a twinkle de Gaulle said, *"Voilà, Soustelle.
I did not know you were a ventriloquist."*

The increasing thunder on the Right failed to swerve him
one degree from his charted course.

In the midst of all these political difficulties de Gaulle
suffered a terrible personal blow. His only living brother,
Pierre, who was also his last intimate friend, had a heart attack
while visiting with the General at the Élysée at Christmastime,
and was taken to the American Hospital at Neuilly. Late in
the evening of Sunday, December 27, de Gaulle was notified
that Pierre had suffered a relapse. He dashed to the hospital
with motorcycle sirens screaming, and reached his brother's
side moments before he died.

Pierre de Gaulle was the baby of the family, dear to his
brother in childhood, perhaps dearer in later years when his
never-failing loyalty and the memories they shared drew them
close together.

As always de Gaulle's grief was publicly apparent only in his
stony expression. Alone with Yvonne, he wept.

The final blow of the ill-fated season was almost mortal
—for France. Late in January 1960, General Massu in Algeria
gave a most indiscreet interview to Hans Ulrich Kempski of
Munich's *Sueddeutsche Zeitung*. In it the brave but flamboyant
paratroop general said, "The Army does not understand de

Gaulle's Algerian policy. . . . . But he was the only man at our disposal. Perhaps the Army made a mistake." (Massu later denied the latter statement, but confirmed the former.)

When the news reached the Élysée, de Gaulle was literally staggered. Maurice Schumann, the President of the Assembly's Foreign Affairs Committee, said, "The General had suffered a great shock. As always in a crisis his mind sought an analogy in history. 'Dreyfus, Pétain, and now this,' he said. 'You know, Schumann, I have always loved the Army but when it makes an ass of itself, it's the biggest!' "

The situation was somewhat like that of President Truman and General Douglas MacArthur, though the danger was far greater. Like Truman, de Gaulle acted swiftly to assert the civil power over the military. Against the advice of most of his ministers, including Premier Debré, and the passionate pleading of Jacques Soustelle, he ordered Massu back to Paris, and there relieved him of his command. His action touched off the Algerian powder barrel and brought the great Rightist conspiracy to a head—prematurely.

On Sunday, January 24, the mob came out in Algiers again. The sun was shining hotly, a lovely day for a revolution. Pierre Lagaillarde, the flaming extremist of May 13, swarthy Joseph Ortiz, and Robert Martel from the hilly vineyards of Mitidja, harangued the crowd in the Forum. The home guards, armed against the F.L.N. terrorists, joined the mob. The barricades went up.

Toward dusk, a thousand men of *Gendarmerie Mobile* charged down the broad Avenue Laferrière to disperse the crowd. In the confusion somebody lost his head and both sides started shooting. Twenty-five people were killed and 141 wounded. Their blood, flowing darkly on the roadway, roused such passions as had never appeared in the bloodless coup of May 13. This was civil war!

Back from the Sunday peace of Colombey, de Gaulle raced through the foggy January night. He reached the Élysée at 11:45 P.M. to be greeted by Premier Debré, resignation in hand. "You will not resign," ordered de Gaulle.

Then he sat down at his desk and dictated a message to General Maurice Challe, Commander of the French Army in Algeria, ordering him to clear out the rebels, who were barricaded in the University and the buildings across the Avenue Laferrière.

Finally he dictated a message to the Algerians calling the riot "a low blow against France," and beseeching "those who are rising against their country, led astray as they may be by lies and slander, to return to order."

But it was not so easily done as that. For the Army was wavering. Challe sent word that his men would not fire on their fellow Frenchmen behind the barricades. Indeed, the next day the paratroopers, who were surrounding the besieged rebels, fraternized with them and allowed their wives and sweethearts to pass through the lines bringing food and, as some said, ammunition. It was an odd scene, a sort of military picnic with the gay printed dresses of the girls and women mingling with the improvised, dirt-smeared uniforms of the rebels and the battle dress of the *Paras*—a very matey little revolution.

But it was no joke. The crux of the matter lay, not in Algiers, but in Paris, where the small Rightist armies were waiting for the word; while their leaders waited for the sign that France was turning against de Gaulle.

There were two disciplined political parties in France, the Army, which had re-entered politics on May 13, and the Communist Party. The Army was wavering. Chief-of-Staff General Paul Ely was loyal to the Government. So was General Challe in Algeria. But the hot-headed younger officers were a question mark. The Communists were also a question mark. But one that did not long remain unanswered.

The Communist Party had fought de Gaulle on every issue since the Liberation. True, they had been howling for African independence for years and it would be logically difficult for them to take the side of those who opposed independence for Algeria. But logic or truth has never been known to hamper the Kremlin if they were contrary to its policy. There was a much more important consideration.

The moment news of the fighting in Algiers reached Communist party chief Marcel Thorez, he got on the telephone to Khrushchev in Moscow. The master of Russia was no fool. His mind quickly assessed the situation. At that time Khrushchev was still hopeful of gaining de Gaulle's cooperation at the Summit Conference. He was due in Paris within a few weeks, and he wanted a nice friendly reception there. He did *not* want to deal with a military dictator or even with a shaky popular front Government. Within minutes the order flashed back from Moscow to Thorez, "Back de Gaulle!"

Early Monday morning when the Communist press hit the streets of the French cities, it was, to everyone's amazement, for order and authority. The disciplined ranks of the Party, which had always formented revolution and chaos to profit by the confusion in the minds and loyalties of men, closed solidly behind de Gaulle.

All the other Paris papers also backed de Gaulle, with one exception, which took a vaguely opposition line.

But that was not the end of the trouble, far from it. Indeed, the Communist position exacerbated the fury of the ultra-conservatives and even threw some fence-sitters on their side. On Monday and Tuesday Paris, shrouded in mist and dreary drizzle, looking on the surface as gelid as the winter's day, was seething. At the key points of bridges and public buildings little groups of gendarmes and steel-helmeted security police stood huddled in the rain fingering their automatic weapons and waiting for the intricate complex of streets and alleys of the old city to spew out the torrent of revolution, as they so often had before.

At the council meeting in the Élysée on Monday, the cabinet was almost evenly divided between giving way by promising the Algerians that they would remain forever French, and standing by de Gaulle's promise of a free vote on independence. The General listened to each of them attentively, but even if they had all been against him, he would have done what his sense of honor commanded. He said, "I must do what is right for France."

By afternoon passions raged more fiercely. Over at the Ministry of the Sahara, Soustelle, who was so emotionally involved with the Algerian French, sat at his desk muttering over and over, "The senseless slaughter. The senseless slaughter." He was distraught.

In his spacious apartment on the Avenue Kléber the only living Marshal of France, Algerian-born Alphonse Juin, was torn between his love and loyalty for de Gaulle and his sympathy for his fellow Algerians. He alternated between deep melancholy and furious anger, saying, "He does not understand. . . ."

But at the Élysée things were much as usual. The black Citroëns of government officials were parked in neat rows in the courtyard. Footmen in livery waited on the broad steps of the portico, and the *Gardes Républicaines* stood like statues at their posts. The atmosphere of dignity and splendor made the tenant of the Élysée appear as solidly based as the residents of Buckingham Palace.

A visitor to the President that afternoon found the same tranquillity within as without. De Gaulle greeted his visitor at the entrance to his splendid office with his usual gentle courtesy. His clear skin glowed with health, his face was fresh and his eyes unshadowed. When he was seated behind his uncluttered table-desk, he began to talk in his soft, clear voice about the philosophy of Gaullism and the future. There seemed never a doubt in his mind that France would fulfill her great destiny. He was serene.

On Tuesday, as a matter of courtesy, de Gaulle received Marshal Juin. Of course, no one knows exactly what these old comrades-in-arms said to each other; but it is known that the tone of their conversation had no asperity, rather a gentle melancholy. Of course Juin urged the Algerian point of view and the wisdom of compromise. De Gaulle listened, saying little.

Naturally, he escorted the Marshal to the door, and so their final words are known. Juin said, "You are old now, you should not engage in folly."

Very thoughtfully de Gaulle replied, "Yes, I know I am old; that death is lying in wait for me. But I have never in my life been so determined."

The situation continued in hair-trigger balance throughout the week. In Algeria, General Challe was unable to do more than maintain the status quo, while Delegate General Paul Delouvrier, shattered by strain and lack of sleep—seven hours in seven days—was visibly disintegrating. The Army grumbled. Paris quietly seethed.

(On Friday, January 29, de Gaulle prepared to stake everything on the people of France, whom he always trusted.) With his customary dramatic symbolism he put on his blue dress brigadier general's uniform, decorated only with the Cross of Lorraine, and sat down at his desk before the television cameras and microphones, while all France and Algeria gathered in homes and bars and public buildings to listen.

(Speaking as always from memory, having destroyed the handwritten copy of his speech, he said, "If I have put on my uniform today to address you, it is in order to show that it is General de Gaulle who speaks, as well as the Chief of State.")

(Then imperiously he stated his unequivocal position: "I, in the name of France, have made the following decision: the Algerians shall have free choice of their destiny. . . . This is the only policy that is worthy of France.) . . .

"There are two categories of people who do not want any part of this free choice. First, the rebel organization [F.L.N. terrorists], which maintains that it will cease fire only if I negotiate with it beforehand. . . . This I will not do.

"On the other hand, some persons of French descent demand that I renounce the ideal of self-determination. . . . This I will not do either."

Then addressing himself directly to the men listening in the besieged buildings of Algiers, he said, "Frenchmen of Algeria! How can you fail to see that . . . you are destroying yourselves and at the same time running the risk of making France lose

[260]

Algeria at the very moment when the decline of the [F.L.N.] rebellion is becoming evident? . . ."

His voice rose to the bugle call of command as he said, "Next, I speak to the Army! . . . As you know . . . it is I who bear our country's destiny. I must therefore be obeyed by every French soldier. . . . Law and order must be re-established. . . . Your duty is to bring this about. I have given, and am giving, the order for it."

Then his voice softened to an intimate, seductive tone as he addressed France herself, speaking as though to a person and not a people: "My dear old Country! Here we are together, once again, facing a harsh test. . . . While the guilty ones, who dream of usurping power, take as their pretext the decision I have made concerning Algeria, let it be known everywhere . . . that I do not intend to go back on my decision. To yield . . . would be to make the State bow before the outrage that is being inflicted on it. Thus France would become but a poor broken toy adrift on a sea of chance. . . ."

Then in a final ringing echo of his great speech of June 18, 1940, he said, "Once again, I call upon all Frenchmen, wherever they are, and whoever they may be, to reunite with France.

"Vive la République!

"Vive la France!"

De Gaulle was right in putting his trust in the French people as no politician had dared to do since the days of the Revolution and the guillotine. Almost to a man they responded to his firm summons with evident relief. Even before his speech they had begun to show their loyalty. In the next few days an avalanche of letters and telegrams of approval almost buried the Élysée—the total was said to be some 300,000. Had a referendum been held that next week, de Gaulle would have won 95 per cent of the vote.

The other 5 per cent, the irreconcilables, retired grumbling to their hideouts. Under the overwhelming pressure of public opinion the Army stiffened. Only in Algiers was there open dissidence.

In Lagaillarde's headquarters in the embattled University, weary men with dull eyes and half-grown beards listened in glum silence to de Gaulle's speech. Equally exhausted girl revolutionists burst into hysterical weeping. There were a few cries of, "De Gaulle to the gallows!" But beyond the barricades, the *Paras* were standing at attention as they listened.

Then it was all over. Hastened by a dispiriting rain the crowds melted away. In answer to an order from General Challe, the home guards began straggling over the barricades to turn in their arms and accept amnesty. Finally, Lagaillarde and a little band of 300 utterly worn-out men marched out between the lines of government troops, who paid them the final tribute of snapping, unordered, to attention.

Once again de Gaulle had won through sheer moral strength. Whatever their politics, whatever their class, the people of France felt that here was one man whose integrity was absolute, a leader whom they could trust.

And when de Gaulle announced an inspection trip that would take him to the dangerous, dissident heart of Algeria almost everyone agreed with the Paris taxi driver who said, "Like him or not, that is a man!"

From its nadir, the graph of de Gaulle's prestige soared steeply upward. At a meeting with General Norstad the relations of France with NATO were negotiated in a fairly satisfactory manner based on the ideas de Gaulle had outlined at the Élysée.

Khrushchev came to Paris, where he was heavily guarded by tens of thousands of security agents and escorted by a battalion of the *Garde Républicaine* representing a curious compromise of traditional and modern in helmets, white breeches and jackboots, mounted on motorcycles. The Russian used all his wiles, which are numerous and beguiling, to wean de Gaulle from his alliance with the "Anglo-Saxons." With perfect courtesy, de Gaulle did not give an inch.

Then de Gaulle paid his third visit to the United States,

where he was received with enthusiasm which expert observers agreed was unequaled since Ike had come home from the war. Whatever reservations there might have been on his side and that of our people were melted by the mutual warmth of that meeting. "Second only to Churchill in the history of modern Europe," was the American opinion.

Only a month later Americans were justified in their enthusiasm. At the disastrous Summit Meeting in Paris, where President Eisenhower was handicapped by a hopelessly invidious position, and Khrushchev raged in barbaric fury, and British Prime Minister Harold Macmillan sat sad-eyed as a spaniel, de Gaulle was staunchly loyal. Dignified, unfailingly courteous to all, even to Khrushchev, he was wise in counsel and unyielding in principle. Of all those leaders of nations, only he emerged with enhanced prestige.

Gloomy but astute Joseph Alsop wrote from Paris: "General de Gaulle's emergence as the leader of the West . . . was far from the least important result of the explosion at the Summit.

"A much greater debt is owed to the French President than most people understand. His untroubled perception and icy imperturbability in a moment of potential danger prevented an even uglier result in Paris. . . . De Gaulle was like a rock. . . ."

Thus in foreign as in domestic affairs, de Gaulle, without the biggest battalions, but by sheer moral force, raised France once more to a position of leadership among the great powers.

Because of human mortality, reliance on one towering figure represents a daily danger to any nation. Even de Gaulle's most bitter enemies ask in awe, "After de Gaulle, what?"

What are the chances for the survival of the Fifth Republic? They are frankly dubious. But far from hopeless. To the question if its constitution was impermanent because it was designed by and for de Gaulle, alone, Maurice Schumann answered, "In the days of the French Revolution, the members of the States General debated modeling the constitution of the First Republic on that of the United States. The idea was rejected on the grounds that the American Constitution was tailored for one man—George Washington—and that it would be abandoned when he died. It would seem they were in error."

"Our constitution is like a brand new car," he added. "It runs roughly because it needs to be broken in."

Almost everyone agrees that the division of power between the Premier and the President is unsatisfactory—"A two-headed monster," François Bundy, editor of *Preuve,* calls this system.

How to resolve the difficulty is the subject of passionate debate. The parliamentarians like René Pleven hope that, after de Gaulle, the power of the Assembly will gradually increase—as it probably will if there is a weak President. But men like Malraux, Schumann, and de Gaulle himself would prefer to work toward the American presidential system. "The people here who say the United States Constitution is not democratic are fools," Schumann says.

And of course there are always the undercover authoritarians who dream of the *Sixth Republic*—or Fourth Empire—and the Communists plotting for a soviet France.

What then of de Gaulle himself?

Certainly, whatever happens, he has played a magnificent role in the history of his country. The Virgin granted his youthful prayer that he be allowed to do "something great for France."

When his seven-year term is over, will he retire to Colombey? Even he does not know. Yvonne can always hope.

Despite his long thoughts about age, the General is in magnificent health. His visual difficulty is temporary. As soon as the cataracts that cause it "ripen," they will be removed and he will see better than he has in a long time.

So the matter resolves itself into a question of duty—the best interests of France and the world, as he sees them. In 1960, the free world, and especially the United States, feels that it needs de Gaulle badly. American opinion has gone a long way from Roosevelt's deep distrust of the "would-be Joan of Arc." In fact, since the fulminations about NATO in January, 1960, it has made a complete about-face.

Now Walter Lippmann approvingly quotes de Gaulle's far-sighted vision of the eventual unification of all Europe—East and West: "Only in equilibrium can the world find peace," de Gaulle said. "On our old continent the organization of the Western group may one day, without risk of independence and the freedom of each nation, and taking into account the probable evolution of political regimes, establish a European entente from the Atlantic *to the Urals*. Then Europe, no longer split in two by ambitions and ideologies that would have become out of date, would again be the heart of civilization."

Lippman comments, "Only a man who believes that the people of the Soviet Union are more Russian than they are Bolshevik, and that they are more European than they are irreconcilable, could have said that. It required a man who is above demagoguery, who is too proud to pander to vulgar prejudice, and who is too great a patriot to be a jingo."

Indeed, that a proud nationalist, so soon after being exposed to Communist vituperation, should be able to envision a European confederation that included the Russian people is surely a wonder. And one that people might reckon another paradox of de Gaulle's complex character.

But all of the man's paradoxes are only apparent. He is a lover of simple country life who keeps a more magnificent establishment at the Élysée than anyone since the Emperor Napoleon III. But there he is France. A great mystic, his realism often shocks the most materialistic of his ministers; but that is because he never confuses the desirable with the possible. Utterly inflexible about matters of principle, he still understands the other person's point of view, and once said to Schumann, "I suspect the cant of those who judge people by principle rather than by character."

One paradox that is hard for Protestants to understand is the fact that de Gaulle, a devout Catholic, is completely uninfluenced by the clergy. In 1944, President Roosevelt had the brilliant idea of sending (then) Archbishop Spellman to Algeria to induce de Gaulle to agree to some policy. When the Archbishop arrived de Gaulle kissed his ring with the utmost reverence and then said, "Now your Excellency, to get down to business, I know what you have come for, and I am afraid you are going to be disappointed."

And when the Mass of Thanksgiving was celebrated at Notre Dame on Liberation Day, de Gaulle actually ordered the Archbishop of Paris not to attend in his own church because he had received Pétain there a few months before.

This is not a paradox of de Gaulle's character. It is a truly Gallic attitude toward the Church of Rome. Frenchmen may accept its teachings with complete faith, while refusing to allow its chosen instruments to meddle in the affairs of state.

There are numerous other apparent paradoxes about de Gaulle: that of the great traditionalist who is more progressive than the radicals because he sees that the way to preserve the best of a tradition is to adapt it to changing conditions; and the ruthless soldier who can forgive and even make an alliance with his former enemies when their interests become similar to those of France. And again, the great nationalist who is working toward a European confederation because "under present conditions it depends solely on Moscow or Washington whether or not a large part of humanity is wiped out in a few hours.

"In the face of such a situation France thinks that there is no territorial disagreement or ideological dispute that has any importance in comparison with the necessity of exorcising this monstrous peril. . . ."

Viewed thus, in the light of understanding, the paradoxes of de Gaulle resolve themselves into a simple formula of idealism modified by common sense. "The Sphinx of the Élysée" gives up his riddle to anyone who takes the trouble to probe into his character, his ideals and his logical mind. As to his character, to paraphrase Winston Churchill, whatever he does . . . at his worst and his best, he is always the essence of France. In this he is very much like Churchill himself, who is always England.

De Gaulle's ideals are truly mystical, but his statesmanship is that of "doing what is possible in the right direction." His genius lies in knowing just how far he can push his ideals without going over the brink.

And his power over his fellow countrymen comes from the simple but tremendous moral force of a character that both friends and enemies know will never betray his honor or the honor of France, which in his mind are the same thing.

All this is not to imply that de Gaulle never made a mistake. Frequently he has been unnecessarily harsh or stubborn, and often, especially in the days of Free France, he was much too touchy and suspicious. In those days, too, he was apt to be inhumanly callous of the feelings of others and absurdly sensitive about his own ego.

But these faults were born of his virtues. Had he been otherwise, he could not have accomplished his great task.

As to the State he has built in France with such great effort, no one knows better than de Gaulle, the realist, that it is very precarious. Those who believe that, with all its faults, it is likely to prove the most satisfactory system of government France has ever known, also think that if de Gaulle remains Chief of State long enough to get the machinery running smoothly, and to give the regime the stability of popular acceptance and the inertia of tradition, that it will endure.

De Gaulle is fully cognizant of his present indispensibility. In Normandy in the summer of 1960, a group of politicians were talking with him. Their leader, André Bettancourt, voiced the question that troubles all Frenchmen. *"Mon Général,"* he said, "we understand and approve your policies, but they are dependent on you and you alone. For the present we fear nothing, but we worry about the future."

There was a short silence that seemed a long time to the men waiting for a reply. Then de Gaulle's lips twitched and his eyes sparkled with that quick flash of humor which is always surprising. *"Voilà, Messieurs,"* he said. "You must find another de Gaulle."

INDEX

(Prepared by Elsa Wagner Nugent)

INDEX

INDEX

THE AUTHOR AND HIS BOOK

ALDEN HATCH, *who was born in New York City on September 28, 1898, has been a contributor to many magazines on political, military, naval and sporting topics and on some of the world's leading contemporary personalities.* He has appeared in the Saturday Evening Post, Collier's, Harper's, Woman's Home Companion, Ladies' Home Journal, *and* Look. *He is a graduate of the Horace Mann School in New York and the University of Chicago Extension and the Blackstone Institute. His many books include:* Gaming Lady *(Farrar & Rinehart, 1931),* Glass Walls *(Dial Press, 1933),* Full Tilt *(in collaboration with F. P. Keene) (Derrydale, 1938),* Bridlewise *(Messner, 1941),* Son of the Smoky Sea *(in collaboration with Simeon Oliver) (Messner, 1941),* Back to the Smoky Sea *(Messner, 1941),* Glenn Curtiss: Pioneer of Naval Aviation *(Messner, 1942),* Heroes of Annapolis *(Messner, 1943),* General Ike *(Holt, 1944),* Young Willkie *(Harcourt, 1944),* Woodrow Wilson: A Biography for Young People *(Holt, 1947),* Franklin D. Roosevelt: An Informal Portrait *(Holt, 1947),* American Express: A Century of Service *(Doubleday, 1950),* George Patton: General in Spurs *(Messner, 1950),* General Ike, Revised Edition *(Holt, 1952),* Young Ike *(Messner, 1953),* Red Carpet for Mamie *(Holt, 1954),* Ambassador Extraordinary *(Holt, 1956),* Remington Arms in American History *(Rinehart, 1956),* Crown of Glory *(in collaboration with Seamus Walshe) (Hawthorn, 1958),* For the Life of Me *(in collaboration with Robert Briscoe) (Little, Brown, 1958),* The Miracle of the Mountain *(Hawthorn, 1959), and* The Circus Kings *(in collaboration with Henry Ringling North) (Doubleday, 1960). He is married to Allene Pomeroy Gaty and they make their home at "Somerleas," Cedarhurst, Long Island.*

THE DE GAULLE NOBODY KNOWS *(Hawthorn, 1960) was designed by Sidney Feinberg and completely manufactured by the American Book-Stratford Press, Inc. The body type was set on the Linotype in Baskerville, a modern reproduction of the types cut in 1760 by John Baskerville of Birmingham, England, reflecting the style of stone inscriptions.*

A HAWTHORN BOOK